MOTHER OF THE COMPANY

Williams-Ford Texas A&M
Military History Series

MOTHER OF THE COMPANY

Sgt. Percy M. Smith's World War II Reflections

Edited by Philip M. Smith

Texas A&M University Press

College Station

Library of Congress Cataloging-in-Publication Data

Names: Smith, Percy M., 1914–1985, author. | Smith, Philip M. (Philip
  Matthew), editor.
Title: Mother of the company: Sgt. Percy M. Smith's World War II
  reflections / edited by Philip M. Smith.
Other titles: Williams-Ford Texas A&M University military history series.
Description: First edition. | College Station: Texas A&M University Press,
  [2022] | Series: Williams-Ford Texas A&M University military history
  series | Includes bibliographical references and index.
Identifiers: LCCN 2022021590 (print) | LCCN 2022021591 (ebook) | ISBN
  9781648430664 (hardcover) | ISBN 9781648430671 (ebook)
Subjects: LCSH: Smith, Percy M., 1914–1985—Correspondence. | World War,
  1939–1945—Personal narratives, American. | World War,
  1939–1945—Campaigns—Western Front. | United States—Armed
  Forces—Non-commissioned officers—Correspondence. | LCGFT: Personal
  correspondence.
Classification: LCC D811 .S58224 2022 (print) | LCC D811 (ebook) | DDC
  940.54/1273—dc23/eng/20220513
LC record available at https://lccn.loc.gov/2022021590
LC ebook record available at https://lccn.loc.gov/2022021591

*Unless otherwise indicated, all photos are from
the author's personal collection.*

For his grandchildren,

Molly

Andrew

Lucy

"One reason soldiers' and sailors' letters home are so little to be relied on by the historian of emotion and attitude is that they are composed largely to sustain the morale of the folks at home, to hint as little as possible of the real, worrisome circumstance of the writer. No one writes: 'Dear Mother, I am scared to death.'"

—Paul Fussell, *Wartime: Understanding and Behavior in the Second World War*

CONTENTS

PREFACE

In early 1966, Warner Brothers released *Battle of the Bulge* starring Henry Fonda and Robert Shaw. I was not yet old enough to drive, so my father drove my date and me and dropped us off at a theater to see the movie. Unknown to me, Dad parked, bought a ticket, and watched the movie from the back of the theater. At the end, he left quickly and picked us up at the curb. On the drive home, Dad said nothing about having been in the battle himself. He made no comments about the film. I knew he was a veteran of the war, but I had only vague notions of his wartime life. He did not talk about it. He did not boast, and he was never specific. I once heard my father say that what he did was done by thousands and thousands of others, and he had nothing to say that was important, nothing more than any other veteran. After reading this book, you might disagree with him.

In the spring of 1943, my father, Percy Smith, was drafted into the army. He left his wife and home in Jacksonville, Florida, for army training at Camp Shelby, Mississippi, entering service as a private. Within six months, he rose to the rank of first sergeant of a heavy weapons company in the 69th Infantry Division. At 5 feet, 6 inches tall and 120 pounds, Dad was not an intimidating physical presence, but he learned how to keep order, get results from his men, and satisfy the demands of the company commander.

A year later, during the fighting in Europe, a captured German soldier of equal rank told my father, through an interpreter, that they both had the same function. In the German Army, the rank was *Hauptfeldwebel*, the senior noncommissioned officer in a company. The soldier explained to my father that the *Hauptfeldwebel* was also known as the *Mutter der Kompanie*—the mother of the company.

My father remained in training camp until the summer of 1944, when he was sent overseas as a replacement to fill in for a company that had lost its first sergeant. By September, he was in a replacement depot in France, awaiting assignment to a new company and a new division where he would be surrounded by strangers and on the front lines of the war.

On 4 October 1944, Dad was assigned to an infantry company, Company G of the 317th Regiment, which was part of the 80th Infantry Division. The 80th had arrived in France in July and became part of the Third Army as it advanced across northern France. When my father arrived at his post near the town of Sivry, Company G had suffered badly the day before, and Dad became their new first sergeant.

As he left training camp, my father began writing letters to his wife, my future mother, Elizabeth. Over the next 15 months, he wrote 214 letters to her, and a selection of these letters form the main structure of this book. Letters he wrote during wartime tend to be shorter and do not contain information that would alarm his wife or trigger censors. After the war, Dad stayed in Europe for six months on occupation duties, and these letters are longer and contain more observations, opinions, and some flashbacks to events during wartime.

Smith during training with the 69th Division at Camp Shelby, Mississippi, 1943

Many years later, my father discovered the saved letters in a box stored in the garage. Mom had asked Dad to get a supply of canning jars, but he found the letters instead and read through them until she called out, "Percy, where are my canning jars?" He read though the old letters, and then edited and typed some of them with this introduction: "What you will read are impressions that were either written during the action or in retrospection shortly thereafter. The letters were not written under ideal conditions and usually by the light of a burning sock in a bottle of gasoline or a sputtering candle. The letters were usually written during a rest stop in the shell of a house or building or any place out of the weather." With one exception, the letters were all written in longhand on a variety of different kinds of paper, including V-Mail, Red Cross stationery, German writing paper, and other random paper found along the way in occupied buildings.[1] My mother's letters to him did not survive.

This is not strictly an epistolary book. My father also wrote memories about his wartime experiences in story form. In 1947, the *Saturday Evening Post* solicited brief accounts from veterans. Dad submitted several, but none were published. Three decades later, he wrote longer memories as stories, and they are inserted here among the letters in the time sequence of events they describe. Occasionally, a single story has been divided into segments in order to align events in the story with the dates of the letters. Also included are a few excerpts from correspondence between Dad and a comrade he knew during the war, who he reconnected with in later years.

Together, the letters and stories give readers different voices from the same writer about this soldier's wartime experience. Letters written at the time of the events are immediate impressions. The longer stories were written over thirty years later, after he had time to reflect. They enrich the overall narrative and tell us what stayed with him, what he wanted to preserve, and perhaps what memories left mental wounds that Dad still needed to work through.

The letters are filled with repeated messages of affection and longing to be home with his wife. It is easy to imagine these battlefront professions of love as potentially his last words, aware as he was that each letter could be his last. Some of the repeated endearments were removed for this book, but many still remain as evidence of the way my father expressed himself. We might wonder if such profuse expressions of love put a burden on my mother by creating unrealistic expectations of an idyllic home life after the war. Of course, we read them all together in this volume, but my mother received them one at a time and sometimes without having heard from Dad for long periods of time—so perhaps each letter made her smile and reassured her about his feelings.

Soldiers longed for reassurance that their loved ones were waiting for them, and—even with some of the emotional language omitted—Dad's letters are evidence of that yearning. As his company's first sergeant, who was married and a bit older than most of the soldiers, my father consoled men who were brokenhearted by letters from home with news of infidelities, separations, and divorce, and surely this influenced the way he wrote home. My mother herself erased or cut out some intimate passages that she apparently felt were not appropriate to share with family and friends—or that she did not want to be seen by anyone in the future.

In a key scene in the movie *Saving Private Ryan*, the main character, who is older and married, speaks frankly to his men about his desire to return home.[2] His deep desire to return home sustains him on the mission to save Private Ryan. This is a sentiment that my father expressed over and over in his letters. One is only left to ponder: If they do survive, do soldiers always find the comfort they expect at home?

In the novel *All Quiet on the Western Front*, Erich Maria Remarque portrays front-line soldiers who can never truly go home again. Home, as a place of security and comfort, no longer exists for these characters. The home they left seems superficial compared with the life they share with other soldiers amid the dangers of war. In Remarque's novel, German soldier Paul Bäumer only feels at home with comrades who shared hardships and had little hope for survival. "They are more to me than life, these voices, they are more than motherliness and more than fear; they are the strongest, most comforting thing there is anywhere; they are the voices of my comrades."[3]

My father's wartime experience was not as grim or prolonged as the trench warfare of the First World War, but his memories reveal similar instincts in the comfort he provided to those around him. Even though Dad sometimes wrote with a wry tone, I am sure he carried trauma and loss with him for the rest of his life. When I first read his letters and stories, I was surprised to learn that the man I knew as a calm and gentle father had been in such distress and danger. I did not see symptoms of a troubled mind in his fatherly care for me, but I was young. When I look back on his life, I do recognize him as the man in these letters and stories for whom empathy and comforting others came so naturally.

In his later life, there were, I suppose, some telltale signs of avoiding full engagement with the present, such as using alcohol more than my mother approved of. Dad always seemed kind and empathetic, but perhaps distractions were his way of managing his feelings about the past. Writing about his memories was most likely a form of therapy for him. At age sixty-one, a stroke left Dad with limited use of his right side, including his right hand. Soon after the stroke, he began to write longer stories. He said that typing was good therapy for his weaker hand, but I think writing was far more emotional and mental than physical therapy.

Percy M. Smith Jr. was born in Nashville in 1914. When he was two years old, his father shot his wife—my grandmother—then took his own life. My grandmother survived and moved with her young son to live with her mother, a second-generation immigrant from Germany, in Waycross, Georgia. They stayed here until my father started grammar school.

In 1922, my grandmother and her son moved farther south to Jacksonville, Florida. The owner of a bakery where she worked had relocated there, and a girlhood friend from her Tennessee youth now lived in the north Florida city. To help support his mother, my father worked for tips as a drug

Elizabeth
and Percy
shortly
after their
marriage in
1940

store curb hop after school, then at the soda fountain in a pharmacy. In high school, Dad was attracted to a group of teens who liked to discuss poetry and literature, but this came to an end when many of them went to college. By then, his mother had remarried, and there was a new baby sister, so Dad kept working to help his family. The Great Depression was a hard time to begin a career, but after high school, my father eventually found steady work with the Southern News Company, a newspaper and magazine distributor.

My mother, Marion Elizabeth Camp, was born in Atlanta in 1918 and moved to Jacksonville in the late 1920s with her divorced mother and three sisters. Both her family and Percy's lived in rented rooms and apartments, moving frequently. In 1937, their families lived next door to each other, and Percy and Elizabeth were married three years later. During the war years while her husband was away in training and in Europe, Mom was one of many working women employed at the Naval Air Station in Jacksonville—in her case, as a supply office clerk. The letters in this collection were addressed to the apartment where my mother lived with her mother during the war, a public housing project called Brentwood.

After the war, Dad returned home in December 1945 and stepped off a troop transport ship in Boston. He then traveled by train to Camp Blanding in Florida, where he was discharged. I have often wondered what his home-coming was like. In my mother's later years, I asked her if she remembered the first time she saw Dad after the war. Where did they meet? What was it like? What did she wear? She had forgotten the details and could offer no answers to my questions. How Mom understood her husband's wartime life is a bit of an unknown. Dad's sister, Betty Sue, did share one homecoming memory. She said that after hugs and a short visit, her brother said, "You'll have to excuse us. I just got home, and my wife and I haven't had too much time together yet."

After the war, my father worked for a fledgling small business, and then found lasting civil service employment with the Duval County government in Jacksonville until he retired. One can draw comparisons between the role of a first sergeant and some of Dad's roles coordinating and documenting the functions of county-level elected leaders. He could utilize many of the same skills as his army job required to fairly and effectively respond to public demands, all while treating elected officials with kid gloves. Dad did not seek positions of power but excelled at making complicated systems run smoothly without rankling constituents or supervisors.

He was a good father and a caring soul, but I am sure that he concealed his own feelings or perhaps did not know how damaging his memories were, much less how to treat them. My father died in 1985.

In another collection of my father's writings, not included here, Dad recounted his experiences in army training camp. In one of those stories, he told of bumping into a fellow soldier from Camp Shelby ten years after the war. Standing on a street corner in Jacksonville while waiting for the light to change, Dad recognized the face of a man he had known in training camp. Up to that moment, my father had not encountered anyone he had known in the army. Delighted, my father said to him, "Red, Red, it's me, Percy Smith. I'm so glad to see you." A woman with Red clutched her companion's arm. Then, leaning on a cane, Red snapped, "You're the bastard that sent me overseas. And I got injured bad." Dad said, "No, I didn't choose who went. Heck, I was a replacement, too." Red limped across the street as the woman with him looked back with a scowl. Why did he remember this and write it down? Dad appeared to have a solemn and respectful attitude about his military service, but was this little incident evidence that disorientation and even alienation were part of it as well?

In the decades following the war, veterans' associations formed and held annual reunions, where aging veterans could meet up, bringing along their spouses and sometimes children and grandchildren. My father never attended, but during his last years, Dad corresponded with a few of his old comrades. After my father's death, I contacted some of the men who served with Dad, and I attended reunions of the 69th and the 80th Divisions. My mother went with me to one reunion, and she was touched by the memories shared by men who knew my father and by their regard for their old sergeant.

Dad mentioned some of these men by name in his writings, so I felt like I knew them when I first met them. I was eager to ask them if they remembered events as my father had in his stories. They did. In fact, after reading one of the stories, one of them broke down in tears as he spoke with me about it. In addition to confirming the memories of Dad's comrades, the army's Morning Reports for my father's company and After Action Reports for his battalion provided some of the strongest sources for verifying the names and events presented herein. These reports provide exact locations and confirm details that Dad mentioned in his letters and stories.[4]

My father wrote from memory, without access to official military records; however, his memory of events and people and even the spelling of complicated names was largely correct. Perhaps this is because one of his duties as first sergeant had been to submit daily information about the status of the company and its men as part of the Morning Report process, and many of the names stayed with him all those years. In a 1981 letter to a former comrade, Dad explained, "Each day I used a worksheet to make up the Morning Report. It contained where we were, if I knew, lists of replacements and lists of what happened to each man, 'from duty to hospital,' etc. And there was a Record of Events in a few words. The report was sent to the Battalion by runner and then passed on to the Regiment. The clerk typed the reports, and sent a copy back to the Company. They were kept in a field desk in the cook or supply truck until we had a break."

Dad's war experiences exposed him to a more diverse group of men than he had encountered while growing up in the American South. His company's daily Morning Reports list replacements, sick, missing, wounded, and those killed in action. Names of the men in the company represent the diversity of American life. Anglo surnames like Smith, Lamb, and Pawley appear alongside Pedro Enriquez, Salvador Estrada, Teodoro Guiterrez, Gustavo Felix, Benancio Garza, Guadalupe Saenz, Mike Damkowitcz, Thaddeus Jankowski, John Kremposki, Vincent Anuskiewicz, Marcel Milewski, Dukas Tramontanis, Felix Cistolo, Dom Palmietto, Umberto Torassare, Liborio Cacicio, Morris Silverberg, Frank Israel, and Kingsley Wong. Wong, the son of a café waiter in Ogden, Utah, was wounded several times and was one of the few soldiers in the company awarded a Silver Star for heroism.

Although army units were racially segregated and Dad had limited direct interaction with Black soldiers, he would have been well aware of Black soldiers in service and support functions. And certainly he later became aware of famous Black units such as the Tuskegee Airmen, the 761st Tank Battalion, and the 92nd and 93rd Infantry Divisions, as well as the Black female 6888th Central Postal Directory Battalion that ensured the vital flow of mail to soldiers. My father knew that to get home safely, he relied on Americans from all walks of life.

ACKNOWLEDGMENTS

The narrative in this book is the work of Percy M. Smith Jr. Other than send-ing a few short items to a magazine soon after the war, my father probably never dreamed that his letters or stories would be published. It has been difficult for me, his son, to judge the merit of my father's writings beyond their place among family treasures. Therefore, I have had to rely on the wise advice of others to help me understand these writings' significance for a wider audience.

In 1995, as the fiftieth anniversary of the end of World War II approached, I sent samples of Dad's writings to National Public Radio (NPR). Producer Robert Malesky responded, and he encouraged me to create a script. Bob's fa-ther was also a veteran of the war, and he had been considering an appropriate feature to mark the anniversary. The story we settled on took the perspective of the children of veterans looking back at their parents' wartime lives. The feature was broadcast on NPR's "Weekend Edition Sunday" program on 7 May 1995, the anniversary of the German surrender. Many years have passed since then, but Bob Malesky's encouragement and wise advice are a major reason this collection is now published. The original feature can be heard on NPR's website at https://www.npr.org/1995/05/07/1005590/-sgt-smith-letters.

This book would not have been finished without the kindness of readers who gave heartfelt responses, and others who have shared their insights about history, memory, and family. I thank Andrew Adkins, Paul Book-binder, Vivian and Lawrence Brooker, Walter Buenger, Archibald Carey, Margaret Parker Cowart, Edith Cowles, Marian Eide, April Hatfield, Renate Heinrich, Charles Hosmer, Gregory Lamb, David Lubin, Holly Mandelkern, Betty Sue and Earl Sapp, and Bradford Wineman. Kelly Crager and Stephen Sloan provided comments on an early draft, and editorial help from Thomas Lemmons, Katie Duelm, Nicole duPlessis, and Rachel Paul was essential and encouraging. And a singular thank you to Jennifer Holman.

No one encouraged me more than Harriet Vardiman Smith. I am grateful for her editorial expertise and for sensitively nurturing a son's emotional journey through his father's memories.

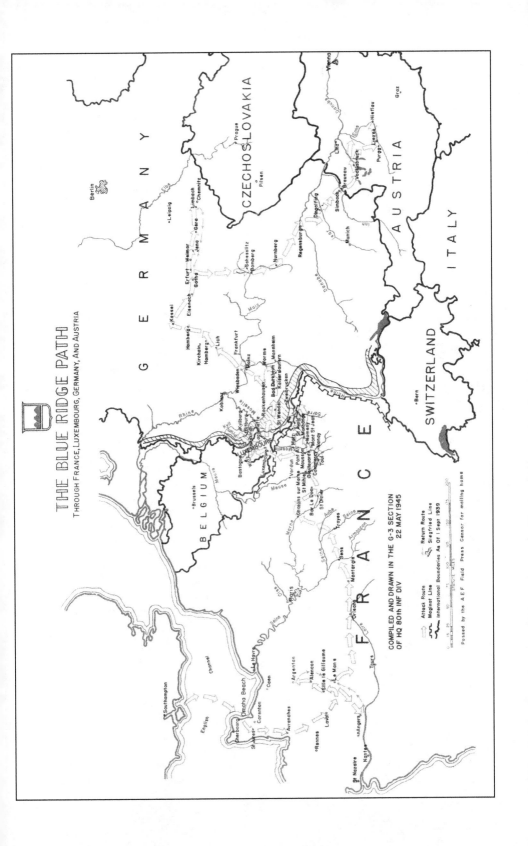

THE BLUE RIDGE PATH
THROUGH FRANCE, LUXEMBOURG, GERMANY, AND AUSTRIA

COMPILED AND DRAWN IN THE G-3 SECTION
OF HQ 80th INF DIV   22 MAY 1945

Attack Route
Maginot Line
International Boundaries As Of I Sept 1939

Return Route
Siegfried Line

STATUTE MILES

Passed by the A E F Field Press Censor for mailing home

MOTHER OF THE COMPANY

Smith (right) at Camp Shelby with John Amabile, 1944

1

EN ROUTE TO THE EUROPEAN THEATER

This can't be happening to me.

In early August 1944, my father left Camp Shelby, Mississippi, where he had been in training with the 69th Division since the spring of 1943. He had expected to be sent overseas with the 69th Division. Instead, he became a replacement for another division, and in the process left behind many friends, including John B. Amabile, pictured here with Dad at Camp Shelby. They never saw one another again, but they must have had a strong friendship. When I was a child, I looked forward to the birthday cards "Uncle John" sent to me every year.

The letters begin after my father left Camp Shelby by train for Fort Meade in Maryland, where he waited to move on to a point of embarkation to the European Theater.

———————————————

13 August 1944
Ft. Meade, Maryland
My darling,

Dear, I expect to leave very soon and as yet I don't know where. I think I mentioned it in another letter that I've increased your allowance to $125 a month. They told me I couldn't have it sent direct to the bank because they were afraid it would be some kind of mix-up and it may take several months to straighten out. Maybe it would be better just to deposit the check and let it go at that.

It is hotter here than it is in Mississippi, can you beat it?

Darling, it's such a mess here, I don't know whether I could get a letter from you or not. While I'm here my address is

1st Sgt Percy M. Smith 34784201
Co "A"—11th Bn—3rd Regt
A.G. F. R. D. #1
Ft. Geo. G. Meade, Md.

I don't have a Company yet, as we are still in a pool—there are one hundred and fifty non-commissioned officers in all and about fifteen are 1st Sgts. They are pretty pitiful, not having anybody to "boss around."

I bought me a watch in Washington, as I was getting the "willies" not knowing what time it was. It cost me twenty-five bucks, and it seems pretty good. Made in Switzerland. I spent about $10 here in Washington and half of that was for taxi and bus fare. The accommodations here are worse than Camp Shelby, and it takes some time to get into town each time you can get a pass. Washington is like Atlanta—it takes too darn long to get anywhere on the busses and street cars.

Things are awfully high here—it cost me a dollar for a haircut. Isn't that ridiculous? The people in Hattiesburg could learn a few tricks from these people.

Darling—don't forget that I love you and think of you all the time. I sure hope this war ends soon so I can come a running to you.

Lots of love dear
your little husband
p.s. I love you xx

———————

7 September 1944
Dearest Wife—

Hello honeybun—I was so glad to hear from you today. It took a week for the letter to reach me, but I was sure glad to get it.

Dear, we have another party in our letters now—a censor—I guess we could kinda look on him as an in-law that has come to live with us. Your letters aren't censored—just mine. I mustn't give out any military information.

Dear, you are always in my thoughts and I'll be rushing to you as soon as I can. I miss you so much dear.

Lots of love
Your little husband
p.s. I love you.

Provisional Company "M"

A memory in story form, written circa 1979–81[1]

It was several hours until daybreak, and the area was dimly lighted as soldiers stood at ease with full field equipment and crammed duffel bags. The men were gathered behind a wooden stake bearing the letter "M" on an assembly field at Fort Meade, Maryland.

A cadre sergeant asked, "Are you Sergeant Smith?"

"Yes," I replied.

"Here's the company roster," he said, handing me a sheaf of paper. "You wanna call the roll?"

"Yeah," I muttered, reaching for my flashlight. "Let's have a look." I snapped the flashlight and peered at the papers. "ATTENTION MEN ATTENTION," I shouted. "Let me have your attention." When the men became silent, I called out, "Stand at ease. As I call your name, sing out with the last four numbers of your serial number. Got it? Okay, listen— ADAMS."

On the vast assembly field, groups of soldiers were standing behind stakes lettered "A" through "M." Each provisional company contained two hundred soldiers.

The cadre sergeant stood by as I called the roll by the light of the flashlight. "Hey," I exclaimed, "I'm short some men—a lot of men. There's more names than men. What's up?"

"Oh, they're aboard the train," answered the cadre sergeant. "They loaded earlier."

"How come?"

"They were quartered near the siding," he replied. "Here," he said, tendering me a form to sign. "Don't worry, they're aboard and under guard."

I scribbled my name. "I don't like to sign for something I can't verify."

"It's okay."

There was a rumbling noise as a convoy of trucks pulled up to the assembly area. The cadre sergeant tugged my arm. "Move the troops to the end of the convoy. Your trucks are marked with an 'M' in chalk. Good luck."

A troop train chuffed up to a railroad siding with its coach window curtains drawn. The trucks ground to a halt near the end of the train. I tapped a staff sergeant on the arm. "Say, sergeant, move the troops to the last coaches marked with a chalked 'M'."

"Okay," the sergeant replied.

"All right—all right—MOVE IT," the staff sergeant bawled, and the grunting and cursing men climbed from the trucks, staggering under their loads. A cordon of MPs surrounded the last coach. I thought, "What the hell?" I called to the staff sergeant, "Start loading, three men to a double seat. I'm going to see why the last coach is under guard."

"Okay, Sarge."

"Oh, another thing," I said. "Keep them out of the compartments—they're for the first three grades. Oh, and save me a space."

"Gotcha," he said, and started shouting at the waiting soldiers.

Daylight was breaking as I made my way to the last coach. One of the armed MPs pointed out the sergeant of the guard.

"I'm Sergeant Smith," I said. "Provisional Company M. The cadre sergeant said some of the men in Company M were already on the train."

"Yeah," he grunted. "We got 'em—they're all aboard."

"How come they're under guard?"

"You mean to say the cadre sergeant didn't tell you?" he asked.

"Nope," I replied. "All he said was that they were aboard the train. What's up?"

"You've got fifty prisoners," he told me.

"Fifty prisoners!" I echoed. "What the hell?"

"Yes, fifty prisoners," he reiterated. "Guys that have 'screwed up,' court-martialed and then assigned to overseas duty."

"Yeah, but why me? Fifty prisoners—"

"Gosh, I dunno—maybe because you have the last company in the provisional battalion. All I know is they're mean bastards."

"But how can I handle them?" I wailed.

"Don't worry. We'll take care of 'em until they're aboard ship."

"Then what?"

"They're yours."

"Damn."

With drawn curtains and under strict security, the troop train huffed and chuffed out of Fort Meade. The train stopped and started as it was shunted to various sidings, provoking cries of "Where the hell are we?" A soldier pulled a curtain aside and exclaimed, "Hey, we're in New York—I recognize the station."

"Aw, you're crazy," a voice cried. "We're headed south, not north."

The following afternoon, the train chuffed to a halt on a siding in a military reservation. Swearing soldiers clambered off the train, burdened with their gear, and straggled a short distance to their quarters. The hutments seemed crude after leaving the barracks at Fort Meade.

"Where are we?" I asked a guide.

"Camp Myles Standish," he answered.

"Camp Myles Standish?" I repeated. "Where is that?"

"Massachusetts, I think."

"Hey," I cried out, "we brought some prisoners. There's fifty I'm told. Where are they?"

"Oh, the MPs will move them to the stockade," replied the guide. "Hold up—this is your quarters."

Camp Myles Standish was a port of overseas replacement camp. During our stay, we underwent physical examinations, received immunization shots, and our gear and clothing were inspected. This would be our last inspection in the United States. The inspecting officers were assisted by a team of soldiers. They were combat veterans that had been rotated from overseas duty. They appeared different from the other soldiers. They were quiet and never joked or horsed around.

However, they were credited with one of the classic rumors of World War II. "Somebody said" that the soldiers rotated from overseas duty told "somebody" in camp that soap, especially toilet soap, was in short supply in Europe. "Somebody" also said that soap was ideal to barter with, especially with females. Like wildfire, the rumor spread and was believed by all as gospel. Excited soldiers eagerly told each other, "Show a French girl a bar of soap and you're in like Flynn." Fired up by the spine-tingling rumor, the eager soldiers launched a mad buying spree, making it impossible for the post exchange to keep soap in stock.

A sad, pathetic side of the ridiculous soap rumor was revealed sometime later. In November of 1944, Company G was reorganizing in a small French village. A work detail supervised by the Supply Sergeant was opening and emptying duffel bags. I happened to be passing and asked, "Say, Sergeant Donato, whatcha doin'?"

He glanced up from a mound of clothing. "Oh, hello, Sergeant Smith." His smile waned. "We're short of clothing, and we're opening duffel bags that belonged to casualties. We need the blankets and clothing."

"It looks like it's quite a stack of duffel bags," I observed.

"Yeah," agreed Sergeant Donato, "about eight hundred."

"Eight hundred!" I repeated soberly.

"Well, maybe a few less, but it's close to eight hundred."[2]

I watched as the men separated the clothing into piles. Personal items, including pens, correspondence folders, hair oil, shaving items, and photographs of loved ones, were piled together. Another contained a huge mound of soap bars. I thought of the line of men buying soap in the post exchange. Judging from the size of the pile of soap, the rumor must have been alive in all port of embarkation camps.

That afternoon, following final inspection, the troops consumed a farewell steak dinner at Camp Myles Standish. Then, shrouded in secrecy, the men swearing and staggering under their load of gear, we all boarded a waiting troop train. No one knew our destination, and no one asked. Everyone heeded the warning, "Loose lips sink ships," and with curtains drawn, the dimly lit train chuffed forward.

Throughout the coach, several poker games were in progress. The swaying coach made me drowsy, and I dozed. I awakened as the train jolted to a stop and then began to back up. When it rolled to a halt, the coach doors opened and a voice bawled, "Okay, everybody out!" I peered out the coach door and saw that we were on a huge covered dock. Moored on the other side of the dock was a huge ocean liner. Soldiers lined the dock, waiting their turn to mount the gangplank. I could hear snatches of music. Somewhere a band was blaring spirited martial tunes.

On signal, the personnel of Provisional Company M hefted duffel bags and shuffled single file toward the ship. As we drew close, I noted the name, USS *Mount Vernon*, on the bow. A sailor, clad in denim work clothes and a white cap, guided us to our quarters. I gazed around the huge room. Formerly, it had been a luxurious ballroom, and now it held tiers of bunks five high.

I sighed and dumped my gear on a lower bunk. "Hey, don't take that bunk," a voice cautioned.

I looked up—it was the sailor. "Why not?" I asked.

"You wouldn't want to be underneath if the guy above you starts '-urping,' would ya?"

"Oh, hell no," I cried as I hurriedly tossed my gear onto a top bunk. "Thanks, thanks a lot."

This wasn't a cruise ship, and the passengers were called on to do the cleaning. A daily chore was sweeping the converted ballroom. As the ranking noncommissioned officer, it became my responsibility to furnish a cleaning detail. After breakfast, I stationed myself by the exit and bellowed, "Everybody out! The last twelve men are on cleaning detail!" I grabbed the last twelve men as they scrambled to the deck.

"Okay fellas, grab a broom," I cried. "Start at this end and sweep the compartment. Do a good job, and if it passes inspection, you're free—move it!"

"Sergeant," said a slightly patronizing voice, "the men could do a more efficient job if they hitched up the lower bunks."

I stared at the soldier, who was wearing a GI sweater and a wool cap. "What did you say?"

"Here, let me show you," he said, pushing back the gear on a lower bunk. He raised it and secured the bunk by a loop chain.

"See?" he said brightly. "Now it's easier to sweep under the bunks."

"Where's your broom?"

"I don't have one," he replied.

"You don't have a broom?"

"No."

"Well, if you haven't got a broom, go ahead of the sweepers and raise the bunks. That's a good idea you had."

He pulled off his wool cap and stared at it. He started to speak, "But, but—I—I—"

"Let's go," I shouted. "Get moving so's we can get through. Move it."

His face took on a baffled expression. When he saw me advancing with balled fists, he yanked on his wool cap and commenced raising the bunks. The sweepers followed, and soon the area was tidy.

As the men straggled by to the deck, I said, "Good work, men." The soldier wearing the sweater and wool cap climbed past. "Hey, you had a good idea," I called to him. "Damn smart—you're officer material."

The following day, I stood by the exit to "nail" the cleaning detail. I was herding twelve stragglers when the same soldier entered the compartment, but this time he wore twin silver bars of a captain.

"Holy smoke!" I called out. I had put an officer—the Officer of the Day, no less—on a detail. I snapped to attention and saluted, "Sir, please accept my apology," I stammered. "I didn't know—"

He returned the salute, "It's all right," he said with a wave of his hand.

"No apology necessary. My fault, really. I failed to fasten the insignia on my cap."

Five days after weighing anchor in Boston harbor, the USS *Mount Vernon* docked in Liverpool. The crossing was uneventful, except for my experience in the shower. At home in Jacksonville, I lived about twenty miles from the seashore, and romping in the surf is fun provided that you shower afterward. Aboard ship, there were hot showers, but it was salt water. I knew better, but put my faith in the special soap, hoping it would neutralize the salty water. Nope, it didn't, and my one and only shower left me covered with an itchy salty film and in a terrible mood.

Debarking followed the opposite order of embarking. Provisional Company M, one of the last groups to board ship, was among the first units to get off. A British troop ship docked alongside the USS *Mount Vernon*, and scuttlebutt had it that a contingent of British troops was being rotated home on furlough after a tour of duty in Africa.

While we waited on the order to debark, we watched the last section of British troops as they smartly snapped to attention and, arms swinging, marched into the streets of Liverpool. Bands blared in the distance and cheers greeted the soldiers. Out of sight of the crowds, ambulances stood by to move the wounded and dismembered.

At last, our file shuffled toward the gangplank. Each soldier toiled under the weight of a full field pack, a crammed duffel bag, and a weapon. I had

USS *Mt. Vernon* (AP-22), off Boston, Massachusetts, July 1, 1944. Catalog # 80-G-237855, Naval History and Heritage Command, National Archives.

an additional load—a box of service records for the men in Provisional Company M.

Something stalled the shuffling column. "Damnation!" Staggering under my burden, I stepped out of line and pressed forward. I can't recall what I said, but it was punctuated with yells and curses. Prodded by my salty imprecations, the column started moving. As I looked up, I saw a British soldier in a wheelchair. "I say there, Yank," he called to me. "That's telling 'em." Puffing and grunting, the men trudged across the dock to a waiting troop train.

Later, when I joined my company in the combat zone, you can imagine my chagrin when I was told to leave my gear with Supply. My combat attire was limited to a uniform and field jacket. The field pack was dumped and replaced with a raincoat, one blanket, and K-rations.[3] My razor and toothbrush went into my pocket. "Pissed off" described my feelings after hauling all that gear some two thousand miles—for what?

A Provisional Company, as the name implies, is a temporary unit. The soldiers remain together until they reach a replacement depot and then are redeployed to replace casualties in the committed units. Replacement spare parts, so to speak. There was barely time to form friendships; however, some of the soldiers were quite voluble and hailed one another by name. As I listened to their loose talk and obscenities, I realized they were the ex-prisoners. Sure, they knew each other—bound to—they had shared time in the stockade for months.

The British railway carriages seemed small compared with American railroad coaches. The interior was shoddy and worn, but the train movement was the same—move forward then back and delays at every siding.

A shout in the railway carriage aroused me. A soldier, one of the ex-prisoners, was cursing out the carriage window. Somebody had called from the siding, and the soldier responded with an obscenity. I peered out the window. An elderly man was standing beside the carriage. "I came to greet you," he sputtered, "and you—and you—"

The soldier replied with a string of curses.

I leaped to my feet, acutely embarrassed, "Shut up, you dumb bastard!" I cried. I wrenched the vestibule door open and stepped out on the platform. "Hey, mister," I called to the man. A man leaning on a cane turned and looked at me. "Mister," I called. "Please accept my apology for our rudeness."

He threw his shoulders back and stood straight, "I came down to bid you welcome."

"Thank you, sir," I said. "Forgive us—we're not all profane."

"Thank God."

I re-entered the railway carriage. The soldiers remained silent under my murderous stare. I looked around the carriage. As I took my seat, there was some inaudible muttering.

Soon, a British vessel ferried us across the English Channel. The deck swarmed with soldiers while white, wispy vapor trails followed the bombers high in the sky.

My attention was attracted to a burst of laughter. I glanced up to see several British Marines clowning around with a young man in a naval officer's uniform. The young man's uniform was much too large, almost comical. I did a double-take—the lad appeared to be very young. I guessed his age to be thirteen, maybe fourteen. A laughing Marine called something, and the young man grinned and gestured with a fist. "What," I wondered, "is this kid doing in a naval officer's uniform on a troop ship in a war zone?"

My question was answered later.

As the ship approached the shore, I saw that it had been the site of amphibious landings. A row of ships was sunk in a line near the shore to form a breakwater. The breakwater prevented the landing craft from capsizing in the surf. Still visible were patches of angled irons and barbed wire protruding from the surf. Debris, gear, and wreckage following the bloody assault in June had been cleared, and engineering personnel had constructed a temporary dock.

The ship's bell jangled, and commands rang out. Horseplay ceased. The British Marines became alert. The young man wearing the oversize uniform shrilly called a command, and a rigid Marine barked, "Yes, sir." This young man was definitely in command of the vessel. He scampered up the ladder and took charge of steering the ship. His shrill commands evoked crisp "Aye, aye, sir!" from the naval personnel. Cautiously and expertly, the young man maneuvered the ship alongside the breakwater. Chains rattled as the ship came to rest some two hundred yards from shore. On signal, the troops clambered over the ship's side and down rope ladders to bobbing landing craft.

A voice called out, "Where the hell are we?"

The Marine at the helm of the landing craft replied, "Omaha Beach."

From the bobbing landing craft, the beach appeared quiet and peaceful. The sections of barbed wire on steel frames partially submerged in the surf and a blasted concrete pill box with a door hanging open were grim reminders of the struggle that took place on the 6th of June.[4]

The Replacement Depot had no facilities and was nothing more than a large field. A series of slit trenches formed the latrine. Word was out that after the noon meal, there would be a formation for soldiers who wanted to take a bath in a nearby stream. A bath? Damn right I wanted a bath—one miserable shower in salt water in over a week—I was ready. But first we had to pitch tents.

"How come they call 'em pup tents?" a soldier muttered. His buddy looked up from pounding a tent peg, "It beats me, unless it's 'cause soldiers live a dog's life."

After tents were pitched and the gear stowed, a formation was called and rations issued. The rations, called C-rations, were in small cans. One contained stew or something similar, the other can held crackers, several pieces of hard candy, two cigarettes, and a small package of toilet paper.

Those who wanted a bath were to assemble at 1300, undressed and wearing just their raincoat. The group of soldiers in raincoats and clutching towels trudged about a half mile to a wooded stream. One thing, for sure, September in France is not the same as September in Florida. I plunged into the stream and promptly turned blue in the icy water. I gasped for air. When I regained my breath, I exclaimed, "Damn, damn, and double damn!" My next bath was a shower in a public facility in November, then another at a field shower facility in January. Three baths in eight months.

Back in the States, we'd call a camp like this a bivouac. We did, however, have reveille and formations that the ex-prisoners ignored. The malcontents set up camp some distance from the balance of the Provisional Company and were aloof and uncooperative. My commands to "FALL IN" were greeted by jeers and unprintable language. I conferred with the provisional captain, and he shrugged and said, "Don't sweat it. Leave 'em alone—we'll all be reassigned soon."

"But, sir," I said, "maybe I should talk to them."

"Suit yourself," he said, and he resumed reading a book.

Despite their lack of cooperation, I felt a degree of responsibility for the ex-prisoners. Later, I learned a simple definition of my military job's classification, and of all things, I heard it from a German prisoner. After a skirmish in a German village, a group of German soldiers surrendered. As the riflemen herded the frightened prisoners into a barn, one who was obviously a noncommissioned officer spoke with authority to his men.

I asked our interpreter, "Hey, Decker, what's that guy telling 'em?" Corporal Decker listened to the conversation and told me, "Aw, he's just calming them down. They're scared crapless and believe that we kill our prisoners. He's explaining that they're prisoners of war, and if they do as they're told, they won't be executed."

This man had lost his helmet and his overcoat was unbuttoned. "Say, Decker," I shouted, "ask him his military rank." Corporal Decker turned to me, "He has the same rank that you have, the German equivalent of First Sergeant." At that moment, I felt a kinship with the prisoner because we had the same responsibilities. I shook hands with him as Decker explained that we both held the same rank. The man spoke as Decker listened. "How about that," blurted Corporal Decker. "He says you guys both serve as the mother of the company."[5]

Looking back, I guess I had a maternal attitude about my ex-prisoners in Company M. They stared at me in silence when I strode into their midst. "Okay men," I said, "I understand you've had a hard time. Maybe you brought it on yourselves, but that's over. Whatever you've done, you've paid for it. Let's start over. You're soldiers—now act like soldiers. Okay? Reveille will be at oh-seven hundred—be there."

My plea for cooperation evoked a string of obscenities of which "son of a bitch" was the mildest.

It was obvious that simple words were helpless. Maybe the Captain was right. Leave the bastards alone. I tried—let them make the next move, if any. But, then, a plan came to mind.

Each morning, during the reveille formation, a supply jeep arrived with the day's rations. In addition, each soldier was issued two packages of cigarettes. I don't smoke cigarettes, so I tossed them into my duffel bag. My pup tent mate was a nonsmoker, so he tossed in his ration, too.

I thought about the group of malcontents. "Okay, you bastards, it's time for a new deal—no formation, no supplies." The following day, the group of ex-prisoners scorned the reveille formation, and I told the jeep driver to return their rations to the supply dump.

"Return it?" the driver asked. "What's up?"

"Aw, just a misunderstanding," I told him. "One of the platoons doesn't care to stand reveille. Maybe they'll change their minds in a day or so."

The following day, the malcontents scrounged around and made do with parts of rations left from the previous day. Few had cigarettes to share.

The next day after that, a soldier exclaimed, "Say, those guys over there are frying eggs and they have bread."

"Yeah," said his companion, "I saw a couple of Frenchmen with bicycles talking to them—they must have bartered something to get fresh eggs."

There was no training program in the Replacement Depot, but there were things to do while awaiting assignment. For one thing, there was a huge stack of enemy ammunition and equipment for the soldiers to examine. German hand grenades had wooden handles and were carried in waterproof aluminum containers that resembled an overnight case. "Very neat," I thought.

The display of German equipment and weapons was impressive. Their accouterments, I noted, were made of leather, whereas ours were made of webbed canvas. A crude target range occupied some of my time as I "zeroed" my carbine. A feeling of unreality crept over me as I lay prone and powed away at the target. "This can't be happening to me," I thought.

The fourth day after my encounter with the disenchanted collection of ex-prisoners, I was on my knees folding a raincoat. A twig snapped. I glanced up to see one of these men walking toward me. I didn't know what to expect, so as I stood, I picked up my entrenching tool, a small folding shovel. He was heavy-set and outweighed me by at least thirty pounds. His field jacket was unbuttoned, and he wore a wool cap. I gripped the entrenching tool as I stood and watched him. "All right, you sonofabitch," I thought. "Start something and you'll get this shovel in your teeth." He hesitated several feet from me, fidgeted, and appeared ill at ease. I calmly stared at him.

"Sarge," he began. "Can I talk to you?" Maybe I had misjudged him. He didn't sound belligerent.

"Sure," I replied. "Anytime." To be on the safe side, I held on to the entrenching tool.

"The fellows, we talked it over, and they asked me to, well, you did come over and talk with us, and, and nobody has ever done that before—you seemed like . . ."

"Yeah, yeah," I said. "What in hell are you trying to say?"

"We've had a rough time." He looked sheepish. "We've given you a hard time, not standing formation and all that, but we thought you seemed fair, and we want to ask a favor."

"Okay, okay," I said. "Ask away. If I can help you, I will. If I can't, I'll tell you. Okay?"

"Fair enough," he said, and then blurted, "We're out of cigarettes. . . ."

"Oh, that's no problem," I interrupted. "Each morning at reveille, cigarettes are passed out, two packs for each man."

"You mean—that's all we gotta do is stand reveille?" Say, you ain't gonna make it tough like everybody else?"

"No, no," I said. "Why should I?"

"You mean you ain't sore at us?"

"No, I'm not sore. Now listen, whatever you guys have done, you've paid for it. Your sentences are over. Damnit! You're soldiers—you understand—it's time to start acting like soldiers." As I spoke, he straightened his shoulders and stood more erect.

"It was tough," he said. "We were pissed off and couldn't help it."

"Okay—forget it," I said. "Now, you said you're out of cigarettes, didn't you?"

"Yeah," he said unhappily, "and it's tough."

"Tell you what," I blurted, "I don't smoke cigarettes, but I saved my ration—if you guys want them, they're yours."

"Want them?" he answered eagerly. "Hell yes we want them!"

"Golly damn," he exclaimed as I dumped the duffel bag. "That's a pile of cigarettes. Gee, thanks, Sarge—thanks a lot."

"That's okay," I told him.

He hastily scooped up the cigarettes and then turned as if to leave. He paused and looked back, "Say Sarge, you're the first guy to treat us human—that's no crap—and cigarettes—thanks, thanks a lot."

"Just be in formation," I said, "and you'll get the same treatment as everybody else."

"From now on," he promised, "we'll be there—I'll guarantee it."

At oh-seven hundred the following morning, I stood in the assembly area and yelled, "FALL IN." The soldiers scurried to their positions. The Fourth Platoon, the former prisoners, moved smartly to their places and snapped to attention. No jostling or squirming. For the first time, Provisional Company M stood in formation with its full complement of men. As the surprised captain took the report, he asked in sotto voce, "What happened?"

"Sir," I answered, "they ran out of cigarettes."

Thus the ice was broken, so to speak. Henceforth they welcomed me to their group. They excelled as scroungers and briskly bartered with the natives. One time, they acquired several bottles of wine and invited me to share. I was leery of homemade wine and said, "No thanks—make mine coffee."

I lolled around the campfire, listening to their stories. There, I learned that they were from the Pacific theatre of operations. While none were criminals, they had been convicted of serious infractions of army regulations. Instead of prison terms, they were reassigned for duty in the European theatre of operations.

One thing was evident—they craved recognition. Their sulfurous cursing was a clamor for attention. Whereas most admitted that they were the cause of their own troubles, it didn't alter their views of military justice— those were unprintable. But what really pissed them off was their treatment by the army. I agreed it was severe.

Following their courts-martial, they were herded together and shipped to the United States. It was not a hero's homecoming. There were no bands or cheering crowds. It was night, and they struggled down the gangplank in chains. The guards hustled them onto troop trains to be sent across the country. The stockade at Fort Meade was the collection point. They became more bitter when they were denied permission to contact their families. One soldier said the train sat for two hours in his hometown, and he would have jumped off had he not been handcuffed to the seat.

I only heard their side of the story, and I realized they were rebellious misfits. However, I sympathized with them.

"Say Sarge," one asked, "What's gonna happen to us?"

"Gee, I don't know," I replied, "but I'll see what I can find out."

The captain of the Provisional Company didn't know either, but he offered to confer with the camp chaplain. From the chaplain, we learned that it was the custom to separate the men and assign them to various units. "This will give them a fresh start," he explained.

"Men," I told the group, "the best information I have is that you'll be split up and assigned to units according to your military specialty. Offhand, I'd say it's a good deal. This way, you guys will have a shot at starting over."

I paused and looked at the group around the campfire. "Well, fellows," I said, "It's time to say 'so long'—I'm pulling out in the morning."

They crowded around. "Hey, where are you going?"

"It beats me," I replied. "A large group—one hundred and forty-seven—were put on alert. We leave tomorrow."

We exchanged "so longs," and several said that they'd miss me. I shrugged and said, "Aw, I'll be seein' you guys around."

With the assignment of troops to various units, Provisional Company M ceased to exist. Normally, this would be the logical place to conclude the episode, but there was an aftermath.

On Wednesday, 4 October 1944, I joined Company G, 317th Infantry Regiment, along with a group of replacements. I soon discovered that the unit was in the 80th Division of the Third Army.

The war raged on, and the 317th Infantry hurtled through France, Luxembourg, Germany, and Austria. We moved on foot or by truck. As we slogged along, I was recognized by some of the former prisoners. One was with engineers repairing a bridge, another was a jeep driver for an artillery observer, one was with a communications unit, and another was in a quartermaster unit. I didn't recognize them, but all of them hailed me and identified themselves. We laughed and slapped backs. All had attained ratings.

At one point, a Military Police sergeant was directing our trucks past the rubble of a shelled village when he spied me. "Hi, Sergeant Smith," he called.

"Hi yourself," I yelled back. "Who are you?"

He held up his hand, and our truck ground to a halt. He grinned, "We were together in the 'repple depple,'" he said.

"Say," I called, "I see that you've made sergeant—and in the military police. How about that?"

"Yeah," he grinned. "You know," he said, "there was a time I hated the bastards—now I'm one of 'em. Ain't that something?" He waved his hand and called, "So long."

As the truck jerked forward, I called back, "So long."

Later, I attended a church service held in a village barn. The chaplain's assistant hailed me. "Hi Sergeant Smith," he said, "It's good to see you."

"Hi," I responded. "Don't tell me—I'll bet we were together at the 'repple-depple.'"

"Thass right," he grinned as we shook hands.

"Whatcha doing now?" I asked him.

"Oh, I drive the chaplain's jeep and help him set up for services."

"Damn," I exclaimed, "I've bumped into you bastards all across Europe—and it's been damn nice."

He gestured in mock horror. "Watch your language," he said piously. "Don't forget, you're in a place of worship."

---

19 September 1944
France
V-Mail
My darling wife—

My dear—here I am in France thousands of miles from you but you are with me in all my thoughts and dreams.

I was in England a short time and it is very pretty, but too crowded for comfort. I haven't seen much of the place yet.

Dear, I love you more each day and can hardly wait until we start for home again. Take good care of yourself, dear, and don't work too hard.

Lots of love dear
Your little husband
p.s. I love you.

---

24 September 1944
France
V-Mail
My darling wife—

Just a little note to let you know that I'm always thinking of you. I love you more and more every day. This V-mail system isn't too good, but maybe I'll be some place that I can buy some airmail envelopes soon.

I am quite a distance into France now and the damage to the cities is terrible. The poor natives are really having a time. I've been moving so fast and so much that my mail hasn't caught up with me yet. I had my first bath in three weeks today. I nearly froze. It's getting winter time here.

Darling, take care of yourself, and don't forget that I love you.

Your little husband

p.s. I love you, dear.

---

29 September 1944

France

My darling wife—

Darling, I think of you all the time if I haven't mentioned it before. I have had a nice trip through France on an open flat car. I saw Paris from a distance but everything is off-limits to the G. I. Joes, so I couldn't get you a present. I've got so dern much stuff to carry I don't know where I could put it anyway.

Darling, it's getting harder to write every day so don't worry if my letters get kinda far between. A lot has happened in two short months. I'll sure be glad to get back to you dear—this is too far away to suit me.

I just had an ice cold bath in a stream. The country is beautiful but the water is like ice. France looks just like it does in the movies. Old stone houses and hardly anything modern. It reminds me a lot of St. Augustine.[6]

What has my little angel been doing? Have you gone back to work? Dear, I'll be looking forward to getting some letters from you.

Lots of love dear,

Your little husband

p.s. I love you.

---

1 October 1944

France

My dear wife—

Well dear, it's a nice rainy day and I'm flopped on my stomach in my little pup tent thinking about you. They have a very nice variety of mud here. Nice and cool and sticky. The weather here is very unpredictable— one minute it's raining, the next it's not.

I managed to get some airmail stamps today so I guess this letter will beat some of the letters I've written previously. I'll write as much as I can dear—each place we go makes for harder writing. But every opportunity I have I'll write to my honey.

Dear heart, I love you more and more every day. No matter what happens I want you to know that. Boy! Will I be glad when this mess is over. Darling, take care of your sweet self 'cause I'll be back someday.

Lots of love dear

Your little husband

p.s. I love you.

2

THE RHINELAND CAMPAIGN

15 September 1944–21 March 1945

Maybe the war will end by Christmas.

On 4 October 1944, my father was assigned to the 80th Division as the First Sergeant of Company G of the 317th Infantry Regiment. Infantry companies were about two hundred soldiers, plus or minus 10 percent. The entire 80th Division had an average of twelve thousand soldiers during its months in action. It was one of more than forty infantry divisions and many other armored and airborne divisions in the Third Army under the command of General George Patton.

In other words, Sergeant Smith was a tiny speck inside a giant military machine.

The 80th Division had arrived in France in early August 1944, and took part in the Northern France Campaign. By the time my father arrived, the division was nearing the Maginot Line in northeastern France and getting close to the German border.

The day before Dad arrived, Company G fought in the town of Sivry. German artillery had fallen on them constantly during the night before, and an enemy infantry counterattack at dawn completely surrounded Company G. By nightfall, American troops were ordered to withdraw. The After Action Report for this day reads, "Germans pressed attack on Sivry and at 1530 remnants of our Co G were forced to capitulate to the German force of about 400 men."

A few days later, the company Morning Report listed forty-one men as MIA at Sivry and my father became the new First Sergeant of a devastated and restructuring company. For the rest of the month of October 1944, the

Regiment consolidated their positions west of the Seille River, waiting for the right moment to cross the flooded river that had swollen to as wide as five hundred yards.

My father remained in Company G for the rest of the war, except for a brief transfer to Company E in February and March 1945.

―――――――――――――――――

4 October 1944
France
My darling wife—

Hello dear—well here I am at a new camp, so I guess I'll be here long enough to write you a letter. I haven't had any mail and I don't think we will have any, for it takes a long time to receive it when we are moving around like this.

It's hard to predict when this will all be over—but it is a pain in the fanny to everybody concerned, so I really can't see why we don't call it quits. I'm not particularly impressed by the French. Their towns are unprogressive and probably haven't been cleaned up in ten or fifteen years. Win Catherwood likes 18th century France.[1] I'll bet he would give it up if he could see this filthy place. Our camp is very near a large town but instead of letting us put up in a barn or something, we camp out—phooey!

Darling, I miss you so much. I love you more and more every day. You are my inspiration, dear, as I don't know what I would do without you. No matter where I go you will always be with me in my every thought.

Dear, tell all the folks hello for me as from now on it's going to be hard to write to all the folks—so you tell them for me.

Lots of love, dear
Your little husband
p.s. I love you

6 October 1944
France
V-Mail
My darling wife—

Dear, as you can see I have a new address. It looks like each day I get further and further away from you. But no matter how far away I am, I always think of you.

I am getting down in the dumps over the war. It looks like a long, drawn-out affair.[2]

Now take care of yourself and tell everybody hello for me. We are having tough going but I'm sure everything will turn out okay.

Lots of love dear
Your little husband

20 October 1944
France
My darling wife—

Dear, don't worry if I don't write too often as it's hard at times. I haven't received any mail yet but I suppose it will be several weeks yet. I'm really dirty now, with the exception of a dip in a freezing cold stream I haven't had a bath since I left the U.S. I've got everything I need except cigars. The men all have plenty of cigarettes here but no cigars.

We are in a section of France that was old Germany, so you can see we are almost there. The land is pretty but it rains and the mud is terrific. Sometimes my feet look like a couple of pillows.

How are all the folks? Tell Mother that I'm well and not to worry. I think of you all the time, dear, and hope for the day when this is all over.

With all my love
Your little husband
p.s. I love you.

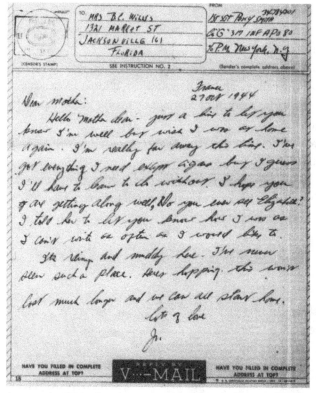

An example of V-Mail—a letter to Percy's mother. His mother always called him "Junior."

28 October 1944

France

V-Mail

Dear little wife,

Hooray! I got my first letter from you today, the one you wrote Sept 15th. Maybe my mail won't be so slow now that it's finally started to come in. I can't tell you how swell it was to hear from you. It sure pepped me up.

Dear, I know you will do what you can for the folks and I sure appreciate you looking in every now and then to see if everything is okay. I wrote Betty Sue to come see you often. I know you can straighten her out.[3]

Lots of love darling

Your little husband

p.s. I love you

2 November 1944
France
V-Mail
My darling wife—

Hello honey—Boy did I hit the "jackpot" today. I received nine letters from you today. Gee! But I love you dear and will be so happy to get home to you.

Dear little wife—I think of our good times together. I think of you all the time.

Don't worry about me. I'm sure everything will work out okay. Tomorrow I'll try to answer the letters so they make sense. Good night darling. I hope we can all be home soon so I can really tell you.

> Good night dear
> Lots of love
> Your little husband

p.s. I love you.

---

5 November 1944
France
V-Mail
My darling wife,

Hello honey—I thought about you so much today. It's Sunday and I was thinking about the Sundays we used to spend together. Dear, I enjoy your letters so much—I still have a pocket full, and I've read them so much they are almost worn out.

Gosh! I love you dear, and I hope and pray the war will soon end so I can return to you. I think of you all the time, dear. I don't know what I would do without you as you are my inspiration. Dear, if you can find a box of cigars, send them to me wrapped up good so they won't get "squashed." Write to me airmail—it's faster.

> Lots of love dear
> Your little husband

p.s. I love you.
Don't forget the pictures.

Crossing the Seille River

A memory recalled in a letter to a comrade in 1981

On 8 November, my father and all three infantry regiments of the division attacked, crossing the flood-swollen Seille River.[4] This is from a 1981 letter Dad wrote to a fellow veteran.

The day I joined Company G of the 317th Regiment, there was another First Sergeant there, a man named John Farmer. I was assigned, and he was attached. Shortly thereafter we crossed the Seille River—that was my first experience under fire. We had to wade waist-deep. Our objective was to cross the river and cut across a road a short distance from the river. As we raced for the road, German artillery fell at random. I spied a hole and started for it—then I remembered Farmer loping along with me. As he was attached, whatever that means, I considered him a guest and waved my hand toward the hole. Farmer jumped in the hole while I raced forward and dove into a drainage ditch beside the road. Almost simultaneously, shells fell all over the field. Farmer was hit. A shell hit a platoon a short distance from me. The sight made me ill, and I was sore pressed to get my breeches down in time. My constipation was cured.

——— ———

18 November 1944
France
My darling wife—
Thanks for the sweet letters dear—they are coming in regularly now and they really give me a lift to hear from you.

Dear, don't worry about me as everything will turn out okay. I'm in Patton's Third Army but I don't think it wise to tell any more. Business has been very good lately, but the war is still not over yet. The Germans are very stubborn.[5]

Darling I am sure thankful for all the nice times we've had together, and they are my most treasured memories.

The other morning I woke up and my foxhole was covered with snow. The first time I'd ever really seen snow. That is, really thick snow. Dear, I'll write every time I have an opportunity so don't worry if my letters are sometimes far apart.

I have everything I need except cigars, but I guess they are hard to get anywhere now. Little jars of jelly would be nice, too. But anything you send must be packed real good as they really beat them up.

Dear—I think of you all the time and only living until the time we are reunited again.

> Good night darling
> Lots of love
> Your little husband

p.s. I love you.

Sarge, Are You Married?

A memory in story form written circa 1979–82

It was rainy and cold in France in November of 1944. The rumbling of artillery made bright splotches in the sky. This moonless, drippy night, I shared a dugout with Moors and McAllister.

Sergeant McAllister's swearing jolted me awake. "Mac," I asked, "What's eating you?"[6]

"It's the damn telephones," he muttered. "They're not working—the platoons are supposed to check in on the hour. They didn't—the line must be broken."

I moved to avoid a dripping leak. "Hey, Mac, what time is it?"

"It's a few minutes past 2200," he answered, "I'll take a detail and trace the wires."

Sergeant Moors spoke, "You want me to help?"[7]

"No, Moors, you stay with the telephone. I'll give a call when I find the break." He fumbled around for his tools and then said, "See you later."

There was a faint glow in the dugout as Sergeant Moors drew on a cigarette cupped in his hands.

"What's up, Moors? Can't sleep?"

"Oh, nothing—nothing wrong. I've been thinking and just not sleepy."

"Well, Moors," I said, "if you can't sleep, rest. In this business, you gotta rest when you can."

"Yeah, Sarge, I know. But it's that I've got something on my mind. Say, can I ask you something while McAllister's out?"

He sounded urgent, so I said, "Sure, Moors, what's on your mind?"

"Well, it's personal, but I need advice—I gotta talk to somebody."

"Okay, Moors, I'm all ears." A trickle of water dribbled from the dugout roof, and I squiggled closer to the wall.

"Sarge, are you married?"

"Sure, I'm married," I replied.

He said something, more like a mumble, and then he spoke. "Well, what I wanted to ask is what it's like to be married."

"Moors," I answered, "I think marriage is wonderful. It really is. Hey, are you planning to get married after the war?"

"Gosh, I don't know—that is, maybe."

"Well, you should know if you're in love."

"I do—I am, but I don't know about her. That's why I wanted to talk to you."

I pushed aside the shelter-half. The rain had stopped, but the night air was cold.

"Moors, where did you meet the girl? Have you known her long?"

"I met her back home—that's Philadelphia, you know. It was at a USO. She came with a group of women to help entertain the servicemen. I stared at her, and she looked at me and smiled. I asked her for a dance, but I'm clumsy. I finally confessed I was a poor dancer, and she said she didn't dance that much either. We sat in the lounge and talked and laughed a lot. I'm shy and not a ladies' man, but I felt comfortable with her. I wanted to be near her."

"Moors, it sounds like you're in love."

"Yeah, I believe I am," he sighed. "I only had four days of my furlough left, and we met every night at the USO." He paused, then continued, "She told me that she didn't have a steady boyfriend and she liked being with me. I felt so happy when I was with her and told her so."

"Sarge, we didn't even hold hands, yet I felt close to her. I asked if I could correspond with her, and she said yes and gave me her address. I started to write her several times, but I tore them up—I don't know what to say or how to say it."

"Moors, it sounds like you've found a nice girl."

"But how can I tell if she cares for me? Maybe she was just being nice to a lonesome G.I."

"Well," I said, "being married doesn't make me wise in the ways of women, but I'll tell you what I'd do. I'd write and tell her just what you told me. Tell her you like to be near her. Go ahead and tell her how you feel about her. You're a decent fellow; you'll know what to write."

"Oh golly," he murmured. "I don't know—but one thing I'm sure of—I'm crazy about her."

The field telephone made a faint buzzing noise. It was Sergeant McAllister. "The damn wire was broken," he explained. "I'm gonna double back and run two wires to each station—that oughta do it."

"Okay," I said, and shoved the telephone into its case.

"Another thing," said Sergeant Moors, "I haven't said anything about the girl to my folks."

"Moors, if you are sincerely fond of her, write and tell her. And, if you love the girl, your folks will, too."

Sergeant Moors sighed. "Thanks, Sarge, thanks for talking with me. I'll write as soon as we get a break."

"German resistance seems to be falling apart," I said. "Maybe the war will end by Christmas."[8]

---

22 November 1944

France

My darling wife—

Hello dear—I had letters from you today, and I sure enjoyed them. The one about Dagwood not shaving made me laugh 'cause I had to let my whiskers grow for a week or so not long ago, and I sure looked awful.

We are resting in a little town we took by storm the other day, and will spend our Thanksgiving here.[9] We have a little house that reminds me of one of the old houses in St. Augustine. The mud is everywhere and the stable is right in the house. You can step out of the bedroom and fall over a pig. Boy does it smell sweet.

I don't know how much longer the Germans are going to hold out, but when President Roosevelt told them we would fight for an unconditional surrender, it seems to make them fight harder. Personally, I think we would be better off with an ordinary surrender, and then dictate peace terms. If we could stop them from fighting, we could dictate our own terms. As it is, I don't see how they can hold out too long, as we are really chasing them.

You asked me in some of your letters where I was and so forth. I can date my letters, but I can't tell you anything except what you read in the papers about the Third Army. I'm writing this letter by candlelight. I'll bet it looks and sounds screwy.

Dear, I just dream of the times we used to have together and relive every minute of them. Your allotment of $125 per month should start soon. I know how things are back home, and a dollar doesn't go anywhere. I hope to get to a big town someday so I can buy some presents, but the towns I see are in pretty bad shape.

Darling, it's time for me to turn in so I'll say goodnight.

> Lots of love, darling
>
> Your little husband

p.s. I love you, dear.

First Snow

A memory recalled in a letter to a comrade in 1985

In a letter to a fellow veteran from Company G, my father noted that one of their old comrades had moved from St. Louis to Florida to get away from the snow. The letter continues:

Speaking of snow brings to mind that I never saw snow until the war. You see, I've always lived in the Deep South. It was November 1944 and Company G was poised outside a village occupied by our German cousins. We dug in and prepared to attack on the morrow. McAllister and I dug a hole and bedded down for the night. At dawn, we were covered with a blanket of snow. I was entranced by the sight and exclaimed that the snow was beautiful. McAllister didn't talk much, but he was so moved by my remark that he swore for about five minutes.

On another occasion, we were in Luxembourg climbing steep hills that looked like mountains to me. McAllister was stringing wire and lugging field telephones. It was so steep we handed our weapon and packs to the man ahead of us, and they helped pull us up. I paused to look back, and McAllister demanded to know what the hell was holding me up. I told him the scene below us reminded me of a Christmas card, all the trees and snow. I knew that McAllister was exhausted, but he was able to express himself with a flood of curses that included all of the Ardennes and Central Europe and the war in general.

Mike, I've Got a Little Task for You
A memory in story form written circa 1979–82

It was raining as I made my way through the drippy woods to an open area where officers of the 2nd Battalion stood in a semicircle holding their map cases. I sidled up beside Lieutenant Damkowitch.[10]

Colonel Perdue paused and lit a cigar. He puffed several times, withdrew the cigar, and regarded it with a frown. "Day before yesterday, the 319th took St. Avold. They are waiting for us to relieve them. It's possible we'll remain there through Christmas. We're scheduled to take special training to crack the Siegfried Line. Any questions? If not, the 2nd Battalion will proceed to St. Avold, about twelve kilometers from here." Colonel Perdue looked around, "Mike, where are you?"

"Here, sir," responded Lieutenant Damkowitch.

Colonel Perdue shifted his cigar and grinned, "Mike, I've got a little task for you. Shouldn't be much to it. We bypassed a German camp called Teting Camp. The G-2 people say it was used to hold political prisoners. They think a small force was left when the garrison pulled back. It shouldn't cause a problem."[11]

"Sir," called out Lieutenant Damkowitch, "Where is the camp?"

"It's just out of St. Avold. Here, look at the map. See the juncture of these two roads? That's it, about two kilometers from St. Avold. Got it?"

"Yes, sir," replied Lieutenant Damkowitch, circling the juncture of the two roads on his map.

Colonel Perdue grinned, "Good luck, Mike." He viewed his soggy cigar and flung it to the ground, muttering, "Damn German cigars taste like burnt paper."

Teting Camp—I visualized an installation similar to Camp Shelby in Mississippi—rows of drab wooden hutments with minimum security. As we reached the gate, I was amazed to see that it was constructed like a fort with barred buildings and formidable concrete walls. A steel and concrete pillbox commanded the courtyard.

Sergeant Oswald, leader of the advance patrol, said later, "We could have taken the camp easy, without firing a shot. The patrol slipped up on the camp undetected. The gates were open and a group of Krauts were sitting around in the courtyard—several had their shirts off sunning. We had them easy, but the guy on point got trigger happy and before I could stop him he started firing. That did it."

As the shots rang out, the startled German soldiers fled, some to the pillbox, others disappearing into the buildings. Several German soldiers fell to the ground, wounded.

All opportunity of a surprise capture evaporated—there was nothing to do but attack. Sergeant Oswald yelled, "Let's go!" and his patrol dashed through the gates, firing as they ran. The balance of George Company followed and fanned out with rifles held at high port. They raced across the courtyard yelling, "Hey! Hey!" at the top of their lungs.

The machine guns in the pillbox sounded like tearing canvas as puffs of dirt appeared in rows on the ground. I ran toward a building, gasping for air. At each burst of the machine gun, soldiers tripped, stumbled, and lay sprawled on the ground.

As I ran, the horizon moved up and down with each step. A doorway loomed and I frantically twisted the knob. The door was locked. I turned to run and an automatic weapon chattered. I looked back and saw an irregular pattern of holes appear in the door—splinters popped up. Somebody was firing wildly through the locked door with a tearing, vibrating sensation. My body trembled.

From the corner of my eye, I spied McAllister. He was sidling along beside the building, clutching a grenade. As I scurried around the corner of the building, I heard the tinkle of broken glass followed by the muffled explosion of a grenade. The automatic weapon firing ceased. I took a deep breath, then realized my left leg was cold, sticky, and wet. My left boot squished and a wave of nausea swept over me as I crouched against the building.

Sergeant McAllister sprinted past the doorway and crouched beside me. His breathing was labored. He shook my arm and gasped, "Say, you all right? Your face is gray."

Shouts, clattering rifle fire, and muffled explosions filled the air. "I don't know," I faltered. "I think I've been hit. My leg—it feels like it's bleeding."

"Let me take a look."

"Yeah," I said. "Funny, I don't feel any pain."

"Boy, you were lucky," exclaimed McAllister. "Your pack is demolished and your canteen is riddled—that's what wet your leg."

"Thanks, Mac," I sighed.

Abruptly, there was silence. Patrols cautiously searched the buildings and collected the German soldiers that failed to make it to the pillbox. The seventeen terrified prisoners were questioned by Corporal Decker, the company interpreter. Decker then told us they were a service unit ordered to remain after the garrison withdrew. They were told that we were bloodthirsty and killed our prisoners. They were awaiting orders when we arrived.[12]

Two medics clad in white helmets with conspicuous red crosses stood by with field cases of first aid equipment. Corporal Decker selected eight of the prisoners, laid down his own rifle, and they all edged cautiously into the courtyard waving a white handkerchief. The pillbox was silent. Two medics ministered to the wounded. Corporal Decker cupped his mouth with both hands and shouted in the direction of the pillbox. After a slight pause, the hatch opened and a white flag appeared. The German soldiers filed out, helmetless and holding their hands behind their heads.[13]

It was drizzling when George Company finally arrived in St. Avold. The original plan was to quarter the troops in a row of modern, well-furnished houses formerly occupied by officers of the German garrison. But the retreating Germans correctly diagnosed our plans and took measures that would have had dire consequences if we had not been warned. Loyal partisans reported that the Germans had installed time bombs, and several houses lay in shambles. Soldiers crowded into homes occupied by civilians. Sleeping cramped on the floor was preferable to a bomb scare.[14]

Chester Pierorazio, the mess sergeant, moved the field kitchen into a building next to an apartment building, and the chow line formed in the courtyard.

---

1 December 1944

France

My darling wife—

I hope you haven't been worried as I haven't been able to write much lately. We are moving around so much we don't have time for anything. We are on foot and you can imagine there's little time for the things you would like to do. I'm in the field and it's hard to write unless we find a farm or something. Tell Mother and all the folks you heard from me.

When we are on the move we eat K-rations, but they are not so bad. For breakfast they have a little can of eggs and some sort of meat, a fruit bar, crackers, cigarettes, and powdered coffee and sugar—the box is made of wax and we use that to heat the coffee—now that's not bad, is it? Of course, I would rather have my little wife fix breakfast, but this K-ration isn't too bad.

Dear, the country is very pretty but it's raining again and it sure is a pain in the neck.

Darling, I don't know when this terrible war will be over but I've sure prayed a lot since I've been here. I feel sorry for both sides—most of the prisoners we take think we are going to shoot them and are really pitiful. They have given me a pretty hard time but I still don't hate them.

All of us are hoping the war will soon end, but it's hard to say just when because the Germans are making us fight for every inch. I guess it will come as a complete surprise to both sides. Most of the prisoners look ragged and underfed, but I guess we look pretty rugged too.

I'll be so glad to get home to my little wife and lead a normal life again.

Lots of love

Your little husband

p.s. I love you dear.

———— ————

3 December 1944

France

My darling wife—

It's Sunday morning here and I can't help thinking about how we used to sleep late and eat breakfast together.

Dear, I wish I could be home with you for Xmas. We'll have to celebrate our anniversaries and holidays after the war. I wish to goodness this foolish war would end. I'm afraid it will be a lot longer now since some of our fat-bottomed congressmen told the Germans that we wanted unconditional surrender. Now the German prisoners tell us "what the hell" we are going to lose everything anyway so we may as well fight to the finish. If we would give them terms, they would quit now—when they give up, we could tear up the agreement. That's the way they do it. Maybe a lot of wives and sweethearts and mothers will get busy with Washington soon and get some action.

Honey, how are you getting along? Take good care of your sweet self, dear, and don't let anybody steal you away from me while I'm away.

Every time I see these old buildings, I think of Win Catherwood—I'll bet he would be disgusted if he could see the mud—even the main streets are covered with mud. The big churches are pretty but drafty and cold. Personally, I prefer steam heat and a little comfort. The water in France is very bad, and our engineers have to haul our drinking water a long distance. The houses have old-fashioned pumps in the kitchens. I can see my honeybun wife fussing if we had an apartment here. I don't know what the people do as I haven't seen a johnny yet. The soldiers have a trench and use that.

I had a pass when we were near Nancy and went to town. At one of the restaurants I had to go, and the men and women went into the same johnny—that beat me—the women went into the toilets and the men use the urinals. Men and women use the washroom together? I had to get out of there—phooey. Every now and then you see a French couple walking down the street, and if the man has to go, he just pulls up by a building and pulls out his dong and goes to it—the women don't pay any attention. The only thing wrong with that is that after several hundred years the towns smell like pee. Of course, some of the places are modern and progressive, but I'm talking about the little villages that I've seen.

The big towns are all behind us and are off-limits. The villages are all close together, and every one has a big church with a bell in the steeple that they ring when we arrive. Then the Germans knew where we were—it didn't take long to stop that. Our Company has taken several towns, and we can't trust the people at all. We put all the civilians in the cellars and don't let them out after dark. All the people speak German even though this is still France.

We took a town the other day and the German soldiers didn't even have time to pack. Dinner was still on the stove and clothes soaking in buckets. We wounded a German soldier, as there were bloody bandages in the hall and his gun was laying there where he dropped it. I guess he got away since none of our prisoners were wounded. Too many of these folks here have relatives in the German army to suit me.

Dear, I wish I could tell you some good news, but all I know is the war. That's why you mean so much to me—No matter how rough it is, I think of you and the nice times we used to have.

Dear little wife, I've got some work to do so I better get at it.

Lots of love

Your little Husband

p.s. I love you dear.

3 December 1944

France

My darling sweetheart—

Dear, I'm glad you like your work, and I'm very proud of you—you are the smartest wife there ever was. I'll be so glad to get home to you. I think I'll swim when they finally let me go.

Wartime workers at the Naval Air Station in Jacksonville. Elizabeth is on the right.

We just fought a big battle the other day, but I don't think it will have anything to do with ending the war soon. The enemy is resisting too strongly. All the prisoners seem to think we are going to shoot them. Too bad we all don't live in peace. The Lord has certainly looked after me, and I'm really going to be a good boy from now on.[15]

I have plenty of warm clothes, but laundry is out of the question. We get clean sox every day when we draw our rations, but we wear the rest of our clothes for several weeks at a time.

Honey, I don't think you would go for France so much. Quaint or not, the stable is right in the house and boy does it smell up the joint. This is beautiful country though, pretty hills and trees that look like pictures. During a battle the other day, we had to climb a hill and I couldn't help but stop to admire the place—it sure is too bad we have to be here under these circumstances.

I'm sorry to hear they are going to give Jesse sea duty—but maybe they will change their minds. I guess Albert will be over here with me soon. We are really glad to see the air corps when they come out to give us a hand. In fact, the artillery men, tank men, and all get along swell over here.[16]

I still have my pen you gave me—it sure comes in handy. Most of my personal belongings have been scattered all over France, but I managed to hang on to my pen and notebook and pocketbook you gave me.

Lots of love dear

Your little husband

p.s. I love you, kid.

——— ———

4 December 1944

France

My dear little honeybun—

Hello honey—just a little note to tell you I love you. Did you know it? It's raining and dark as pitch outside. The Germans could get right in with us and we would never know it. One of the men is fixing something on the stove for us to eat. He calls it foxhole pudding. It's made out of parts of K-rations—crackers, fruit bar, lemon powder, caramel candy all put together in a can and heated with a little water. It makes a pudding that tastes something like apple sauce—pretty good, too.

We had a treat today. The special services officer brought the moving picture machine and we saw "Phantom Lady." The soundtrack broke down several times, but it was good anyway.

I went to church in a barn across the street. We sang some Xmas carols, sure made me homesick. I haven't been to any of the church services in the big churches as they are all Catholic and I'm afraid I wouldn't understand it.

Just stopped for a minute to eat my pudding—it hit the spot. The men spend a lot of time messing around with their rations experimenting— guess they will drive their wives crazy fooling around the kitchen when they get home. I'm writing by the light of a rag stuck in a bottle of gasoline and it smokes and flickers so I can hardly see the paper.

Dear it's about time for me to turn in so I'll tell you good night for now.

Lots of love,

Your little husband

p.s. I love you.

Whispering in the Dark

A memory written in 1947

Company G made a night approach by compass through a heavily wooded area near St. Avold, France. We had captured several German prisoners

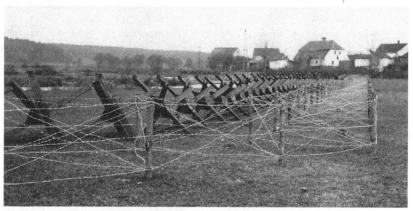

Captured German photo. It was mailed to Elizabeth with these words on the back: "More obstacles that make our visit to Germany interesting. About where the camera was in the picture a German machine gun is usually dug into a hole in the ground. When the men bunch up to get over it, they shoot us down."

that were on patrol. We were operating independently and couldn't spare a man to take the prisoners to the rear. They were taken along on the attack at the end of the column.

A short time later, the company entered a thickly wooded section of the forest. It was so dark that each man held onto the pack of the man in front as we moved in single file. When the column was ready to move, each man whispered to the man in front, and when word reached the head of the column, the men moved cautiously forward.

Various messages went up and down the column, "Moving too fast," "Hold up, somebody has broken the chain," "Keep a sharp lookout," etc.

The column stopped, and a message came down the line, "Barbed wire ahead." Then another, "Pass up wire cutters." Wire cutters were passed forward. While we waited, another message came back, "Where in hell did those wire cutters come from?" The reply, passed man-by-man, "We lost ours, so we borrowed a pair from the prisoners."

———

11 December 1944
France
My dear little wife,

Gee, I missed a couple of days writing you. I hope you'll forgive me honeybun.

We moved into a fairly large town for a rest and the town is really beautiful. I was surprised as most of these little towns are pretty dirty. We are in the same houses the Germans had, and the house I'm in has steam heat and the barn isn't next to the bedroom. Of course, I have to sleep on the floor but I don't mind—it's swell.

We have a clock on our wall that chimes every quarter hour and is sure pretty. I'll hate to leave here.

The building and houses close by were all occupied by big German officials. The Germans put time bombs under most of the houses they used, and really made a mess of things. The house we are in had some civilians living in the cellar, so we think it is safe. I can't tell you how nice these houses are—modern too. The Germans, according to the civilians, ran all the people out of the houses or made them use the cellars when they were here. Nearby is a large concentration camp where the Germans used to keep political prisoners and the big officials lived across the street from where I am.[17]

The news is not much, but the air is full of rumors of an early peace agreement. They can't agree too soon to suit me—I'm ready to come home to my little angel.

Good night dear heart
Your little husband
p.s. I love you, kid.

———— ————

12 December 1944
France
My darling wife—

I just received your sweet letter you wrote me on 2 Dec—you know, the one where you described the hit parade—I haven't heard a popular tune in so long I don't know what I would do if I heard one. Every now and then when we are a good distance back, the Red Cross comes up with some old records and a record player. We listen to some old jitterbug music while we eat a doughnut and drink coffee—nice, huh?

The town we are in is swell—mainly because we are quite a distance from the front right now and secondly 'cause it's the only town we've occupied that we didn't have to capture ourselves. Our sister regiment took it for us. This writing paper came from a Nazi headquarters we took over. Nice, isn't it? I can't get over how nice the houses are here. Modern and everything, that is, if you don't mind a few shell holes. The artillery really plays the dickens with houses.

Dear, I sure am proud of you—being promoted to a supervisor. You are the smartest wife there ever was. You are everything a man could ever wish for.

Lots of love
Your little husband
p.s. I love you, kid.

13 December 1944

My dear little wife—

There isn't much news here that I know of—you know how it is—the closer you are to the thing, the less you know about it. One of the men who speaks German in the company has been talking to the civilians here, and they said this was quite a propaganda center for the Germans, and the Gestapo had their headquarters here.[18]

According to some of the stories he picked up, the civilians were treated pretty rough. A lot of them were forced to go to Germany with them. The German soldiers made a census of the town and took all the men and put them in the German army. One of the stories he picked up was about a family that lived down the street from here—when the Gestapo men came to their house and wanted to know if they had any men there, the women said "no." So they looked in a book and said they lied—that they had a son old enough to be in the army. The son was hiding in a closet. The Gestapo men grabbed his grown sister, one of them cleared off a table and a couple of the Gestapo men laid the girl on the table and then they asked where the boy was—nobody said anything so they took off her pants and they held her legs apart and stuck a candle in her tallywhacker and lit it. After a while the hot wax made the girl pretty nervous so the boy tried to slip out and they caught him. Pretty bad isn't it?

Dear, it's time for your little husband to hit the hay, so I'll say goodnight darling—

Lots of love dear

Your little husband

p.s. I love you, kid.

I've Got Plans after the War Is Over

A memory in story form written circa 1979–82

Our Battalion was scheduled to breach the Siegfried Line, and all troops took special training on orders from headquarters. Each day, George Company hiked a short distance to an abandoned fort and practiced storming fortifications. Demolition experts demonstrated the use of explosives. To warnings of "fire in the hole!" teams of soldiers practiced placing satchel charges of dynamite. Mortar sections fired grappling hooks and rope over the fort walls. Soldiers with slung rifles climbed up and over. It was a grueling exercise.

Each afternoon, a messenger delivered classified intelligence reports from Battalion. The reports contained the daily password, a summary of the situation, and other intelligence information. On the 13th of December, there was information of enemy activity above the Ardennes Forest. Not fully known to us, German troops were moving, and armored units and trucks were massing along the edge of the forest.

Enemy activity in the Ardennes was far from us. We were south of that area, and it wasn't in our sector. All was quiet in St. Avold, and rumors that we would stay quiet through Christmas were comforting.

Replacements arrived. One of the newcomers was a Sergeant Weatherby. As we shook hands, I said, "Weatherby, leave your gear here. You'll remain with Company Headquarters."

I turned to Sergeant Moors, "Joe, I'm assigning you to the first platoon. There are a lot of new replacements in Sergeant Anuskiewicz's platoon, and he'll need your help."[19]

"Okay, Sarge," responded Sergeant Moors, "I'll grab my gear and report to him." He smiled, "I'll miss you, Sarge, and thanks for everything."

"It's okay, Moors. I'll be seeing you around."

Some days later, I was standing in the chow line next to Sergeant Moors. We paired off and ate together.

"We're getting along swell, me and Anuskiewicz," Moors said between bites. "He leads the platoon, and I act as platoon guide, bringing up the rear. I don't want to take too many chances," he grinned. "I've got plans after the war is over."

"Oh," I exclaimed. "You got a letter from the girl in Philadelphia?"

"Three," he said with a dreamy expression. "I did as you suggested—I just told her my feelings for her. Then I sweated out her reply. When her letter came, I was so nervous I dropped it several times when I tried to open it."

"I started breathing again when she said she felt the same way about me. She said she never knew anyone like me and confessed that she had been afraid that maybe I didn't like her. Imagine that." Sergeant Moors's eyes sparkled, "She told me about herself—she's been married and has a little boy. Her husband died at Pearl Harbor. I'll write my folks tomorrow and tell them about her." He looked at me. "Thanks for urging me to write to her."

It was the 15th of December, 1944.

3

THE ARDENNES-ALSACE CAMPAIGN

16 December 1944–25 January 1945

Smitty, all hell has broken loose.

On the 16th of December, German forces attacked through the Ardennes region to begin what became the Battle of the Bulge. The bulge in the lines was north of where my father and the 80th Division were located in St. Avold.

Two days later, General Patton made a commitment to his superiors, Eisenhower and Bradley, to move the 80th and two other divisions to meet the German attack. They had been moving in an easterly direction, but by the 22nd of December, the division turned to the north to intercept the breakthrough and relieve overwhelmed American troops.

Before Christmas, my father and the 80th Division met the German attack in northwest Luxembourg. It took several weeks to defeat the German offensive, and my father's company finally crossed the border into Germany on 12 February 1945.

---

18 December 1944

My darling wife—

Dear I received two letters from you today, and I was so glad to hear from my little angel. I guess one reason you have been having trouble getting my letters is 'cause the big Xmas rush is jamming up everywhere. We passed our mail depot the other day, and you never saw such a mess. Packages all over.

I sure love you dear and wish I could be with you tonight. The guys are singing, "I'll be back in a year, little darling," and the place is in an uproar.

Honey, when this war is over, I'll sure rush to you. I get the willies being separated from you.

I couldn't locate any stationary so I had to use this—it's out of a German office—but it will have to do.

Dear, I sure love you. I can't tell you how much in a lifetime, but you are everything to me. I think of you all the time and you are with me in all my dreams.

Dear I sure would like to be with you this Xmas—I'm about as far away as I could possibly get—almost around the world. And I'm just living until I can get back.

    Good night dearest

    Your little husband

p.s. I love you, kid.

Original 18 December 1944 letter written on German ledger paper

The Bastards Are Freezing Us, Frightening Us, and Hiking Us to Death

A memory in story form written circa 1979–82

On the 16th of December, Special Services installed a generator and movie projector in the St. Avold local cinema, and *Gaslight* was the afternoon feature. Lieutenant Damkowitch was talking on the field telephone as I walked into company headquarters. The communications sergeant was monitoring a radio message. Something was amiss—I could feel it. An air of urgency permeated the room. Lieutenant Damkowitch said, "Yes, sir" several times. "Yes, sir, I understand. We'll be ready, sir." He returned the telephone receiver with a stunned expression. He removed his helmet and ran his fingers through his hair.

"Smitty, all hell has broke loose. The Germans have penetrated our lines and they're racing toward Paris. All is in confusion. They made a break-through somewhere north of us. We're on red alert to move out tomorrow morning."

On Sunday, 17 December, at 0745, George Company was standing at ease in the staging area. Everybody was wondering what had happened. Soldiers were clad in field uniforms, overcoats, two bandoliers of ammunition, and rifle. Their field pack contained K-rations, a blanket, and a raincoat.

The colonel's jeep rolled to a stop at the staging area shortly before 0800. "Hey, Mike," he called, "the trucks are on the way." Mike asked, "Any news about where we're going?" "Not yet, Mike," was the reply. "Everything is confusion. The entire front is fluid. We'll proceed north and receive instructions by radio."

The truck arrived, and chains rattled as the drivers released the tailgates for troops to clamber aboard. The truck motors raced, gears shifted, and bodies swayed as we left St. Avold behind. For thirty-six hours, the rumbling trucks followed a zig-zag course, sometimes doubling back. A solider exclaimed, "Hey, that road sign, I've seen it twice—the same sign." Steadily the convoy moved, pausing only for rest stops or to take on fuel. Snowflakes were softly falling as George Company detrucked at the outskirts of Luxembourg City.

The Ardennes Campaign commenced in a mélange of confusion that turned into a series of forced marches, pitched battles, tank skirmishes,

artillery duels, rumors of atrocities and gas attacks, and bewildering ma-
neuvers to maintain pressure on the enemy.

Soon, George Company was in a holding position on the side of a hill.
The Germans were on the opposite side of the hill, unable to advance; nor
could we. Tanks had been called for but had not arrived. To bolster morale
during the impasse, the colonel ordered the kitchen train to prepare two
hot meals a day, breakfast and supper. A jeep delivered the hot chow under
cover of darkness. Usually it was something that could be held in the hand
and hot coffee.

Our dream of Christmas in quiet St. Avold, and an early end to the
war was dashed by the stunning German breakthrough. What followed
was a nightmare of confusion, hardship, endurance, and sheer terror. The
Ardennes Campaign raged on with no end in sight. In the snow-covered
forests and mountains, the 2nd Battalion collided with an enemy clad in
white suits and parts of American uniforms. In our sector, the front was
shifting and fluid, marked by blitz attacks and sudden withdrawals. Artillery fire caught us with devastating results. Sergeant Bailey expressed
everybody's sentiments when he said, "The bastards are freezing us, frightening us, and hiking us to death."

Dry Socks and a Hot Cup of Coffee

A memory written in 1947

When the German Army attacked through the Ardennes, our company
was in a rest area near St. Avold in France. We received the alert order,
and we immediately loaded on trucks and set out to intercept the German
breakthrough.

Forty-eight hours later, we were in the vicinity of Luxembourg City and
set out on a forced march in driving snow to the high ground outside the
city. When we arrived at our sector, we found that it covered almost two
thousand yards, a distance too great for us to control effectively except by
patrols.[1]

On one of the patrol routes, we noticed a deserted chateau. We entered
a large room on the first floor and built a roaring fire in the huge porcelain
stove in the corner. We were unable to remain until our overcoats could
dry, but we each washed out a pair of socks and hung them by the stove to

dry. One of the men had a can of powdered coffee, so we put on a pot of water. When we returned in a couple of hours, at least we would have dry socks and a hot cup of coffee.

On our return trip, the fire was still burning brightly, but in place of the pot of coffee there was a pot of simmering water and on the line by the stove, still damp, were the same number of freshly washed socks, German issue.

---

22 December 1944

V-Mail

My darling wife—

Just a note dearest to tell you I am thinking of you and wish I could be with you for Xmas. It's snowing here and the whole countryside is covered. It looks like an Xmas card.

Dear, I love you more and more every day and can hardly wait until I can return to you.

The women here really have to work hard. Every day we see them working in the fields and scrubbing and washing. I'm glad my little angel lives in the USA. At least you don't have to plough.

I have no news except we all hope and pray for an early peace agreement.

> With all my love
> Your little husband

p.s. I love you, kid.

A Sign of Home

A memory written in 1947

A company of American soldiers got off a truck in a wooded area somewhere in Luxembourg. They adjusted their packs and fell in silently on each side of the road. This was the farthest point that could be reached by vehicle, and from there on, movement would be on foot.

Orders were passed down that the company would continue the march until the enemy was contacted. This was a solemn occasion—the soldiers had been transferred from another active sector and the strain was visible on their faces. There was never enough time to sleep. Faces were covered with one, two, three weeks of stubble. And with the exception of socks, their clothes hadn't been changed for a month. Each man carried a full belt of ammunition and across each shoulder was slung a full bandolier. Two hand grenades hung on the hooks of their pack straps. The older men were chain-smoking as they trudged down the road. It began to sleet, and the prospect of spending another night in the slushy cold mud was depressing.

Thoughts turned to home, a cheery fire, steam heat, home-cooked food, loved ones.

Around a turn in the road was a small deserted inn that had been partially destroyed by artillery. There was a familiar sign on the wall. Each homesick man gazed at it as long as he could, and somehow it seemed to pep them up. Within a few minutes I was abreast of the sign, and with a curious lump in my throat read an old familiar slogan in German: "Trink Coca-Cola."

The Ravine

A memory in story form written circa 1979–82

On 19 December, Company G detrucked in Luxembourg City and set out on foot toward Bastogne. It was a forced march—hike fifty minutes and rest ten. On 23 December at 2130, the 2nd Battalion was trudging across an open field near the village of Neiderfulen, then stopped as scouts probed the woods ahead. Exhausted, the soldiers flopped in the snow and dozed.[2]

At the sound of automatic weapons, the soldiers became wide-eyed in terror. They frantically slithered toward a depression in the ground as tracer bullets seemed to float across the field. In the moonlight, I saw Lieutenant Coputo blindly stumbling around holding out both hands. I raised up and yelled, "Hey, Lieutenant! Over here!" I reached out to take his arm, causing him to cry out, "No, no, let me hold your arm. I can't see—what's happening?"

I shoved him into a slight depression and shouted, "They waited until we were spread out in the field, then they opened up with machine guns." He clutched my arm as we crawled to a safer dip in the terrain. "Lay low," I cried. "Let's hold up here."

Over the shouts and cracks of rifles, I heard Sergeant Anuskiewicz's shrill voice scream for the First Platoon. As the crouched men rallied, I saw Sergeant Moors struggle to one knee and look around. He spied me and as he moved forward he called, "See you later, Sarge." Tracer bullets whined as the First Platoon slogged through drifts of snow shouting, "Hey! Hey!" and firing their rifles into the wooded area.[3]

"What happened to 'Sergeant Weatherby'?" I asked.

"I don't know," replied Lieutenant Coputo. "When the machine gun opened up, I felt him lurch and stagger, and I lost my grip on his arm. I can't see at night—he was my guide." Brave Lieutenant Coputo. The bullets that cut down Sergeant Weatherby exposed his night blindness, ending his career as a combat troop leader.[4]

Waves of soldiers surged toward the wooded area. They ran forward then flopped prone in the snow. Then forward again, but some did not get up as cries of "Medic! Medic!" from the wounded filled our ears. I scurried along with Lieutenant Coputo clutching my arm. Somebody was shouting for the mortars. A Browning automatic rifle was thunking. What was left of the First Platoon huddled behind a swell of land short of the wooded area. Sergeant Anuskiewicz was directing the fire when his voice was cut off in the middle of a command.

Four medium tanks, grinding and screeching, rumbled up behind a snowdrift and halted. Soldiers scrambled to shouts of "Fall in behind the tanks!"

Derisive, mocking cries came from the wooded area. A loudspeaker blared in English, "Come on, you American bastards—death will set you free." Our tanks responded with a deafening salvo. Firing point-blank into the woods, the tanks clanked forward followed by crouched soldiers with tense stomach muscles.

Bullets whined and pinged as they ricocheted off the tanks. Suddenly, I saw clusters of stars. My helmet was ripped from my head by a ricocheting bullet. The landscape flipped upside down as I stumbled into loose barbed wire. The end of the barbed wire wound around a tank tread and I felt my body being dragged behind the tank. From afar, I heard Lieutenant Coputo pounding on the side of the tank yelling, "Stop! Damnit, Stop!" Somebody—I think it was McAllister—snipped the wire and helped me to my feet.[5]

"You all right?" he cried.

"Sure," I replied. "I bleed more than this when I shave."

The Germans had carefully chosen the terrain to make their stand. Concealed from the tanks, there was a deep ravine at the edge of the woods. As the tanks tottered on the brink, Panzerfausts blasted the tank treads. Automatic weapons cut the tankers down as they attempted to leap from the disabled tanks. I shoved Lieutenant Coputo against a large tree as bullets thunked against the trunk.

Shouts and jeers rang out from the German soldiers as flames engulfed the tanks. With shouts of "fall back," we set up a perimeter defense. Behind a swell in the ground, soldiers fell to hacking slit trenches in the frozen earth. The plaintive cries of the wounded were mingled with the sounds of entrenching tools and the whumps of exploding shells in the flaming tanks. The light of the dancing flames revealed a dead unarmed medic, his body sprawled across a moaning soldier.

I paused in my digging and called to Sergeant McAllister, "Say, Mac, you think they'll attack?"

"Naw, I don't think so," he replied, leaning on his entrenching tool. "They'd be crazy. They picked the terrain, hit us in the dark, and pulled back. My bet is the main body has pulled out and left a token force to harass us."[6]

The next day was Christmas Eve, 1944.

Dawn found the 2nd Battalion in a perimeter defense to stave off a possible attack. I nervously peered around. Soldiers were dug in a large circular pattern. Company H had mounted the heavy machine guns in sections. A soldier flopped by me and said, "Say, can I borrow your entrenching tool?"

"Where's yours?" I asked.

He shrugged, "I don't know. How about it, can I use yours?"

"Yeah, I guess so," I answered, and when I turned my body to unhook the shovel I heard a sound like an angry bee. I turned back to see the kneeling soldier staring into space with sightless eyes. Frantically, I peered into the wooded area but couldn't determine where the shot came from. I winced and recalled a saying, "You don't hear the bullet that gets you."

A squad of infantry made an assault toward the woods. Horrified, I watched as soldiers twisted or partly turned as they were picked off by snipers. My eyes rested on a soldier studying the terrain through binoculars when he abruptly stood, twisted, and fell into the snow. Our heavy machine guns sprayed the woods with bursts of six. As machine gunners were picked off, another would pull aside the body and take his place.

I was digging out my emergency chocolate ration when Private Koedam, lugging a bazooka, flopped beside me. He was excited, "Sarge! Sarge!" he hollered, "I found 'em, I found 'em—them guys."[7]

"Calm down, Koedam," I cried. "Whatcha trying to say?"

"Them guys shooting at us—I know where they are."

"You do?" I stared at the excited soldier, then yelled, "Come on, Koedam!" I pointed, "Lieutenant Damkowitch is over there. Follow me."

Crouched low, we scurried across the open space to Lieutenant Damkowitch's slit trench. He listened to Private Koedam then said, "How'd you happen to see them?"

"I had to go," he explained. "You know, nature called. I looked around and spotted a ravine. I crawled to the ravine, slithered across, and climbed into the woods. While I was squatting, I looked up and saw part of a building through the trees. Later, I eased closer and saw 'em."

"Where are they from here?" asked Lieutenant Damkowitch.

Koedam looked back, "I was over there—that's the ravine—you can't see it till you're right on it." He pointed, "I crawled into the woods about there. The building is about a hundred yards thataway."

"Can you guide us?"

"Yes sir, no sweat—there's the ravine. That's where I crawled into the woods to take a—"

"Okay, Koedam," Lieutenant Damkowitch waved his hand. "Hey, McAllister," he called to the communications sergeant. "Round up a squad of riflemen—have 'em follow us," he said, pointing toward the ravine. "We'll need ammo bearers and a BAR team," he added.

"Yes sir," replied Sergeant McAllister.

Lieutenant Damkowitch pointed to the bazooka, "Soldier, can you fire that?"

"Yep," said Private Koedam. "I qualified on the range."

"Okay, okay," interrupted Lieutenant Damkowitch. "Hey, Smith, let's move it! Everybody stay low—pass the word."

The detachment—with Private Koedam guiding—cautiously made their way into the woods. Suddenly Koedam held up his arm and pointed. Partly concealed by icy foliage was what looked like a weather-beaten barn. The loft had windows that overlooked the field where the stalled 2nd Battalion was held up.

McAllister was right, I thought. The main body must have withdrawn and left a contingent of sharpshooters to harass us.

Lieutenant Damkowitch signaled with his hands, and the riflemen and BAR team covered the barn. He pointed to a window in the barn, and Koedam nodded his head. Private Koedam, accompanied by his ammo bearer, cautiously worked their way toward the barn.

German rifles cracked. Private Koedam looked back, and Lieutenant Damkowitch waved his hand. Koedam nodded and hefted the bazooka. The ammo bearer unsnapped the rocket pouch and took a position in back of Private Koedam, slipped a rocket into the bazooka tube, then moved aside. Koedam sighted and pressed the firing mechanism. A whooshing noise and the rocket arched toward the barn. A miracle, the rocket went through the window. The barn roof appeared to raise, and a fraction of a second later, there was a terrific explosion.

Flames and smoke boiled from the barn windows. Gasping, dazed, and confused German soldiers stumbled out of the building into the line of fire of the American infantrymen. The BAR team held their weapons hip-high and forced the barrel down with the left hand as they fired. The snow-covered bushes quivered from the muzzle blasts as fleeing German soldiers jerked and turned as the heavy bullets ripped into their bodies. Wary rifle-men crept cautiously into the barn. Parts of bodies littered the floor.

A soldier with a shattered arm was staring at us from the floor. His collar bore the double "S" insignia of the elite troops. He sneered, "Ha, you were observed for two days!" He spoke in English, "If we had our heavy machine guns, all of you would be dead." He expired cursing us.

---

27 December 1944
V-Mail
My darling wife,

Dearest sweetheart—just a line to let you know I'm well and miss you so much. I hope you had a nice Xmas—we had it pretty rough here as you have no doubt read in the papers by now.

Honey, the war news doesn't look so encouraging, but I'm still hoping it will be over soon and I can rush home to you. I believe I love you more and more every day if that's possible, and I think of you all the time.

Good night dearest. I'll write again as soon as I can.

Lots of love dear

Your little husband

p.s. I love you, dear.

———————

28 December 1944

My darling wife—

I love you honey—I miss you more and more every day and only live for the day I can return to you.

I had a pretty miserable Xmas as we were in foxholes and trenches until early Xmas morning, and then we went into a town to get warm. About three o'clock in the afternoon the kitchen brought us up a turkey dinner, for which we were very thankful.

The country is beautiful here—snow-covered hills and fir trees. The ground is frozen and it sure seems funny after living in Florida, where the ground never freezes. I think you would like the country here if we could visit it after the war. This part of the country is much more progressive than where I was before, but the stables are still in the houses.

Honey—I'm sure glad you are getting along so well with your job and I'm sure you'll get a "4" rating, as you are the smartest one. I noticed on my payroll sheet that they are deducting for your allowances and I hope you receive them okay.

I had a letter from Mother the other day. She brought me up to date on the home news. I guess Betty Sue is growing up fast now. It seems like I've been gone for years.

Goodbye for now dear

Your little husband

p.s. I love you dear.

5 January 1945

Happy New Year dear—

This is the first opportunity I've had to write you since the new year started, but I want you to know I've thought about you every minute and though sometimes my letters are quite a distance apart, you are always with me in my every thought. Lots of times it's hard or impossible to write at all.

Dear little wife, I believe I love you more and more every day and I pray each day that the war will soon end and that we may all return home. However, the German prisoners tell us they can hold out two years or more if necessary. They are fighting us from ditch to ditch, hill to hill, town to town. Recently, they've been pushing us around a little, as you have no doubt seen by the papers.

Dear heart, I think of you all the time. We will start our life all over again—it may be a late start but we'll do it.

    Lots of love dear

    Your little husband

p.s. I love you.

---

5 January 1945

My darling wife—

Hello honey. I'm at a rest camp in Nancy for a few days, and it's swell. The building is a girls' school or convent converted to a military rest camp. We have breakfast at 0745 and then we can go back to bed or do anything we want to—it's very nice.[8]

We had been in foxholes for over a week and in freezing weather. The other day, I poured out some water in my cup, and before I could light the heating unit (little wax box) to make my coffee, the water froze solid. I spent New Year's Eve in a hole in the ground. The holidays don't mean much here, I guess.

It's awfully cold here just now and the snow makes everything white. I guess you thought I had forgotten to write, but since Xmas, we've had to stay right out in the snow as the Germans were giving us a hard time, and I'm afraid it will be a long war unless some of our fat-bottomed congressmen get on the ball and offer some kind of peace terms, and when we get our occupation inside Germany to tear up the agreement. That's the way they do it.

Darling, I'm getting tired of this and I'm ready to come home to my little wife. I pray each day that the leaders of each side will soon see that war doesn't prove a thing and it is a foolish waste of time and lives.

Darling little wife—I love you more and more every day and can hardly wait until I can come home to you.

Lots of love dear—

Your little husband

p.s. I love you.

Understrength

This is from a 1982 letter Smith wrote to fellow veteran Gerald Myers. The event described would have occurred on 9 January 1945.

You mentioned the town of Heiderscheid. We didn't make it, and it was partly my fault. Originally, we were to take up a position outside Heiderscheid. That we did—remember the frozen haystacks? Then a captain, the adjutant, showed up. He couldn't raise us on the radio—the transmitter was frozen. Easy and Fox Companies wandered off the course, and there was no contact.

We were understrength and only had one light machine gun. Sergeant Lyles had to use his foot to move the cocking lever. I couldn't pull the bolt on my carbine because it was frozen. The adjutant brought word for us to seize Heiderscheid. We sallied forth across a field and were raked with automatic weapons fire. The Germans were using flashless and smokeless ammunition. My lungs were about to burst, and I laid in the snow to catch my breath. A medic kneeled beside me, and a burst got him. I scrambled from under him and scurried to a draw. Sergeant Lyles was mounting the light machine gun. Other soldiers tumbled into the draw.

Lyles fired a burst of six, and the gun looked like a ball of fire. The Germans must not have had mortars or we'd have been done for. I was scared stiff and told Mike we were crazy to tackle that town by ourselves. He agreed and we had to withdraw a few at a time as Sergeant Lyles covered us by firing sporadic bursts. My urging Mike to fall back to our original position until we located Easy and Fox caused his promotion to captain to be held up. I told him if there was a court-martial, I would be glad to testify—I was pissed off. Gerald, we didn't have forty men, and they wanted us to do a job that required a battalion. Crazy.

---

10 January 1945

My darling angel—

There isn't much news that's good. It gets kinda discouraging. I was looking at my pictures in my billfold today—makes me homesick for you, dear. I received your letter with the photo of you in your new bathing suit—Wow! You'll get me excited.

Dear, I miss you so much. I love you more than I could ever possibly tell you in a hundred years. I'm afraid you're going to have a hard time with my smoking as I've been smoking cigarettes. Everybody gets issued a pack a day so I started smoking them until I can get some cigars. Now I have a smelly old pipe too. Maybe you'll be able to get me in hand when I get back

Elizabeth
in a photo
accompanying
this letter

home to you. A guy really goes to the dickens when his wife isn't around handy, doesn't he? Dear I'm only living until we are reunited, and I pray every day that the leaders on both sides will soon see light and stop this foolish war. All it does is bring misery to everybody. Dear, I wish I could give you a big good night kiss—

Lots of love

Your little husband

p.s. I love you, kid.

---

13 January 1945

Dear little wife—

Hello honey—just a little note to tell you I love you very much. We have just received permission to disclose our whereabouts, so I'll tell you now that I'm somewhere in the Duchy of Luxembourg.

The people here are much more progressive than the French. This place is really picturesque, with high hills and villages in the valleys. Just like a Xmas card. It's really cold here—deep snow all over the place. We have our headquarters in a shell-riddled house, but we managed to scout around and find a stove, only to discover the room didn't have a flue so we had to poke the stovepipe out the window. They really have some screwy stoves here—nothing like ours—we have a helluva time keeping it from smoking. I don't remember if I sent you a piece of French money or not, so I'll enclose a piece of Luxembourg money. It's a facsimile of theirs and printed by us. This piece is worth about 23 cents in our money.

I received a box from the American News Co. They sent shaving stuff, books, candy, and cigarettes. I guess my boxes from home were destroyed by the enemy as our division lost about 6 tons of Xmas packages by enemy artillery fire. While I was in Nancy, the PX truck came by our company, and lo and behold they had some cigars. The men all bought some and saved them for me—now wasn't that sweet?

Good night, honey, and if I haven't mentioned it before, I think you are the most wonderful wife in the world.

Lots of love

Your little husband

p.s. I love you, kid.

15 January 1945

My dearest wife—

I just received two sweet letters from you, long ones too, the ones you wrote the 27th and 29th of December. That's pretty good time, just a little over two weeks.

The Germans really gave us a hard time for a while, and we are still not too sure of the outcome. We had to make a rush trip up here to help hold them off. My division, the 80th, made a 150-mile trip by truck to the Duchy of Luxembourg. Then we marched on foot till we contacted the enemy. We went at it biting and scratching—this old stuff about the Germans running out of supplies is a lot of hooey. They've got plenty. Two days before Xmas, we started an attack, and by Xmas eve, the Krauts had us practically surrounded, so we had to dig little holes on the side of a hill and sit in them until we could slip away that night. New Year's we were in the same fix, but I had a nifty hole dug so I didn't mind too much.

A lot of funny things happen—one of our gun crews captured a Kraut gun and aimed it at the enemy. A Kraut ammunition truck brought up a load of ammunition in the dark, and our men helped unload it. Then the Kraut dashed off for another load—this time after he unloaded his truck we took him prisoner. I'll bet he was disgusted.

Dear heart, this is all very tiresome to me, and I would much rather be home with you (where I belong) than here. Dear, you are my inspiration, and without you I don't know what I would do.

Sure wish I could squeeze you in those striped pajamas. I'll bet you sure look cute in them.

> Good night honey
> Lots of love dear
> Your little husband

p.s. I love you—kid.

---

20 January 1945

My darling wife—

Dear, I have a little time so I'll sit down and have a little talk with my little wife. There's a lot of confusion here so I'll get in a corner and try to concentrate.

Every day I keep hoping a miracle will happen and the war will end—
But it keeps on going—

Our mail isn't coming through so good now—I guess everything is snow-bound. The snow and ice are pretty, but it's a pain in the neck to walk on.

Darling, the light is going out and I'll have to close for now. All the electric plants were destroyed here, and if you don't have a candle, you are out of luck here. I haven't seen by electric lights in a long time. Except when I was in Nancy.

Darling, I'm so glad you are getting along swell with your job. Gee! I sure am proud of you.

Lots of love dear—

Your little husband

p.s. I love you, dear

21 January 1945

A memory in story form written circa 1979–82

I saluted, "The men are assembled, sir." It was 20 January 1945.

Lieutenant Damkowitch glanced up from a map he had been studying. "Are all platoons represented?" he asked.

"Yes sir."

Stubbly bearded platoon leaders, overcoat collars turned up, shuffled around in the shell-torn barn. The farmhouse had been destroyed during the German blitz into Luxembourg, and the barn offered scant protection from the biting cold.

"Men," said Lieutenant Damkowitch, little puffs of vapor curled around his mouth, "men, here's the big picture." He held up the map and pointed. "Here we are in the open area. Over here is the hill. Beyond the hill is the town. That's our objective, the town. The colonel is sending Easy Company around the hill to attack on the flank while the rest of the 2nd Battalion, with Fox Company leading, will climb the hill and mount a frontal attack." Lieutenant Damkowitch paused. "Any questions?"

The men shuffled around. One of the platoon leaders asked, "That hill, is there anything in the wooded area?"

Lieutenant Damkowitch held up an aerial photograph. "The observation plane dropped down close to get this. Two men in Fox Company who are former forest rangers looked at the photo and agree the foliage has been disturbed. It may be a minefield. The former forest rangers volunteered to guide the Battalion so there won't be a problem there."

A voice spoke, "What's the line of march, sir?"

"Fox Company will lead, followed by Battalion, then George and How Companies. Easy Company will flank the hill. They'll make a racket and create confusion while we attack from the hill."

"Thank goodness we won't hit the minefield first," a voice murmured.

Lieutenant Damkowitch continued, "The colonel says he doesn't expect any opposition. Just walk in and take the town. He's already ordered the kitchen train to bring hot chow as soon as we secure the town. No sweat."

"What's the name of the town, sir?"

"Dirbach, or something that sounds like that."

Lieutenant Damkowitch looked around. "Men, that's it. After Fox and Battalion, we'll follow. Okay? Dismissed."

At dusk, the supply jeep brought up K-rations, ammunition, and a sack of mail. Several soldiers received delayed Christmas presents.

At 2200, a jeep lumbered over snowdrifts and rolled to a halt near George Company command post. Colonel Boydstun, the battalion commander, climbed out. He dismissed the driver and announced that he would accompany the troops on foot. One of the traits that endeared him to the soldiers was that wherever he ordered the men, he went too. To Colonel Boydstun, no obstacle was impossible or even difficult. He radiated confidence, leadership, and boundless enthusiasm.

Lt. Col. William
J. Boydstun

"Hi Mike! Hi Smitty!" he grinned as he wriggled into the dugout. He shucked off his gloves and extended his hands toward the little stove filled with burning shell casings.

"Gad, what luxury!" he exclaimed. "Mike, I've talked with the soldiers in Fox Company, the ex-forest rangers, and they confirm that the aerial photos show evidence of a minefield."

"Yes sir," said Lieutenant Damkowitch. "We heard the same thing."

"No problem, Mike," answered the colonel. "McPeters, one of the former rangers, climbed up the hill this afternoon for a look-see. He and the other ranger marked a trail that will lead us through the minefield."

"Good. I hate mines."

"No sweat, Mike," grinned Colonel Boydstun. "Easy Company will create a ruckus on the flank, and the balance of the Battalion will hit them from the hill. Hot chow in town, how's that?"

The frozen shelter half covering the entrance to the dugout rattled and Colonel Boydstun cried out, "Hey Tex, squeeze in. Look what these guys found, a stove."

Lieutenant Clark was the forward observer with the 80th Field Artillery supporting the attack. His wise-cracking and good humor made him popular with the men. He was from Texas, and he let everybody know it. To anybody he met he would say, "Just call me Tex."

Two other enlisted specialists accompanied the artillery forward observer to help with the radio. Tex spoke, "Colonel, we just arrived sir. Where do we fit in?"

"You'll be with me and Battalion headquarters, Tex," replied the colonel. "Let's hit the trail. Fox Company is due any time now," he said glancing at his watch.

The soldiers climbed out of the dugout and stood shivering and stomping as elements of Fox Company slogged past.

A detachment from Battalion headquarters struggled past us, stringing telephone wire. Two soldiers with packs and slung rifles struggled with a heavy reel of wire. They pulled, strained, and stumbled as the wire unwound behind them.

Sergeant McAllister eyed the toiling men. "That's stupid," he snorted. "Those reels of wire are too heavy. They ought to be divided so the men can carry them."

"What did you say, soldier?" asked Colonel Boydstun.

"I—I was talking to Sergeant Smith, sir."

"I know, but I asked you what you said. Speak up."

Flustered, Sergeant McAllister stuttered and stammered, "I said the reels of wire, they're too big. If the reels were half that size they'd be easier to carry. That's all I said, sir."

"That's what I thought I heard," said Colonel Boydstun. "And it's a damn good idea. From now on that's the way we'll do it." He turned to his aide, Lieutenant Coputo. "Make a note to tell the communications people to divide the wire reels."

Then he turned to McAllister. "What's your rank, soldier?"

"Sergeant, sir."

"Mike, promote this man to Staff Sergeant."

"Yes sir," responded Lieutenant Damkowitch. "Smith, see to it."

The air was crisp and cold, the moonlight bright. Lieutenant Damkowitch raised his arm and I shouted, "Let's go! G Company!"

The soldiers fell in on each side of the trail. Men fashioned mufflers from pieces of blanket wound around the face, leaving only the eyes visible. Wispy icicles formed around the nostrils and mouth.

"Move out!" cried Lieutenant Damkowitch. It was 0300. Snow crunched under combat boots. George Company was on the move.

An Infantry Rifle Company is composed of 187 men and officers. Seldom was George Company full strength, and 147 soldiers trudged the trail toward the hill.

Dawn was breaking as the weary soldiers reached the foot of the hill. A turn in the trail brought the soldiers face to face with a German machine gun emplacement. The gun crew were dead, their sprawled bodies frozen and partially covered with snow.

The troops entered the forest and toiled up the hill. The rigorous climb caused the men to perspire, even though the water in their canteens was frozen. They ate snow to quench their thirst. The column moved slowly as advance elements maneuvered steep ridges and soldiers pulled each other up over steep embankments.

Equipment passed hand-to-hand across ravines and other obstacles. At every pause, stinging prickly sensations warned of freezing feet.

At the sound of whistling whumping artillery shells, Sergeant McAllister cocked his head and listened. "It's okay," he said. "It's ours. It's outgoing mail."

A series of muffled explosions halted the column. "That's landmines," observed Sergeant McAllister. "I'll bet the men carrying that reel of wire stumbled."

A message came back along the file of soldiers, "Minefield up front. Send stretcher bearers."

The Germans had developed a deadly landmine. When the tripwire was struck, it bounced waist high and exploded. It was dubbed the "Bouncin' Betty" by the soldiers.

The leading elements of Fox Company bore the brunt of the minefield. It was havoc. The medics moved from wounded to wounded, and the faces of men on stretchers were sickly gray.

Slowly, the column shuffled forward. A sentry warned as the men approached the minefield, "Stay on the marked trail, and you'll be safe." Fearful glances at the crumpled bodies and severed limbs insured that each soldier stepped in the footprints of the man ahead.

The 2nd Battalion passed through the minefield and started climbing more steeply up the hill. Without warning, the German artillery retaliated. Screaming shells crashed on the hill or burst in the trees. Soldiers scurried for cover amid the whistling and whining shell fragments, and the line of march was littered with torn bodies. The air was filled with screams of "Medic! Medic!"

I was frantically digging at the base of a large tree as a medic hurried by carrying a satchel of first aid supplies. He spied me and yelled, "You guys with your guns, you're gonna get us all killed."

He turned and hurried to a crying soldier. "There, there," he said soothingly, "nothing can hurt you now. You're out of this stupid war."

I was petrified by the whizzing whumping noises as I watched the medic with this soldier. I tried to scream out a warning to them, but nothing came out. Soon there was a blinding flash followed by an ear-splitting explosion. Shell fragments tore the tree above me. I peered out, and where the two men had been was only a blackened jagged hole. The medic's white helmet with its red cross rolled across the trail. I vomited.

The German guns traversed and searched. They were systematically shooting back and forth and up and down. A lull, and Lieutenant Damkowitch bounded to his feet, yelling, "Get moving! Get moving! Let's get out of here. Come on, sing out, let's hear it!"

Shouting, "Hey! Hey!" soldiers pressed across an open area.

Slipping and stumbling brought us to another plateau. For a short distance, we saw a level strip of terrain, and beyond that was the densely wooded peak of the hill. Cracking rifle fire signaled that Easy Company was attacking. In the distance, automatic weapons chattered. Could we make it in time? We re-entered the woods and climbed toward the peak.

German artillery found us again as we toiled over the hill. Exploding shells burst in flashes of flame framed in black smoke. Thunderous ear-splitting blasts churned up geysers of dirt, trees, and debris. An acrid smoke odor permeated the atmosphere.

Soldiers dashed for cover. Some crouched in a ravine, others buried facedown in the snow. Wump! Wump! Wump! Screaming shells filled the air. Lethal whining shell fragments rained on the terrified soldiers. After each explosion, puffs of smoke swirled in the air. Dead, dying, and wounded soldiers littered the line of march.

Among shrill cries of "Medic! Medic!" I heard a soldier calling for his mama. Over the clamor, he cried in plaintive tones, "Mama! Mama!"

Suddenly there was a lull as the bursting shells moved to another sector. Medics carrying first aid scurried to attend to the wounded. I cautiously peered from my place of refuge, a slight depression in the ground. The soldier crying "Mama" was a few feet from me. It was Private Alfred Miller. He lay on his back, helmet missing, and his face streaked by smoke. His legs had been ripped from his body, and his overcoat was soaked with blood. I stared at the dying soldier. His bleary eyes flickered. He saw me kneeling and cried, "Mama! Oh Mama, thank God you came."

Private Miller, a new replacement, had been court-martialed for disciplinary reasons and transferred to Company G. Eagerly, he grasped for my arm. He missed but succeeded in clutching my overcoat sleeve. His voice became shrill and pleading, "Mama, Mama, please don't leave me and sister again."

I attempted to free myself, but his grip on my sleeve tightened, "Mama, don't leave me, please." The dying soldier became a frightened little boy. I heard my voice saying, "There, there, take it easy."

"Oh Mama," he whispered. "Why did you leave us? Sister cried 'n cried 'cause she was hungry." Then he added like a little boy, "But I found something for sister and me in garbage cans. That man said he wasn't our daddy. He was mean to us. We cried but you didn't come back. A lady came and said sister would have to go to the orphan home."

The shelling returned. I was gripped with fear as the whistling wumping shells screamed and burst in the treetops. I burrowed in the ground. The air was filled with whizzing and whining shell fragments. I quaked in terror as shell fragments ripped my pack and overcoat. Ice oozed from my punctured canteen.

Another lull. Private Miller was babbling, "Mama, Mama," he cried. "Me and sister won't have to go to the orphan home now, will we? Will we, huh?"

I swallowed a lump in my throat, "No, you won't have to go anywhere—ever."

Private Miller's voice grew weak, "Mama, I'm sleepy. Good night sister, good night Mama."

I was freeing my overcoat sleeve with my trench knife when Lieutenant Damkowitch waved his arm and yelled, "Let's go, G Company, move it!"

Abruptly, the shelling shifted to another sector. Lieutenant Damkowitch scrambled to his feet. He thrust an arm through the sling of his carbine and flung his gloved hand in the air. "Hey Smitty," he called to me as little frosty wisps of vapor puffed from his mouth. "Smitty, I'm going forward to check with Battalion."

"Good idea," I responded, stamping my feet and waving my arms. "Yeah, let's get moving. It's freezing."

With his carbine hanging from his shoulder, Lieutenant Damkowitch slogged through the snow toward the Battalion command post. Telephone lines lay along the line of march, making the trail easy to follow, and snow had been flattened by the boots of the soldiers that had gone ahead.

The "Crump! Crump! Crump!" and smothered explosions were farther away, and I continued to wave my arms and stamp my feet in the snow. Presently, Lieutenant Damkowitch came slipping and sliding back down the trail. He propped his carbine against a tree and rubbed his hands. "Smitty, Battalion command post is a few hundred yards up the trail. I talked to Colonel Boydstun, and he . . ."

"Yeah, what's the hold-up?" I asked. "We gotta keep moving before the shelling comes back."

"Yeah, I know," said Lieutenant Damkowitch, "but there's been a change in plans."

"What?"

"A change of plans," he explained. "Originally, Easy Company was to skirt the hill and attack the town on the flank." I nodded my head. "Then we would climb this hill and make a frontal attack on the town."

"And now that's not the plan?"

"No, Easy Company bogged down. They hit heavy resistance. A radio message reported heavy casualties and that Captain Jenkins had been killed. Then it cut off mid-sentence. Looks bad."

"Sure does," I agreed.

Lieutenant Damkowitch waved his arms and clapped his gloves together. "The colonel thinks Easy Company has been annihilated. He's calling a conference, and I'm going back. As soon as Fox and How Companies report, the colonel will give us orders."

"Okay Mike," my teeth were chattering. "As long as we get moving—this is murder."

Lieutenant Damkowitch turned to leave. He grabbed his carbine but then paused. "Say, Smitty, get a strength report. Bring it to me at the colonel's command post."

"Yes sir," I replied. "I'll get Sergeant McAllister on it right away."

Lieutenant Damkowitch was about to leave but he crouched low. Did I hear something, or was it a premonition? I clutched Lieutenant Damkowitch's arm, "Hold up, Mike! Down! Get down!" There was a low rumble in the distance and it grew louder. The projectile was from a heavy artillery piece or possibly a big railroad-mounted gun. The eerie whooshing-whumping sound could be heard for seconds that seemed an eternity.

I yelled, "Down! Down! Heads down!" The shell exploded on one of the peaks with a deafening, ear-splitting roar. The crash was like a head-on collision of two thundering locomotives. The ground trembled and shook. Shell fragments whizzed and whined. The air was filled with debris, tree limbs, dirt, and smoke. Terrified, we burrowed in a depression in the ground as shell fragments whistled and ricocheted in the trees.

Another whooshing-whumping screeching sound heralded one more huge shell. It exploded in a burst of flame and smoke on the peak occupied by Colonel Boydstun and his staff. The explosion hurled us sprawling in the snow by the force of the blast. Burning trees crackled, I stumbled around dazed and confused. My body trembled, and I couldn't control my agitation. I fell to the ground and rolled to a fallen tree to burrow against it. Lieutenant Damkowitch huddled behind a boulder. Smoke blacked our faces.

The exploding shells shifted to another sector, and the wooded hill had been reduced to smoking shredded tree trunks. Lieutenant Damkowitch was unsteady as he pulled himself to one knee and shook his head like a downed prize fighter. I raised my head and gazed back down the line of march. The German guns had created havoc. Slain soldiers littered the path through the woods. The bodies lying helter-skelter resembled bags of crumpled laundry.

Cautiously, soldiers began to stir about. Without panic or confusion, the able aided the wounded. Medics in white helmets with painted red crosses circulated, administering first aid. Tedious training was paying off.

"Hey, Mike," I called. "You all right?"

He looked at me with a blank stare and then his glazed eyes cleared. Sanity returned.

"Gee, yeah," he stood and shook his head. "Yes, I'm okay, just shook up. How about you?"

"I'm okay, I think."

"The colonel!" Lieutenant Damkowitch blurted. His eyes were apprehensive. "That last shell, it landed close to the colonel's command post." He looked around and found his carbine. A shell fragment had gouged the stock.

"C'mon," he yelled. "Let's get going." We made a turn on the trail, and Lieutenant Damkowitch stared at the shambles of Battalion headquarters. Flames danced and crackled as they licked burning trees. The air was filled with the acrid odor of burning flesh. Bodies of soldiers and pieces of equipment were scattered over the ground. Body parts dangled from tree limbs.

Wounded soldiers of the headquarters staff wandered around dazed and incoherent. A soldier was holding his intestines. Another was looking at his arm laying on the ground. Colonel Boydstun was reclining in a half-sitting position at the base of a tree. An arm was missing, and he was bleeding from multiple wounds. The colonel's aide, Lieutenant Coputo, was stumbling around confused and bewildered.

The artillery forward observer stood with his back against a boulder and clutching a radio microphone with a dangling shredded cord. The bodies of both radio operators were sprawled over the smashed transmitter. The stunned artillery observer was calling for strikes that the battery would never hear. He saw us and a silly grin appeared on his lips. He cracked, "It's a helluva life, ain't it?" He coughed and spit blood, "One thing for sure—

you can't get out of it alive." His grin evaporated as he fell forward on his face, dead.

Lieutenant Damkowitch knelt by the colonel's side. Colonel Boydstun's voice was husky. "Don't worry about me," he croaked. "I'm beyond help. Mike, you and Smitty go forward and contact Captain Williams at Fox Company. He's the senior officer." He was speaking now with more difficulty. "Tell him to continue the attack." His head drooped. We stared incredulously. He raised his head, and blood trickled from his mouth. He gurgled, "Damnit! That's an order. Get moving."

Colonel Boydstun beckoned to Lieutenant Coputo. He spit out a mouthful of blood and spoke a message to deliver to his family. Colonel's Boydstun's eyes grew filmy, then closed. He expired in the arms of the bitterly weeping Lieutenant Coputo.

Lieutenant Damkowitch stood straight, shoulders back and heels together. To Colonel Boydstun's final order, Mike's right hand came up in a salute. Lieutenant Damkowitch's eyes were brimming.

The colonel's boundless enthusiasm inspired confidence, and everyone was fond of him. He was loved and respected by the officers and men of his command.

Lieutenant Damkowitch sniffed, swallowed, then said, "C'mon Smitty, you and McAllister, let's go forward and find Captain Williams."

The winding trail grew steep, and advancing soldiers had cut toe holds in the hill. Puffing and red-faced, we toiled past bodies of Fox Company soldiers on our way to the summit. Elements of Fox Company were regrouping in the flat area. White helmeted medics with hypodermic syringes were administering shots and applying bandages.

Looking around, Sergeant McAllister observed, "Fox Company has been hit hard, too."

"Yeah," I agreed. "Maybe we can get out of the woods before the shelling starts again."

Sergeant McAllister glanced up at the overcast sky with wraiths of swirling fog in the air. "This weather will hold up the artillery," he prophesied. "The Krauts don't shoot if they can't see."

"For once, the bad weather is in our favor," said Lieutenant Damkowitch. "They are probably moving their infantry to meet us when we come out of the woods." Then he added an afterthought: "Oh say, McAllister, the strength report—what we got left?"

Sergeant McAllister pulled off a glove and fished around in his overcoat pocket. He took out several slips of paper. "We were understrength at the start, only had one hundred forty-seven men," he said as he straightened out the slips of paper. "Each platoon reported the actual number that they could account for. Let's see, as of now our total strength is sixty-one."

"Dear God," I murmured as I mentally subtracted. "We've had eighty-six casualties. That's more than half of what we started with, nearly 60 percent lost."

"Some may have got lost and will straggle back," said McAllister. "This is all we could account for at the time. The Fourth Platoon was hit hardest. They only had six men left. A shell landed on them and demolished their mortar and most of the men. They've still got the light machine gun."

Lieutenant Damkowitch led the way and we followed. Soldiers were deployed along the trail. Some were digging while others rested and munched frozen K-rations. Lieutenant Damkowitch sang out, "Is this Fox Company?"

"Yes sir," a sergeant responded. "The Third Platoon, that is, what's left of it."

"Captain Williams, where is he?"

"He went forward, sir," the sergeant replied. "He took two scouts and went forward. Then the shells came in." He shook his head, "Don't know. It looks bad."

"We'll take a look," said Lieutenant Damkowitch.

A medic was attaching a tag to Captain Williams's overcoat when we arrived. He was sitting on a log in a draw, babbling and incoherent. Blood trickled from his ears. His weapon and helmet were missing. Lieutenant Damkowitch started to speak, then hesitated. The captain's eyes rolled and saliva dribbled from his mouth.

"It's no use, sir," said the medic. "It's a concussion. He's in a bad way. We'll get him to our rear as soon as we can."

Lieutenant Damkowitch silently patted the weary medic on the arm and turned to Sergeant McAllister. "McAllister, we've got to have instructions. Can you raise Regiment on the radio?"

"Yes sir, I think so. We've got to go back to Company headquarters," he said. "The radio wasn't damaged, and I left it with Private Cordon."

"Cordon is the only man strong enough to carry it over these hills," I added. "He's built like a bull."

Sam Cordon

"C'mon, let's get cracking," barked Lieutenant Damkowitch as he started back down the trail.

I glanced at my watch. It was 1610, and darkness was setting in.

We struggled back down the trail past the wreckage of the 2nd Battalion. Soldiers were digging in, and entrenching tools whacked and thumped against the frozen ground.

Private Cordon, a rough, bulky, powerful man, had gently covered the radio with a blanket. Sergeant McAllister and Private Cordon were friends, and Cordon frequently boasted that he could carry the radio and McAllister. Sergeant McAllister barked, "Hey, Cordon, break out the radio and turn it on. The lieutenant wants to send a message."

Private Cordon grinned at his friend and said, "Okay, Sarge"; he pulled the blanket from the radio and handed Sergeant McAllister the microphone. I noticed a covering on the microphone and so did Lieutenant Damkowitch.

"What's that?" he demanded.

Private Cordon mumbled, "It's a rubber, sir."

"Damnit, I know what they are," said Lieutenant Damkowitch, "but why is it on the mic?"

"Sir, it was Cordon's idea," responded Sergeant McAllister. "You see, moisture forms when you talk and freezes the microphone."

In a flood of understanding, Lieutenant Damkowitch exclaimed, "And if the mic stays dry, it won't freeze, right?"

"Yes sir."

Sergeant McAllister turned his attention to the radio. He twisted dials and called, "George Six to Big Six. George Six to Big Six."

Lieutenant Damkowitch addressed Private Cordon, "Soldier, what's your rank?"

"Private, sir."

"As of now, it's sergeant. Smith, see to it."

"Yes sir."

Sergeant McAllister looked up at Lieutenant Damkowitch. "We've made contact. It's Regiment, sir." He held out the microphone. Lieutenant Damkowitch nodded as he took the mic and pressed the switch. He reported that the 2nd Battalion had been hit hard. There were numerous casualties, including Colonel Boydstun and most of his staff. Before he released the microphone switch, Lieutenant Damkowitch asked for instructions.

We were told to hold fast until darkness and then fall back to our original position. Other units had been dispatched to pass through our unit and continue the attack. Small hedge-hopping observation planes had spotted the German battery, and counterfire would commence the next attack.

Regiment reported there had been no contact with other units of the 2nd Battalion, and we were instructed to pass the word that first aid jeeps and equipment would meet us at the base of the hill. Lieutenant Damkowitch was on the verge of saying, "Roger, over and out," when a voice cut in and asked how we were able to establish radio contact and other units could not.

"I'll have to explain in person," Lieutenant Damkowitch responded. "Over and out."

The air rang with Thunk! Thunk! Thunking! sounds as the soldiers hacked the frozen earth with entrenching tools. Even though we were soon to withdraw, the act of digging foxholes relieved tensions.

Sergeant McAllister cocked his head skyward and observed, "The shelling is over for now. The Krauts don't shoot unless they can see, and they sure can't see in this fog."

It was late afternoon. All around, soldiers were opening K-rations and munching the frozen food. I pulled out a concentrated chocolate bar and hacked off a hunk with my trench knife.

The task of collecting the wounded began. Medics had some stretchers; others were improvised. The walking wounded guided the blinded. Our slain were left for the Graves Registration and burial details.

Tacitly, the soldiers were helping one another. I worked my way back down the trail, telling the men that another unit would pass through our lines and relieve us.

Two soldiers were loading a comrade on a stretcher when the wounded soldier called out to me. "Hi, Sarge, when are we getting out of here?" I recognized Private Buehler. "Hi Buehler, soon I hope. You hit bad?"

"I don't think so, Sarge," he replied. "It's my legs. The medics patched me up and gave me a shot. I don't feel a thing."

One of the soldiers was breaking open the wounded man's pack to get his blanket. A small package fell out. It was a delayed Christmas gift that he hadn't had time to open. Private Buehler spied the package and cried out, "Hey, gimmie my present."

I looked at the men preparing to lift his stretcher. One said, "Oh hell, Sarge, let him have his gift. It ain't that heavy." The other man added, "Yeah, we don't mind."

"Okay," I replied. "Here, Buehler, take the package." Blood was seeping through his blanket.

"Thanks, Sarge," he said as he took the package. "It's from my girl. As soon as the war's over, we're getting married."

"That's great," I smiled.

"Sarge, I'll see that you get an invitation to my wedding."

"Thanks. I'll come, too."

"Say," his voice was animated, "maybe they'll send me to the same hospital where my brother is."[9]

"It happens sometimes," I agreed. "I hope so." The bloody spot grew larger on the blanket.

"Hold on, it's freezing. I'll get you another blanket." I pulled a blanket from the pack of a body lying beside the trail and covered him. The two soldiers slung their rifles, hefted the stretcher, and joined the line of stretcher bearers trudging back down the trail.

Surviving officers of Fox and How Companies converged on Lieutenant Damkowitch. He briefed them on the instructions from Regiment, and it was the consensus to immediately evacuate, stretchers first, followed by walking wounded, then the balance of the Battalion would withdraw in reverse order of the approach march—How Company, followed by George, Battalion, and Fox Companies. Word passed down the column that if German patrols probed the forest, we were not to return their fire.

The officers looked to Lieutenant Damkowitch for leadership. He appeared at ease in the confusion, a natural leader. He called out, "Hey, Smitty, you and McAllister, over here." We joined him near the trail. "How and George Companies are moving," he said. "Smith, you and McAllister stay and check the men. Sergeant Rayburn of Fox Company is bringing up the rear of their group. When he clears the checkpoint, then you follow."

"Yes sir."

"Be careful," he warned. "Be on the lookout for German patrols. They'll try to draw fire, but don't return it."

"Yes sir."

He turned and scrambled back down the trail.

The frigid chill factor penetrated to our bones. We stomped our feet and waved our arms. The withdrawal moved at a snail's pace, and it was past midnight when Sergeant Rayburn shuffled up to the checkpoint. The muffler over his mouth and nose was covered with tiny icicles and his teeth chattered as he mumbled, "Let's get the hell out of here."

I turned to Sergeant McAllister, "C'mon, let's go."

"Hold on a minute," he replied.

"What's up?"

"I want to leave a calling card."

A full moon peeped between the clouds and reflected against the snow. Sergeant McAllister withdrew wire cutters and clipped several lengths of the telephone wire strewn along the trail. I watched as he unfastened two hand grenades dangling from his overcoat lapels then fastened a length of wire between two trees.

"They'll spot that," I observed. "It's waist-high."

"Yeah, that's what they're supposed to do," he replied. "If they walk around that wire, maybe they'll stumble on this one," he said as he fastened another wire to a sapling low to the ground with the other grenade dangling from the wire. "The Krauts gave us a hard time," he said, "and I thought I should do something to show my appreciation."

I nodded my approval. As we climbed down the trail, I was moved to say, "McAllister, you're a devious son of a bitch."

McAllister replied, "If I ever find out what 'devious' means, I might get sore."

The freezing bitter cold was intensified by the chill factor. My thoughts turned to home and Florida, and I mused, "And to think that I used to complain about the heat. Never again."

At night, everything seemed different. A smoky fog hung in the air. Moonlight filtered through the clouds and reflected in the snow. Ripped, torn trees stood like phantom specters. Abandoned stretchers dotted the line of march where wounded soldiers had perished.

Sergeant McAllister grabbed my arm, "There they are. German patrols."

I cocked my head and listened. We could hear the unmistakable sound of German automatic weapons, bursts that sounded like ripping canvas.

"That's Kraut burp guns," said McAllister. "They've lost contact with us, and they're probing trying to draw our fire."

"They don't know how hard we were hit," I said.

In the distance, the ripping canvas bursts continued.

"If they locate our trail maybe they'll stumble over the grenades," said McAllister.

As we pushed down the trail we came upon another abandoned stretcher. In the moonlight, I recognized Private Buehler. His expression was so peaceful. He appeared to be sleeping. Little flakes of snow were collecting on his face. The unopened Christmas package lay in the crook of his arm like a kid holding a teddy bear. I recalled hearing that a sensation of warmth and an overpowering desire to sleep precedes death by freezing. I stooped and covered his face with his stiff, blood-drenched blanket.

The trail led back through the minefield, and we cautiously trod on the telephone lines blazing a safe path. Bouncin' Betty mines had been detonated by stretcher bearers that lost their footing and stumbled off the narrow trail.

"What a damn shame," muttered Sergeant McAllister, looking around at the carnage, "and so close to safety." He shook his head.

As we approached the base of the hill, I thought, "What a disastrous day—and the hell of it was we never got to fight back."

The first aid jeeps were loading the last of the wounded as we came off the hill, exhausted and puffing back to our former positions.

Around the area, the soldiers were clearing snow from their old foxholes and spreading tent shelter halves over the openings.

I turned to Sergeant McAllister, "McAllister, the Morning Report—I've got to submit a Morning Report. Send runners to each platoon and get a list of the men actually present. The balance, I'll list as missing in action. As the lost straggle in, I'll pick 'em up as returned to duty on the next Morning Report."

Sergeant McAllister nodded, "Okay, I'll get right on it."

I pulled the tent shelter half aside and climbed into the dugout. Our stove had been removed during our absence. Lieutenant Damkowitch was on his knees lighting a makeshift lamp, a sock protruding from the neck of a gasoline-filled bottle. The smoking lamp cast dancing reflections on the walls of the dugout.

Lieutenant Damkowitch's eyes were red—he'd been crying. His face and scraggly beard were streaked with tears and dirt. His bloodshot eyes watched as I struggled out of the straps holding my pack. The door covering creaked and cracked as I rummaged for my blanket. Sergeant McAllister wormed himself into the dugout.

"Did you get the lists from the platoons?" I asked.

"Yeah," he replied, pulling off a glove with his teeth. He fished around in his overcoat pocket and produced several slips of paper.

"It was a bad day," he commented as he handed me the platoon rosters.

I totaled the slips of paper. "I make it thirty-six," I announced. "Of course, some may have got lost and will straggle in. We'll take another head count later."

"Thirty-six men left!" exploded Lieutenant Damkowitch, "Oh my God," he moaned. "To think we started with one hundred forty-seven men, and now we have thirty-six. Oh God!" he sobbed. "We've lost one hundred and eleven men." His mood changed, and he cursed and beat the dirt wall with his fist.

"Mike, you did your best," I sympathized. "The artillery, they surprised us, caught us flat-footed. There wasn't anything anybody could do."

He calmed down and blew his nose on his pocket handkerchief, "You know," he said, sniffing and wiping his nose, "we're almost sure to go to heaven."

"Who? Us?'

"Yeah," he said. "We've already been to hell."

"I always thought hell was hot," murmured Sergeant McAllister. "But if hell is anything like we had today—no, I mean yesterday—count me out. I've had enough."

"Smith, how is our average holding up?" asked Lieutenant Damkowitch.

I unfastened my field case and rustled through papers listing our casualties and replacements. I did some adding and subtracting and announced, "Our average is still about a week." In other words, if you were in Company G for more than a week, you beat the average.

Averaging the length of time at the front had become a macabre ritual. We had lived so close to death, we had become fascinated by it. Sergeant McAllister muttered, "Better not start reading any continued stories."

Outside was noisy confusion. "What's the commotion?" asked Lieutenant Damkowitch.

Sergeant McAllister peered out the dugout opening, "Hot damn," he exclaimed. "The kitchen jeep is here. Hot chow."

We grabbed our canteen cup and joined the line. One cook reached into a thermal can and withdrew two pancakes, another cook plopped on a glob of jelly, and a third cook ladled steaming coffee from a thermal can. In the dugout, out of the bitter cold, we wolfed down the food.

I spread my ripped overcoat across my feet and huddled in a corner. Lieutenant Damkowitch squirmed and pulled his wool cap down over his eyes. McAllister was snoring.

I twisted on my side and fell into a troubled sleep fraught with nightmares. I was running and couldn't find my way—I drilled the troops—I shouted commands—I saw Elizabeth, but I couldn't reach her. I cried out but she didn't hear me—I cried and babbled.

Lieutenant Damkowitch roused his head, "Smitty! Hey Smitty, you all right?"

In a daze I prattled on, "Colonel Boydstun isn't going home—this damn war, when is it going to end?—Miller's mama came for him."

I heard a voice from the distance, "Smitty! Smitty! What the hell are you talking about?"

"Just what I said—Miller found his mama today."

"Smitty, stop it! You're talking crazy."

"Huh? What say? Huh? No, I'm not going to Buehler's wedding, there won't be one—Hey! Damnit, quit shaking me—I told you Buehler's wedding—quit shaking me—I'll—" My bleary eyes cracked open, and Lieutenant Damkowitch's face floated into focus. He wore a concerned expression. My head bobbled as he shook me.

"Mike! Mike!" I blurted. "Cut it out! Hey, I was dreaming. Good gosh! Is it time already? I thought . . ."

"You're okay," he sighed. "For a minute I thought you'd cracked up. No, go back to sleep." His head drooped.

Outside, self-propelled guns rumbled through. Another infantry unit was passing by our position. Boots crunched in the snow, ammunition cans clinked, snatches of conversation, muttered curses as the soldiers tramped by.

Overhead, outgoing artillery shells whumped-whumped. Artillery batteries were pumping shells toward the town we couldn't reach. The advancing infantry units were continuing the attack behind the rolling artillery barrage.

Lieutenant Damkowitch snored. The strain of the past twenty-four hours was taking its toll. Company G would lick its wounds, rest, and reorganize. Replacements would arrive along with supplies and ammunition, and Company G would be committed in another sector.

My eyes closed. Silently I prayed, "Our Father which art—which art—in heaven—ur—hallowed be thy—thy—"

I must have fallen asleep.[10]

---

31 January 1945

My darling wife—

I had the nicest surprise today—I received a box from my honey. It was swell. We have just stopped for a few days rest and the box hit the spot. I thought the Germans had got my package but since they are beginning to arrive, I guess everything will be okay.[11]

I've been doing a lot of mountain climbing recently and I'm sure sick of snow and mountains. Don't worry about me dear if I don't write regular, as when we are out in the snow it's next to impossible to write. And now that we are in houses, there are so many men coming in and out you can't concentrate.

Everybody here is cheering the Russians on and hoping the war will end soon—but that remains to be seen. We were all "hipped up" once before and liked to got our ears pinned back.

Everybody lives like communists here—I ate everybody's cookies when my packages didn't come and now they are helping me with mine.

I just received two letters from you, one postmarked Jan 4 and the other Jan 18—I was sure glad to get them as it's been about a week since I had heard from you. I sure am proud you are getting along so well with your work. I know you make the sweetest supervisor there ever was.

Dear, it's time for your little husband to go to bed so I'll say good night dear heart and hope we will soon be reunited.

> Lots of love
> Your little husband
p.s. I love you angel wings

---

1 February 1945

Darling—

Dear—Every time I write to you, I imagine I'm home with you and we are really together. I don't know much what to talk about except I love you more and more every day.

They hauled up a moving picture machine so we all went into a barn and saw Kay Kyser in "Around the World"—it was pretty good.

We are staying in a quaint little town for a few days. The village must be hundreds of years old. It has electric lights—the first I've seen in a long time. The power plant is in a nearby town, and they cut off the juice every morning and turn it on again every night. I guess the natives think we are crazy, as they all gather around to see what we are going to do. When we set up our kitchen, the locals get in line with us and eat with us.

We are having a hard time with our coffee right now and have been using captured German coffee, which is lousy.

My company went down to a shower point and took a hot shower—the first hot shower in a long time—it sure made me feel swell.

The Russians seem to be "going to town" and maybe it won't be too long.

I understand Hitler still wants the Germans to fight on but it looks like a lost cause. We have been pushing as hard as we can to take the pressure off the Russian front, however our side is all hills and mountains and it's hard to move as fast as the Russians. Just as soon as we get out of the mountains maybe we can get moving again.

Well, darling, I'll say good night and hope and pray that I will soon be home with you and we can forget this nightmare.

> Good night darling
> Lots of love
> Your little husband

p.s. I love you, kid.

---

5 February 1945

Dearest angel wings—

Your little husband is writing you a little note to tell you I love you to pieces—did you know it?

The candy you sent was so good. The caramels were like the ones that come in the C-ration cans, and we never get but three or four (just enough to make you mad), so this was one time I ate all I wanted—in fact I couldn't even eat supper.

We are billeted in a little jerk town in Luxembourg that would make St. Augustine look like a modern city.[12] These houses must have been handed down from father to son for years and years. Most of the houses have large piles of straw and manure piled up in the front, which they rake out of the stalls that are next to their houses. Somebody said that's probably how wealthy a family is: the larger the manure pile, the wealthier the people.

The snow is beginning to melt and everything is sloppy and muddy. I guess it will be spring before we know it.

It looks like we finally got the German bulge straightened out—hope they don't get out of control again as it's an awful nuisance to get things under control again. Everybody here cheers the Russians on and the new battle cry of the 80th is "Roll on, you Russians." However, our newspaper keeps harping about us going to the Pacific after the war here—now wouldn't that be heck?

Honey—you are the most wonderful wife in the world and I sure was lucky to get you. Good night precious.

Lots of love

Your little husband

p.s. I love you honey.

Dear Daddy

On Father's Day 1980, my father wrote a long letter to his father, who had taken his own life when my Dad was two years old. These paragraphs are from that letter.

Daddy, I had to go to war. All my life, I was never allowed to have a gun, not even an air rifle. I've never been hunting. I guess I've missed a lot. Daddy, I was in the Army, the Infantry, and I had a gun. It became part of me, and Daddy, I was an excellent shot, a natural shooter.

What? No Daddy, I wasn't an officer, I was a Sergeant—and I tried to be a good one.

Daddy, we operated in small units called platoons. We moved at night or at times when we couldn't be seen. We scrambled through the woods and across streams. And sometimes we'd get caught and I'd be scared half to death.

Once, our group was crowded in a depression in the frozen ground for protection. It was winter and cloudy, we hadn't seen the sun for days. Our aeroplanes were grounded. In front of us was the enemy and they had tanks. Casualties had reduced our group to about fifteen men. We were caught. If we tried to run, we'd be mowed down. If we tried to stand our ground, we'd be run over by the tanks.

Then we heard a voice ring out, "Lay down your arms. Hold up your hands and walk forward. Don't be foolish. Surrender and have hot chow."

The frightened men looked at me. I was so scared my teeth chattered. "It looks hopeless," I managed to say. "If you want to surrender, there's no stigma." I choked up and don't know what else I said.

Then a voice asked, "Sarge, what are you gonna do?" Daddy, I was so scared I could taste vomit. I mumbled something and one of the men said, "I'm staying with Sergeant Smith." I heard some other voices, "Me, too." Several soldiers, about five, looked thoughtful. One said something about having kids. Some called us suckers as they walked down the hill with their hands clasped behind their heads. Daddy, the sound of the machine gun was like tearing canvas—all were murdered. The tank motors rumbled as they moved forward. I stuttered as I tried to repeat the Lord's Prayer.

Daddy, now I believe in miracles, 'cause one happened. Suddenly the sun burst through the clouds for the first time in weeks. The rumbling tanks had reached the open field and were approaching four abreast. Then a beautiful sound—the roar of our fighter planes skimming the treetops as they bombed the tanks. We cheered as we unrolled the orange signal panel that identified us.

6 February 1945

My dear wife—

Dearest, just a little note to tell you I love you, ever so much. I've just received several letters from you and boy, was I glad.

A snapshot
of Elizabeth

By the way—I have a new mailing address now. Company "E" instead of "G". That's the only change—the two Companies are just next door so I'll still get my mail okay.[13]

We are living in one of the "Grand" hotels. Boy is it a mess—all the windows broken, broken furniture, and junk scattered every direction. I had lunch today in the main ballroom—I carried my little mess kit into the dining room and sat down at one of the tables. Just imagine the Roosevelt Hotel dining room turned upside down and you'll have it.

It's stopped snowing now and started to rain—everything is slushy and muddy. Dear, I love you so much and I do hope I can return to you soon. Well dear heart, so long for now.

> Lots of love
>
> Your little husband

p.s. I sure do love you, kid. Say—the snapshot is real cute, kid—wonderful.

Easy Company

This is from a 1982 letter written to a comrade, recalling my father's move from Company G to Company E

On 21 January the 2nd Battalion was practically chewed to pieces by the German artillery. On 4 February, the commanding officer of Easy Company, Captain McDonnell, interviewed me and said, "I'm asking for your transfer to Company E."

"Why me?" I asked.

"Sergeant Geste is back from the hospital and can take care of Company G. I'll need help to reorganize Company E."

At the time, we had pretty good quarters in a former girls' school, or maybe it had been a convent. As I recall, it was good and out of the cold.

I didn't take kindly to the transfer, and went to Battalion headquarters to complain to Captain Sheean, the acting battalion commander. But I never talked to him about the transfer. When I arrived, he was talking to a colonel in charge of medics. The colonel was saying that he was taking over our quarters in the school for a hospital.

"You are?" Captain Sheean seemed surprised.

"Yes," said the colonel. "I thought you knew. The 2nd Battalion is crossing the river into Germany, and we're setting up to handle the casualties."

"I didn't know," confessed Captain Sheean.

"That's right," said the colonel. He turned to an aide. "What's the estimate of casualties?"

"About 30 percent, sir," I heard a voice reply.

Captain Sheean asked, "You'll need all the beds?"

"Yes, and then some," the colonel answered.

Captain Sheean said some stuff about being understrength and short of officers. The colonel apparently was not interested and cut him off by reminding him that he was a colonel.

"Yes, sir," I heard Captain Sheean say as the colonel departed.

I knocked on the door and went in. Captain Sheean's eyes were red from lack of sleep—he looked beat and stared at me with a "What now?" expression. I didn't have the heart to bitch about my transfer.

"About my transfer to Company E," I said.

Captain Sheean's shoulders drooped—he was expecting a protest.

"Sir, I'll do it—yes, sir."

He nodded and patted me on the arm.

On 8 February, I was transferred to Easy Company while we were in the town of Diekirch. On the 14th of February, we crossed the Sauer River and stood on the soil of Germany.[14]

---

9 February 1945

My dearest little wife—

Right now I'm writing you from a hotel room but you would never recognize it as such—looks more like a stable and I sleep on the floor—the main thing is that it has a nice thick roof.[15]

The natives are just returning to this village and it sure is pitiful as most of the homes are battered flat. The women here work awful hard. Most of them run around carrying sacks and bundles that I don't think I could lift.

I can watch the people from my broken-out window. In the restaurant part of the hotel there was a pile of rubble, and I happened to notice some ration books and stamps—I've always wondered what would happen if all the ration books got torn up. In fact, if the whole ration board got bombed.

I'm writing you by candlelight again as the lights are out here. The people really go for feather beds here—most of the time we have to squeeze ten or more men in a room, so when they pull the bed apart it's enough for each to have a part to put under his blanket.

They talk of the beautiful French girls but to me they are not so hot—the soap has been rationed too long I suppose—everyone looks dirty to me.

You are the most wonderful wife a man could have, and not a day passes that I don't thank the Lord that I have you to come home to. You make life bearable until we do come home, as without you I don't know what I would do.

The lieutenant who used to command our Company was stuck in a foxhole with me one day and he told me he found out his wife was untrue to him just before he shipped out—it almost broke his heart and he told me that he often exposed himself more than necessary in hopes he would get hit and end it all—I sure did feel sorry for him. Poor fellow has nothing to look forward to, as he is Catholic and will not marry again and has already divorced his wife. I guess there are many cases like that, as separation is a hard thing to bear.

My little candle is burning low—so I'll soon have to go to bed or rather to go to sleep, as beds are few and far between. It really will feel strange to sleep on a real bed again. After a while you get used to the ground (except when it's raining).

Take good care of yourself dear and don't forget I love you ever so much.

>Lots of love dear
>Your little husband

p.s. you are the sweetest one, Honeybun.

———— ————

18 February 1945
Germany (at last)[16]
My darling wife—

Dearest little angel—just a little note to let you know I'm well and that I love you more than anything in the world.

This is the first time I've had a chance to write in almost a week so I'll have to hurry this one up so I won't get too far behind.

So far, Germany looks like all the other places I've visited, France and

Luxembourg. The fighting is tougher; otherwise it's about the same. I'm in a captured town that we just finished taking. In fact, this letter is written on some German soldier's stationery, as I don't have any of mine here. We slipped into town early in the morning and crept past their guards and got into some of the buildings before they were completely awake. We had a hot time for a while as our German cousins had three big tanks at the other end of town. Thank goodness we were able to capture all the men and only wounded a few. The tanks took off in the afternoon after our artillery started to work on them.[17]

> Darling, I'll have to write a little later as I'm about to go to sleep writing.
>> Lots of love dear
>> Your little husband
> p.s. I love you.

The Non-Fraternization Order

A memory in story form written circa 1979–82

A mud-spattered jeep rolled to a stop in front of a bomb-scarred building. The driver squinted at the tactical marker and called out to the guard, "Hey! Is this Easy Company Headquarters?"

"Yeah," the guard replied, "Through here and up the stairs. It's the room in front with all the wires hanging out the window."

The driver picked up a brown envelope, climbed out of the jeep, and disappeared through the door. Moments later he emerged from the building and drove away, leaving Sergeant Smith holding the brown envelope.

Captain McDonell slowly opened his eyes, "Huh!—what?—huh—say, huh—what?" His voice was gruff. "Smith, I thought I told you not to wake me unless it was an emergency." He pushed back the blanket and sat on the edge of the bed, "Well, what's the emergency?"[18]

"Sorry, Captain," said Sergeant Smith, "The message, it just arrived."

Captain McDonell ran his fingers through his hair. "Well, who's it from? General Patton?"

"No sir," said Sergeant Smith. "It's from Supreme Headquarters, General Eisenhower."

The news brought Captain McDonell to his feet. "General Eisenhower," he said. "Here, let's see what it says."

Captain McDonell tore the envelope and scanned the message, "It's an order from General Eisenhower. I'm instructed to read it to the men without delay. What time is it?"

Sergeant Smith glanced at his wrist, "1530, sir."

"The platoons are scattered about the perimeter of the village. Could we have a Company formation by 1600?"

"Yes sir. Bailey and Sumkis have strung wire to each platoon. We can notify them by telephone, yes sir."

"Well, get with it."

Sergeant Smith returned to Company Headquarters and sang out, "Hey, Bailey, Sumkis, get on the telephone and alert the platoons to fall in at 1555. Have them form in the street, facing the company headquarters. Emphasize the captain wants everybody present, no excuses."

Sergeant Bailey cranked the field telephone.

Two nights before, Easy Company along with the balance of the 2nd Battalion crossed the Sauer River from Luxembourg to Germany. The river crossing was bitterly contested, and the battle for the village has been costly. Another unit, pursuing the retreating Germans, had passed through and relieved the exhausted 2nd Battalion. At present, Easy Company was resting, reorganizing, and awaiting replacements.

"Fall in!" shouted Sergeant Smith. It was 1558. Easy Company snapped to attention. Squad leaders reported to platoon sergeants, the platoon sergeants reported to the first sergeant, the first sergeant about-faced and saluted the captain. "All present, sir."

The captain sang out, "Post!" Captain McDonell surveyed the casualty-riddled ranks, then thundered, "At ease!"

"Men," he began, "when we crossed the Sauer River, we entered Germany. The war is being fought in the enemy's homeland. You are no longer on friendly soil. You must be constantly on guard." He withdrew a paper from his blouse and held it aloft. "This is an order signed by General Eisenhower. I've been ordered to read it to you. Pay attention!"

Captain McDonell read the order, which said in substance that any solder that fraternized with Germans would be court-martialed and fined.

He finished reading the order. "Men, I emphasize, it's against regulations, it's dangerous and unsafe to fraternize with the enemy." Sternly, he said, "Fraternizing with the enemy will not be tolerated in Easy Company." He paused, then added, "Take heed, any soldier suspected of fraternizing with the enemy will be court-martialed, and if found guilty will be fined $60." He stared back and forth balefully, then barked, "Any questions?"

The troops stood wooden-faced and silent.

"Com-pan-ee, TEN-HUT! First Sergeant."

The troops straggled back to their quarters in partially burned, shell-pitted houses.

Captain McDonell pushed open the door of company headquarters and walked in. He was staring at a steaming pot on the stove as Sergeant Smith entered and pulled off his helmet. Captain McDonell yawned and said, "I can't decide whether to have a cup of coffee or go back to bed." He thrust his hands in his field jacket and sauntered to the window overlooking the alley. Idly he gazed out the window. Suddenly he withdrew his hands from his field jacket and placed them on the window sill. "Damnit to hell!" he sputtered, "Look here, Smith."

Sergeant Smith looked up, "Yes sir."

"Come here and take a look, tell me what you see."

Sergeant Smith peeked out the window. Two soldiers were strolling down the alley with two German women. The soldiers playfully put their arms around them. Their intentions were clear.

"Who are those soldiers?" demanded Captain McDonell.

"It's Sullivan and Crews," responded Sergeant Smith. "They're platoon runners attached to Company Headquarters."

"You see what they're doing?"

"Yes sir."

"Just look at those two," snorted Captain McDonell.

Unaware that they were being observed, Sullivan and Crews dallied with the two giggling women. After playfully horsing around, the four disappeared into the building.

"Those men are deliberately disobeying orders," screamed Captain McDonell. "Smith, have those men arrested. They are going to stand a summary court-martial." He hissed, "I'll make an example of those two."

"Yes sir, but—"

"But what?"

"The court-martial manual, the army regulations and forms, they're all stored in the field desk. It's with Sergeant Blackburn at supply."

"Will it take long to get the field desk?"

"Not long, sir. Supply moved up with the kitchen train and will be here while we occupy the village." Sergeant Smith turned to the communications sergeant. "Say Sumkis, contact Sergeant Blackburn at supply. We need the field desk."

Captain McDonell said, "Very good. I'm going to my quarters. When you get set up, let me know." He paused at the door and added grimly, "I'm going to throw the book at those two."

"Yes sir."

Sergeant Blackburn reported, accompanied by two puffing privates bearing the field desk. "Where do you want it?" he asked. "Say, it's covered with mud. I don't think it's been opened since we left the States."

"Put it over there," said Sergeant Smith, pointing to a makeshift table. Two chairs supported planks with an army blanket. A chair was pulled up to the table. The field desk and the imposing volume marked "Army Regulations" lent an aura of dignity to the proceedings.

"Sergeant Sumkis," said the First Sergeant, "get a detail and arrest Sullivan and Crews. And you, Sergeant Bailey, report to Captain McDonell and tell him we're ready."

"Okay, Sarge."

Flanked by two armed soldiers, the bewildered culprits shuffled into company headquarters. A corporal reported, "The prisoners are here, sir."

Captain McDonell acknowledged them with a crisp salute. "At ease, men." The guards fell back and stood at ease, eyes straight ahead.

Bewildered, the prisoners nervously whispered to each other, "But what did we do? We ain't done nothin', have we, Crews?"

Captain McDonell rapped the table. One of the prisoners whispered, "Shush," and pointed.

Captain McDonell assumed a judicial air, "Men, you are charged with fraternizing with the enemy. Are you guilty or not guilty?"

Dismayed and wild-eyed, one prisoner blurted, "No sir, we ain't guilty. We ain't done nothin', have we, Crews?"

Private Crews nodded eagerly, "No sir."

Captain McDonell spoke sternly, "Were you in formation when I read General Eisenhower's order forbidding fraternization with the enemy?"

The men nodded nervously, "Yes sir, we were there, we heard it, yes sir."

The prisoners whispered with each other and then blurted, "Captain, we ain't done nothin', honest, we ain't done no fraternizin', no sir, not us."

Exasperated, Captain McDonell pounded the table, "But damnit, witnesses saw you, both of you."

The prisoners were even more wild-eyed. Their expressions of consternation were genuine.

"Right after formation," roared Captain McDonell, "witnesses saw you walking down the alley arm in arm with two German women. Then you went into a building with them. What do you say to that?"

The prisoners' blank looks evaporated. They looked at each other and heaved a sigh of relief. "Jeez," one murmured. "For a bit I thought we done something."

Captain McDonell looked puzzled. "Well, what do you have to say?"

The prisoners shuffled around and sniggered. They looked up and quickly lowered their eyes.

"Well?"

"Shucks," said Private Sullivan bashfully. "We didn't fraternize, we screwed 'em. That's all, honest."

Private Crews nodded eagerly, "That's right, sir. All we did was screw 'em, just like he said."

Captain McDonell rolled his eyes toward the ceiling and thoughtfully tugged at his ear. "Do you men have any idea what the word 'fraternize' means?"

The two men talked earnestly in undertones. "Crews knows what it means," said Sullivan. "Yes sir, he does."

"Well, Crews, what does it mean?"

Crews stammered, fidgeted, and finally blurted, "It's like, well kinda like if the enemy offers you food, don't eat it, it might be poison. You know, something like that, I think."

"Yes," said Sullivan, "we gave 'em a chocolate bar, but we didn't eat nothin' from them. We were careful, yes sir."

A resigned expression covered Captain McDonell's face. He sighed, "All right men, that's all. Forget this and return to your post. Dismissed."

"You mean we're free, sir?"

"Yes," he waved his hand. "Dismissed."

Captain McDonell and Sergeant Smith silently stared out the window at the two buddies sauntering down the alley avidly engaged in conversation. Their words were unintelligible, and they paused from time to time to face each other and make hand gestures. Captain McDonell heaved a sigh as the two men disappeared behind a building.

"Damnit, Smith," sighed Captain McDonell. "Why the hell bother to read them an order like that when they don't know what the word means?"[19]

Sergeant Smith silently listened.

"I'm going back to bed, this time with a bottle of brandy. Don't wake me until Tuesday." He paused at the doorway. "If a message comes from President Roosevelt, don't wake me until Tuesday, that's an order."

"Yes sir."

———— ——— ————

21 February 1945
Germany
My darling wife—

How is my little angel wings today? I received three packages from you. Now I have plenty of cigars. Oh Boy! I've just finished eating my fruitcake, with some help, and it really hit the spot. I wondered what I had when I saw your toilet water box—but sure was glad it was jam instead of toilet water—can't use that here.

Those cartoons by Mauldin are just about right. I look like that when I can't shave for weeks.[20]

Our German cousins kept us pretty busy when we arrived here. Apparently they don't like us. Most of them are typical Nazis—Big shots when they are in power and cowards when we catch them—then when they find out we are not going to shoot them they get smart aleck again.

Tell Betty Sue I've got the coins she asked for—the problem is to get them sent to her. I'll look up a box and paper as soon as I can. It takes a long time to get a package home, though.

Dearest, I love you more and more every day and can hardly wait until I get home to you. I'll eat you up—and I don't mean maybe. Bet I'll be worse than the guy in the next room to us in Mississippi. [Remainder of the letter was cut out.]

28 February 1945

Germany

My darling wife—

Dear, I haven't written for several days as we've been moving pretty fast and stopping only to eat and change sox.

Dear, I love you so much and you are always with me in my every thought. It doesn't seem possible that soon it'll be two years since I left home. Wow!

Dear, the Germans are having the war brought home to them, as almost every town we've taken was squashed flat. I don't suppose they thought we would get this far. We crossed the river from Luxembourg in little rubber boats, as the Germans blasted the bridges. We pushed the Germans back far enough so the engineers could build a new bridge to bring our tanks over. Then, before they knew it, they were set back on their heels.

Of course, they are resisting every mile. After we take a town, if there are any civilians, we try to herd them to one section of town so they will be out of danger. And also we don't trust them. So far, most of the towns are well stocked with cured meat and dried and preserved fruit so the civilians were not hurting. One of the men picked up a ham and we fried some with some eggs we found. Our C.O. has put an order for the men to leave the civilian food alone but it's hard for the men to resist.

The back of the photo reads, "Street scene in a little town in Germany—note white flags. Tanks were brought up to help us convince the Krauts to go somewhere else. The men are reading *Stars and Stripes*. One lucky guy got a letter." The town was not identified.

Guess what! Our company captured a German First Sergeant. His officers ran away so he surrendered his company. He only had 15 men left. He spoke English and told me he taught school in Berlin before he came into the army. He just came from the Russian front and I think he was glad we caught him instead of the Russians.[21]

I love you more than anything in the world, honey.

    Lots of love

    Your little husband

p.s. You are wonderful, kid.

Heavy Breathing

A memory written in 1947

After entering Germany from Luxembourg, our progress was slow, and every inch of ground was bitterly contested. The German soldiers fell back slowly, making us pay dearly for every advance.

Shortly before dawn after a heavy artillery barrage, we attacked a small village that was strongly fortified by German tanks and infantry. It was drizzling rain, and the mud was abundant, cold, and sticky. By the afternoon, we had driven the Germans from the village. Orders came via radio to move up and take the next village, about one thousand yards distant. We were to launch the attack at 0300 and move into the village under cover of darkness.

That evening, the German patrols became extremely active, and the sound of German burp guns was very near. Several enemy tanks began to shell our positions, making it nearly impossible to snatch a wink of sleep.

At 0300 we started for the village. We had to keep well off the road to avoid shells that came whistling down at frequent intervals. Slowly we made our way, our hearts in our mouths, palms sticky with sweat despite the cold. Every tree became a potential enemy, and at every open space our stomachs tightened as we expected German machine guns to cut us down.

Suddenly out of the dark loomed a huge building. According to a prearranged plan, I took two men and hurried to the rear of the building while another group entered the front. Stealthily creeping along the side of the building, we located a door. With the butt of my carbine, I quickly pushed the door open and crept inside. Immediately I had a sensation of someone else in the room with me. I could actually hear the breathing.

I froze against the wall, knowing that if I fired the flash would give away my position and blind me before I could fire again. The Germans used flashless powder, so there was nothing to do but sweat and wait for dawn.

My nerves were stretched to the snapping point just as the sun rose. As light filled the room, a large docile cow turned limpid eyes on me, then calmly turned its back.

---

10 March 1945
Germany
My dear little wife,

Did you ever receive a letter written on a German typewriter? Well honey here is one for you—they have a few more keys than ours and the "s" and the "y" are interposed; otherwise the keyboard is the same. Of course, if you are not careful stuff like this (öäß) pops up now and then but not enough to spoil the letter.

We've stopped for a rest in a picturesque little village—I guess you could call it cute if you didn't have to stay long. The room I have used to be a "Heinie" supply depot and still has a lot of bread that looks like bricks and about as hard. It's the brown bread and has a sour taste—right now the civilians are eating it, as we do not feed them.[22]

The other night, the movie machine came up and I went to see "Bowery to Broadway." A little corny, but as I have not seen a movie in months, I enjoyed it. The machine breaks down every now and then and they have to stop to change reels but everybody likes them. We use the village schoolhouse for a storage depot, and they let us have one room for movies. It must have been the elementary class as they have real small chairs—can't you just see the little Krauts learning about the Fuehrer?

It's been some time since I've heard from my little angel, but I guess I'll get them all at once.

Good night darling,
Lots of love
Your little husband
p.s. I love you, kid.

Shoulda Been There Yesterday

A memory written in 1947

After some time at the front, unusual events became commonplace. Dangerous patrols and hazardous missions became routine—just another job.

One day, our regimental commander, "Hammerin' Hank"—so named because he pounded his points home by hammering his fist in the palm of his hand—called his First Sergeants to the command post. One question he wanted answered was why more citations weren't being sent back for the men at the front. He pointed out that the casualty rate was terrific, and somebody must be doing something to merit medal citations or we wouldn't be rolling along like we were. If men were due credit, he would see that they got it and the like.[23]

After returning to our dugout, we sent for the men that had single-handedly performed some feat of bravery that might qualify them for a citation. Somebody suggested, "How about that guy that brought in fifteen prisoners by himself?"

"Okay, let's interview him," we said.

In a short while, the soldier reported. A week's growth of beard covered his face; his overcoat was muddy and eyes red from lack of sleep.

"Tell us, how did you do it?" we asked him.

"Well," he replied, "there isn't much to tell. My platoon leader said that since I was the only guy who spoke some German, I should go into the village and tell them to give up. When I got there, they were all packed and ready. They said that according to their intelligence reports, we shoulda been there yesterday."

4

THE CENTRAL EUROPE CAMPAIGN

22 March 1945–11 May 1945

Your husband is getting to be quite a character.

The Central Europe Campaign began as Allied forces crossed the Rhine River and advanced rapidly across Germany. My father's unit crossed the Rhine on the 28th of March, and soon they were moving much faster than before. German resistance weakened, but some cities and towns were still hotly defended.

After crossing through Germany almost to the Czech border, the 80th Division turned south in pursuit of retreating German SS units that were rumored to be regrouping to create a redoubt in the Austrian Alps. The plan had been suggested by senior Nazi leaders, but apparently there was never any substance to it. During the last days of the war, some German government officials fled toward Berchtesgaden in the Bavarian mountains near the Austrian border, but rumors of a fortified stronghold proved false.

Nevertheless, my father's regiment sped south, and when the war in Europe came to an end he was in central Austria, where at the Enns River they met the Red Army.

---

25 March 1945
Germany
My darling wife—
Gotcha picture today dear, and it was a honey. Almost like being home

again. Dear, I enjoy hearing from you so much—I sure look forward for the mail to come in.

I went to church today in a church that was almost a thousand years old—the steps were worn almost round. It was really an experience. I sat in the balcony and on the wooden rail was carved some initials that some little "Kraut" carved during a dull sermon, I guess. The organ had to be pumped—one of the soldiers climbed a little ladder and put his foot in a gadget like a stirrup on a horse saddle and pulled up a box-like contraption that made the wind go through the organ. There were two of these little stirrups, so by the time one was pulled down, the other was up.[1]

Everything is very old in this little German village but very neat and clean. The houses are built to last, but they don't have the "new" look that our homes have. The place I'm staying now has a big pump in the court-yard but no running water in the house. The stable is attached to the house just like they were in France and nearly as smelly. The scenery is beautiful, as the land is getting green. Tonight I ate my supper in a field, and it was like having a picnic lunch in the park.

I really had a break the other day. My Company captured a little town about daybreak and one of the guys came running to me and said, "Hey Sarge, look here"—he had found a German quartermaster supply house. Inside was a huge store of clothing and crap and one of the rooms was filled with liquor and (of all things) German cigars. I got several boxes— all I could carry—and stuffed them in my pack. They are milder than ours but I was glad to get them anyway. I still had some you sent me so I'll hold on to them and smoke the "Kraut" cigars. I don't know where the Germans get their tobacco—I guess from Turkey.

My Division has been very successful and we've overrun several prisoner of war camps and released thousands of Russian and French prisoners. The Germans had them working building fortifications. When we first came across Russians, one of the men saw their fuzzy caps and said, "Holy Smoke, I didn't know we were going that fast, to run into Russia so soon."

I don't see any advantage to being a housewife over here—the women all work like horses. They seem to do everything, especially in little agricultural villages, where they have to work in the fields, too. All the men able to carry a gun are in the army, but they were pretty busy when they were home as almost every house has a mob of little squirts running around. You should see the beds these folks have—about three layers of mattresses and a big feather comforter that looks like a feather mattress. I slept on those beds for a long time until somebody told me that the top mattress is to cover up with. Generally when we arrive in a city and have to shell it before we go in, the people are all gone to a shelter somewhere and we just take our pick of houses. If we take a place by surprise we have to herd the people all to one place before we can take possession of their homes.

I know it seems mean to run the people out of their homes, but it's generally for just a night and they should really be glad as they know as long as we are there, we won't shell them, and when we leave they can move back. They just move in with their neighbors until we leave. I told one guy we should get a job with the sheriff when we get home—kicking people out of their homes when they can't pay their mortgage.

I sent Betty Sue a Nazi flag. I hope it gets home okay—it's a dilly and we had quite a rumpus getting it. It is the Regimental flag—the one with silver trimming. I took the flagstaff and all, only to discover I couldn't send it that way, so I took off the top piece and sent that too.[2]

Dear, I love you more and more every day, and how I'll love to squeeze you tight and kiss you again. [The page was cut here.]

---

25 March 1945
Germany
My darling wife—

Hello honey—I got a chance to write again. My regiment has been moving pretty fast, and we've had no time to do anything. Things look pretty good as we've just about cleared everything this side of the Rhine. For several days, the roads were thick with PWs on the way to the rear. One line must have had a thousand in it—three abreast—and a tank following along at the end. Usually we just send them back down the road without a guard, and frequently you can see twenty or thirty walking toward our lines. Most of them are glad to get captured—the German officers and non-commissioned officers are the ones trying to carry on the war, it seems.

The other day we slipped into a town and captured the entire garrison before they knew what happened. We captured one kid in civilian clothes who was home on furlough. He was only 18 and had been in the army a year. We made our headquarters at his house which was also the local post office. We were very rough and businesslike, as these dopes don't know what it is to be human. That evening, the family assembled in the kitchen next to my room and had family prayers. That got me down, so I sent our interpreter in to tell them that he would be safe and would be sent home after the war. They told our interpreter that he was the last son, as the other two were killed a short time before. The kid was returning to the army the next day. The family felt much better after we explained the situation to them.

Most of the Germans are religious—and then again we find evidence that they have been cruel. We recently overran several prison camps where hundreds of Russians were kept prisoner. The Russian women were farmed out to do house work and farm work, and in several houses we found whips where they beat them. At one of the houses we stopped at, a Russian girl told us she had worked there three years. She said the German soldiers brought them from Russia when they invaded.

The German language is very harsh—it seems like everybody is yelling at one another. I don't know how they manage to make love—but they must as every house has a bunch of kids.

One town had a row of nice houses—all had a housewife and about 8 kids and no husbands. Somebody told us that was one of the Hitler baby plants—some system, eh kid?

As I said before, these people do not understand anything except direct orders. The minute you smile or act human they take advantage of the situation. Hitler sure had these folks regimented. The people are all progressive though, and although their houses are very old, the inside is neat and clean and for the most part very modern. The towns are very close together and you could easily walk across the country, stopping overnight at a hotel when you get tired. Recently we've been going through 10 or 15 towns a day.

Darling, I love you more and more every day—I think when I get home I'll just spoil you. I'll just baby you to pieces.

> Goodnight darling—
> Lots of love
> Your little husband

p.s. I love you

Crossing the Rhine

For chronological reasons, this letter written on 28 April is included here

My darling wife—

... Take a good look at the postcard that has "Mainz" written in the lower left-hand corner. That river is the Rhine and the picture was taken from an island in the middle. The city of Mainz is on both sides of the river and that is where we crossed—we got control of the side of town you see and held it—across the river to the right the Germans held the other half of the town.

The idea was to slip across shortly after midnight and take them by surprise. So we quietly sneaked our boats down to the water's edge and launched them at 0100. The first wave started and in ten minutes another wave of boats left, then every ten minutes until we were all across. When the first wave reached the middle of the river, the moon came out bright as day—the Germans opened up on us with machine guns and anti-aircraft cannons.[3]

That was one of the bloodiest engagements we've had since Luxembourg. Every boat had dead and dying men in it when they finally landed. The bank was a brick sea wall, and those that were able to make the shore were caught in a crossfire of machine guns there. I don't know how we did it, but we gained a foothold and held on till dawn's early light. The Germans fought like wildcats to push us back into the river—they killed every prisoner they took—but the waves of boats kept on coming and by dawn we had built up enough power to go out and drive them back. No matter what happens, when we start, we keep going—I guess even Hitler's supermen get "goggle eyed" at that.[4]

By the time we had control of the town, the Germans reorganized and brought up tanks to push us back. We frantically radioed our artillery support to give us a hand. In a moment, the artillery radio announced "on the way," and the big shells began to rain on the German tanks and they had to back up. The artillery is really our friend, and they never fail us when they are called on. When we are tired and discouraged on long hikes with heavy packs and pass their trucks, they hand us part of their rations and give us water from their canteens when we are too tired to pull ours out. When we are fresh and rested and feel pretty cocky, they tell us they don't think we are so "hot" and give us a good "razzing." They paint names on their cannons and the bigger and uglier the gun the "sassier" the name they give it—"Little Audrey," "Daisy," "Tootsie," and a lot more equally silly. . . .

Respite on the Riviera

A memory written in 1947

One day in late March 1945, just after crossing the Rhine River, our company was marching through a badly shelled German village. It was a raw cold day with sleet and rain. The soldiers' overcoats were wet, and it seemed that the damp penetrated to their bones. After miles of marching across country, their feet were raw and sore.

A messenger came down the column with several slips of paper in his hand. "Sergeant, you are to report to the Battalion Command Post," he told me.

"Why?" I asked. "What's up?"

"Gosh, don't asked me," he said. "They never tell me anything."

We made our way to a charred wreck of a building, and in the one usable room, we found the sergeant-major. "Say you guys," he said, "jump on this truck. You've been selected to go on pass to the French Riviera. I don't have details to tell you. Here's your papers."

In an instant, we were on a truck bound for Luxembourg City, where we took a train to Nice. Our coach was third-class—plain wooden benches and very uncomfortable. Two days later, we arrived in Nice on the southern coast of France.

We were a forlorn-looking group of infantry soldiers. We were taken from the front lines in the miserable cold and deposited on the sunny shores of the Mediterranean. Heretofore, we hadn't given much thought to our appearance, but the glimpses from the coach window of the neat, well-groomed soldiers from other branches of the service made us acutely uncomfortable.

Most of us had shell fragment holes in our overcoats. Our hair was matted from wearing wool knit caps too long without washing. Eyes were red from lack of sleep, and faces stained gray from exploding gunpowder. Our boots were covered with red clay, and our trousers were filthy from keeling and digging. We were still wearing our net-covered steel helmets when we detrained. Each man in the group, conscious of his looks, tried to edge behind a companion.

"What in the hell is this?" cried a good-looking, well-dressed air corps sergeant, his shoes shined and uniform pressed. Then he swallowed hard and turned to a group of air corps men and yelled, "Let's have a cheer for the Infantry, and make it loud!" After the cheer, they rushed up and took our packs and rifles, and carried them for us to our hotel.

"Jesus!" whispered the guy next to me. "This is one of the proudest moments of my life."

---

1 April 1945
Easter Sunday
Nice, France
My darling—

Dear heart—I surely had a big surprise. I had my pack and equipment on my back and my Company was marching down to an attack when a messenger came up and yelled for "First Sergeant Smith" to report to Battalion HQ. When I arrived at the torn-up building they called Headquarters, the Sgt Major told me I had been selected for a week furlough on the Mediterranean Ocean. I hopped into a truck and went to the rear where they gave me a towel, soap, razor, and a carton of cigarettes (that I don't smoke). Thank goodness I had some of my Xmas cigars in my pack.[5]

I slept there that night and then early in the morning, we loaded into another truck and rode almost 200 miles to [censor cut out words]. We arrived about seven o'clock in the evening. The restaurant in the railroad station has been taken over by the army, so we had supper and walked around Luxembourg City for a while. I had never seen the capital of Luxembourg, as we were doing some fierce fighting the last time I was nearby. The station is beautiful and is similar to the railroad stations we have at home. The restaurant was very elaborate at one time, but the army doesn't go in for much decoration.

We got aboard our train about eleven, and you should see the railroad cars or carriages as they are called. Six people occupy a compartment—three facing each other. Each compartment has a door opening outside the car and a narrow aisle runs down one side of the car—it's very uncomfortable. The johnny doesn't have any water and the closet was similar to the farmyard variety. It took us two days and nights to get here. A solid trainload of G.I.s.

I had my pack and full field equipment, so at night I spread my two blankets on the floor between the seats and another guy slept with me. Two on the seats and two, of all places, in the baggage rack overhead. At noon the next day, the train stopped at a feeding point I guess you would call it, a mess hall beside the railroad tracks, and we had a hot meal. We were nearly starved. They also had a lot of helmets propped up like wash-basins, and we washed, ate, and were off again.

About midnight, the train pulled up to another station, and we had sandwiches and coffee. The next day about noon we arrived at the Riviera on the Mediterranean Ocean. The train stopped at Cannes and all the offi-cers got off. One of the army men got aboard with an arm full of envelopes that we bought for 100 Francs (about two bucks). It had the name of our Hotel, meal ticket, guide, and a lot of other crap in it.

This place is classier than Miami, so you can imagine the beautiful hotels. We are put in rooms, three to a room. After we washed, we were given brand new clothes and had lunch in the finest hotel on the prome-nade overlooking the Mediterranean Ocean.

As I was pulled out of the front line, I discovered that I was broke, since I never took any money with me on an attack. So they let me draw fifty bucks on my next month's salary. Gee! I can hardly believe it. The army is providing everything except souvenirs, which are terribly expensive and foolish stuff. We get our hotel room, meals, clean clothes, and free movies and Red Cross entertainment. This is some sort of Lend Lease in reverse or another "quick shuffle" so the American saps will pay the French back in business again. The army provides the food and the French cook it and civilians run the hotels and nightclubs, but the army supervises and pays up the difference.[6]

The only thing is I wish they would have waited until the war was over and then sent me and my little wife here for a vacation. I never did enjoy going anywhere without you, kid. I guess I'll just rest and take it easy—I'll wait until I get home to you to whoop it up.

I asked the bellhop what kind of hotel it was before the war, and he told us it was a very exclusive whorehouse—can you beat that? In the bathrooms of all the hotels, they have a little tub that looks like a bathtub for a midget, and when we asked what the hell that was for they told us that was the ladies' douche bowl. I guess before the war everybody did a lot of screwing around here. The army put a stop to that for the men visiting here. And it's a good thing too, as some of the men don't know when to stop drinking and wind up with some sort of venereal disease and can be ruined for life.

Darling, I love you more than anything in the world and will be so glad when this is over and I can return to you. Say! See where the Third Army is now—it looks encouraging. Maybe it won't be too long.

Lots of love dearest

Your little husband

p.s. Gee! but I love you.

---

2 April 1945

Nice, France

My darling wife—

Hello honey—here's your little husband taking it easy and wishing he was with you instead.

Every morning, I get up about 8 o'clock and have my breakfast in the hotel dining room—most of the meals are very light, French style, and we are served by the French waiters. The food is served out of silver bowls, and they like to make a big fuss over each dish. For the noon meal, we had pancakes with tomatoes in the dough. Tasted good. We had spam fixed like that once also.

The Easter parade was something to see here. Everybody turned out and had a walk up and down the beach. The women all seem to have plenty of makeup and use lots of it. Most of them dress very smart, and you never see a sloppy one. All of them are in a rush and remind me of our sophisticated Avondale set (ha! ha!). None of them are as smart as my little wife, though.[7]

I tried to buy lingerie but have to have points, as the ration system is going full blast. I understand it's quite the "stuff" to be able to say your pants come from France or the Riviera, but doesn't look as though I can make it unless I can find a place that will sell without the points.

The French folks spend a lot of time sitting around in the little sidewalk cafes sipping coffee or wine or something—I guess that's how the war got away from them. Some guy was telling me at lunch there are 150 hotels here—another Miami.

I went to the movies this afternoon. It was for soldiers only and in a beautiful theatre on the promenade that faces the ocean. It was a clever picture called "When Irish Eyes Are Smiling" or something like that. I told the fellow I was with I'd probably leave in about 10 minutes, but it turned out to be very good.

The other two guys are clamoring to go eat, so I'll write you more tomorrow.

Don't forget I love you more than anything else in the world.

Lots of love

Your little husband

p.s. I love you.

—————

3 April 1945

Nice, France

My Darling—

Well I finally got my photos but I don't think they are so hot. But be that as it may, it's your little husband and you are stuck with him, kid. As you can see in the background, "sojers" are running all over the place.

Me and another guy are going to rent a bicycle this afternoon and go sightseeing. The other night, we ran into some sailors that are part of the Mediterranean fleet, and it looked like home to see a blue uniform again.

The hotel ballrooms are redecorated and open again, so I usually sit and listen to the music and watch the floor show until I get sleepy. The men invite lots of French girls they meet to the dances, but I'll just wait until I get home and dance with my little honeybun.

The ballrooms are much more elaborate than anything I've ever seen in America, and they don't have that noisy crowded feeling. Most of them have terrific high ceilings, so I guess that explains it. Around the outer edge of the tables, there are comfortable chairs where you can sit and watch the crowd. That's where I hang out. Then I sit around the beach and read too—just taking it easy.

Sergeant Smith on furlough in Nice: "To my little wife with all my love, Perc"

French cooking isn't so hot—it's too dainty and not enough of it. You should hear the men piss and moan when the waiter pours them a little cup of coffee and serves little plates of food—almost everybody eats two dinners. The French waiters like to make a big show and have the food on hot plates in the dining room—oh! It's very nice but the soldiers are mostly goons anyway, and it's like casting pearls before swine, you know.

The women are wearing shoes made out of straw, and they look pretty smart, too. I guess it's cool and saves leather too. Most of the people are well dressed and look prosperous. Their clothes look as though they have been worn but very good quality. Sometimes you get the impression that they would do without eating to keep up appearances.

Well, dear heart, I must go to lunch and I'll write you again real soon. Don't forget I love you more than anything else in the world.

Lots of love

Your little husband

p.s. You're the sweetest one.

6 April 1945

Nice, France

My dear little wife—

Well Dear, the little vacation is about over. I catch the train to join my Regiment this afternoon. It was nice in a way, but rather tiresome to me in another. It made me homesick to sit in the ballroom of our hotel and hear the orchestra play familiar American tunes. "I Walk Alone" and "Night and Day" I believe are my favorites—"Stardust" used to be my favorite tune.

This is a good place for single men and men who don't get along with their wives—everybody makes whoopee—one of the men in my room has gone head over heels for one of the French girls. He tells me he's going to take her to America after the war. Me and the other guy have been trying to talk some sense into him, but you know how it is—you can't tell anybody anything.

I went to see a stage show put on by "Folies Bergere" from Paris. It was the regular vaudeville we usually see at home, only longer. They don't have too

Taking a stroll along the streets of Nice, France

much tap dancing (I don't care for it anyway) in their shows. The theatres are much more elaborate than anything I've seen in the states. I saw an Andy Hardy movie, but this one was for the French civilians and the characters all spoke French. I've read several books and loafed around, so I don't guess my little vacation was entirely wasted.

According to our Army newspaper, it looks as though Germany will never surrender and we will just have to take over all the territory and tell them the war has ended. No matter how much they are surrounded, they still fight. You have to admire their courage, although it's a "pain in the fanny" to have to bother with them.

I've had to holler and bellow so much in broken German and French to make myself understood, I'll enjoy sitting down talking to you—peaceful like. In Germany, the only thing they understand is a lot of loud rough talk. Of course, you and I won't have to talk too much at first. I'll be like a brand-new husband—nervous and everything. It'll go something like this—your little husband will come rushing. . . . [8]

Lots of love
Your little husband
p.s. I love you.

---

8 April 1945
Luxembourg City
My darling wife—

I'm on my way to rejoin my Regiment and had to stop over in Luxembourg City for the day while we await trucks to take us back to the front. It took two days and nights to get from Nice to Luxembourg City by train—goodness knows how long it will be before we reach our units. I enjoyed my little vacation but I missed having you with me—I can't really enjoy myself without you. It seems like I'm just half there or that part of me is missing. I guess you are a part of me dear—a part that I can never do without.

It was very warm in Nice—here in Luxembourg it's still cold and windy. There is quite a contrast between the people of Nice and the people of Luxembourg. In Nice everybody seems lazy and indolent, while the people in Luxembourg have energy and zip.

I went to see a movie this afternoon and saw an older American film—"Having a Wonderful Time." Ginger Rogers and Douglas Fairbanks Jr.—it was very screwy—no wonder the Europeans think we are a little odd.

Let's see if I can answer some of the questions you asked me in former letters—yes, I received the pecan roll and it was in very good shape and we sure enjoyed it—of course I had to pass it around—and swish, it was gone, you know. I haven't the slightest idea what I'll do after the war.

Darling, I can hardly wait until the day when I can take you in my arms and kiss you and really tell you how much I love you.[9]

  Good night dear heart,

  Lots of love

  Your little husband

p.s. you are a little angel

Buchenwald

In his own wartime letters and his stories written later, my father did not describe direct encounters with victims of Nazi concentration camps. But he kept a postwar anecdote on that subject written by Virgil Myers, a fellow Company G infantryman. Perhaps moved by wartime stories that Smith had shared with him, Myers wrote the following description of an incident that probably occurred on 12 April 1945.

Percy Smith, the first sergeant of G Company, Don Smith, our jeep driver, and I were instructed by Lieutenant Damkowitch, our company commander, around 1600 to see if we could find out where the men in striped uniforms were coming from. We started out in the direction we saw some of them coming from and found Buchenwald about two kilometers NW of town. Men were standing leaning against the fence facing us and they seemed to be in a trance. One of the men who was so thin he could hardly walk held his hand up and walked to one of the buildings, saying something in a language I couldn't understand, but in a short time he came back with a small fellow who said he could speak English if we spoke slow. He told us he was originally from Lithuania and had been in the camp for four years. He said the SS guards had left the night before when they heard the Americans were coming.[10]

As the guards were leaving, the prisoners overpowered and locked several of the guards in a room. He told us that the prisoners had looked forward to this day and had arranged for their own rules and plans to live by until they were freed. Percy took several pictures of the people. We walked between two or so rows of buildings, saw dead people piled outside of the buildings that had been placed there to get them out of the living quarters. We went back to Weimar and reported to Lieutenant Damkowitch what we had seen. He said he was going to call Regiment or Division and let them know what was there. I do know that the next day there were trucks of food, clothes, and medicine for the prisoners.[11]

16 April 1945
Germany
Dear little sweetheart—

The first thing I want to tell you today is that I love you and think you are the sweetest wife in the world—and the second is that you are the smartest wife a man could have.

Your husband is getting to be quite a character—we had to clear some woods on our way to take this town, and our first action took place when we ran into Germans hiding in the woods.[12] We opened fire and kept right on firing as we walked toward them—one of them gave up and walked toward us with his hands up. They passed him on to my section to hold until we took the next town. I looked at him and blinked—"Say," I asked the interpreter, "ask the guy how old he is." He was just fifteen years old. A few minutes later, two more gave up and they were fourteen—a little later another gave up and he was fifteen. He was wounded so badly we couldn't take him with us, so the aid man patched him up and we put him on the road so the first aid jeep could find him, and moved on through the woods. I took the prisoners along with me and they were pitiful to look at—they were so young it made me think of Betty Sue. They were scared stiff, as they had killed some of our men and thought we were going to shoot them.

As we moved through the woods, we gathered more prisoners—these were older though. Our group of prisoners got so big, I had to move them down on the road and line them up. As we were doing that, who should come riding a bicycle down the road but a German nurse. She said she was going to the next town that we were going to attack, to the hospital. So we had to put her in the column of prisoners and take her with us. A little later, a couple of guys in civilian clothes came walking down the road—they were added to our collection. A few more miles down the road, we added a couple of women to our group. A little later we picked up another woman, and I guess she saw her husband in the group of men with civilian clothes, as she started bawling. That was awful rough, but we couldn't take a chance, as a lot of our men have been shot by women snipers and it's better to be safe than sorry. By the time we got to our objective, we had a helluva collection—we had German air corps men, German artillery men, German infantrymen, German tank men, nurses, civilians, and damn if I don't think the kids were German Boy Scouts. We took them along with us and when the town was taken, we took them to the PW cage, as it's called. The women were released and the civilians that could identify themselves were released also. The women were scared stiff of your husband, as I wasn't fooling when I stuck them in with our prisoners. They didn't have any business out there in the first place and knew we were coming by all the shooting we were doing. And another reason is that every time I feel like feeling sorry for these folks, I think about the men I've seen with arms and legs blown off and bodies of men killed by them. Then I say to myself—if it wasn't for them and the Germans that voted and sanctioned the war when they were winning, I would be home with my little wife where I belong.[13]

The guys we like to catch are the S.S. boys—you remember they were the special army that Hitler created and they were told they were supermen. That's the gang that burned Lidice and killed everybody in it. They killed about a thousand Poles and Russians near a town we were in recently. A lot of the men went out to see it and said the bones are still in the lime pit, and you can see hands and feet sticking out.[14]

Most of the S.S. troops we catch don't seem much like supermen when we get close to them. The other day, a section of my Company had to surrender to the S.S. troops, and they shot them all through the head—one of the men saw it and played dead until we could get some help up and push them back. When we catch these bastards, I have to almost threaten to shoot our own men to keep them from tearing them limb from limb.[15]

These Germans brought Russians and Poles back to Germany with them and farmed them out as maids, farm laborers, and used them for all kinds of work. Some of our men speak their language, and they really tell some pitiful stories. We were stopped for a rest at one nice-looking house, and they had about ten Poles and Russians working for them. They give them clothes and feed them, and in turn they have to work for them.

One girl who was a housemaid told us she had been brought from Russia three years ago, and the man they worked for was really mean and beat her and the other girls every chance he got. She said he kept a big whip in the barn, and she took some of the men out and showed them. She said he made them go get the whip and take it to the cellar. He must have been downright mean, as he would tell them to strip and he would be down later. She said she and the other girls used to sit on a bench in the cellar for a couple of hours with nothing on but their dress until he came down to whip them. He had a piece of rope to tie them up with, and when he came down he would make her take off her dress and tie her hands and pull the rope over the beam in the cellar until her hands were over her head, then beat her until she was nearly unconscious. She told us that in January, one of our pilots crashed on their farm and the pilot's leg was broken. This guy, who was the Burgermeister or mayor of the village, kicked him to death. We found him and put him under arrest. Somebody must have beat him up a little, as he looked a little rugged when I saw him.

Not all the Germans are mean to their slave help, and frequently the slave seemed contented to stay. We are going to have a big problem with the Russians we release when we overrun the prison camps—they are like wild people. They hate the Germans so much—they grab guns and go to work on them right and left. The other day when we released several thousand Russians, they were killing their civilian bosses right in the streets, and bodies were all around everywhere. They told us they wouldn't do any more to the Germans than they did to the Russians; then they would smile—so the Germans must have been pretty rough when they had their day. The released prisoners are being sent to the rear as fast as we can get them there, but there are so many. Some of them run loose and loot warehouses and stores. Goodness knows what else they do when they get a little drunk. One of the German prisoners told me that when he was fighting on the Russian front, the Russian soldiers would sneak up on them when they were in their foxholes and throw water on them—it was so cold they would freeze to death. He said he was glad he was captured by Americans, as the Russians were mean.

We must have quite a reputation too, as they tell the civilians we are

"Chicago gangsters." We look the part too. I've never seen such a tough collection in my life.[16] The people in the towns are terrified when we arrive with miles and miles of tanks and the tough-looking soldiers marching along with them. It's quite a sight when the shooting stops and the dust settles and the soldiers move in the houses for a rest and maybe spend the night. Sometimes we have to kick the door down—then we give the civilians fifteen or twenty minutes to clear out—now that sounds rough, doesn't it? Well, it's a case of us being mean or sleeping on the ground in the rain. Then when I start to feel sorry for them, I think about the dead bodies of the men of my Company and the pathetic letters from their wives and mothers trying to find out the details of their death. Kid, this is a rough life, and I'm so glad my little wife is in America.

Do you think any relatives would like to have a small German pistol? They are cute—and all have snappy cases. I can get them a couple if they want them, but it will be sort of hard getting them back, as they don't want us to send pistols home—some of the birds in the rear like to grab them. After the war I don't ever want to see a gun again, but they might like to shoot them. Let me know and I'll see what I can do. I'll send some of the [German] officers' dress knives sometime soon—they are real snappy and will make nice letter openers. I could send a lot of junk if we would get a little time to wrap them up.

I haven't heard from you for a couple of days so I guess my mail got screwed up when I changed Companies again. Did I shock you in the letter I wrote yesterday? Write me and let me know.[17]

    Lots of love honey
    Your little husband
p.s. you are an angel—angel wings

———————

18 April 1945
    Germany
Dear little angel—

Well we didn't move today as we expected to, so I'll write you another letter before we shove off again—this suspense of getting ready and waiting gets me down. I guess that's why everybody in the service gets indifferent after so long a time. Sometimes I feel that if the building across the street should collapse, I wouldn't even walk over to the window to see what happened.[18]

My Battalion controls this town, which is pretty big, so yesterday the colonel decided to have a parade.[19] I guess the Germans were surprised to see the Amerikaners marching down their streets—they all stuck their heads out the window the same as when their Supermen used to march up and down the street. It must be embarrassing as hell to the Krauts to work for years to build up an army second to none and then have a bunch of "Chicago gangsters" come over and kick the hell out of it. It would be too much for me. I think I'd just quit and cut paper dolls or something else.

I just noticed my hair in a mirror today. I've been wearing a little wool cap under my helmet all winter, and my hair sticks out in all directions now. I don't have it cut short, and half of it looks like a porcupine. One of the men in my section is a barber, and he told me that we've been wearing those little caps so long it makes our hair dry. So your little husband jumped in a jeep and went out to a German warehouse and got us all some hair oil. The German soldiers all have a long mane of hair, and most of them have bottles of hair oil in their pockets. This warehouse was loaded with stuff to send the soldiers—pocketknives, sunglasses, writing paper (this is some of it), pictures of Hitler, and a lot of other crap. So your little husband gathered us up a supply and distributed them to our soldiers.

There is a bad feature about this war—while the fighting is going on and after it stops until the military government takes charge, the place is open territory and civilians and soldiers are busy picking up stuff. The civilians usually take valuable stuff and the soldiers try to get souvenirs—I've got a couple of officers' dress knives that would make pretty good letter openers or paperweights and some more junk I'll try to send home soon. I have several pistols too. If I can, I'll send them home too—you can give them away. If nobody wants them, throw them in the creek, as I don't want to see a gun again after the war. About all they would be good for would be to shoot at targets—unless you want to hold up a bank or something.

About the only thing I've seen around here that I've really wanted was some bolts of cloth that we found in a uniform factory. It was really nice, and it was used to make uniforms for the "Supermen," light-brown Palm Beach type of material. You could really make some nice stuff out of it. These bolts of cloth were for the elite guards' uniforms, and they were really snappy—even had snow-white kid gloves to go with it. I looked pretty sorry in my washed and unironed wool shirt and trousers. We get clean suits fairly often, but they are just washed and you can imagine how my shirt and pants look. I don't care though—there isn't any reason that I can see to put on the "dog" over here.

There is one thing I'll have to say for this country—it's beautiful. Really, I've never seen anything like it—the grass is pretty and green and the country is hilly—the farmers just plow one section of their fields and it makes a checkerboard—the trees in the orchards are arranged in pretty designs and rows—the people are all busy and never loaf around like the French. I don't guess I'll ever understand them.

You should see the houses over here—they are all stone and the walls are two or three feet thick—boy, they were made to last generations. The walls are all painted and most of them I've seen look pretty fresh. The beds are short though. I can't figure that out unless they sleep humped up on top of one another—could be, as there are lots of little "Krauts" running around. Maybe we should get us one of these beds—they're piled high with feather mattresses and have huge pillows. They look nice to sleep in, too.

Darling, the candle is playing out, so I better end this before I'm left in the dark.

    With all my love

    Your little husband

p.s. I love you—dear.

---

19 April 1945

Germany

Dear little angel—

Dear little wife, I just received your letter you wrote Easter Sunday—I'm 19 days away by airmail. While I'm writing, I'm looking at your latest picture in your bathing suit. (Oh! la la) What are you doing to me kid—set me on fire? I like it though, kid, so fire me up.

Dear, while you were writing at Easter your little husband was at the Riviera—but he would rather be with you. My vacation was soon over though, and now I feel as though I had never been away.

Elizabeth at Jacksonville Beach, 11 March 1945

Say, kid, take a look at the joint your husband is staying in the past day or so. The place hasn't been hurt too much, just a few panes knocked out. The big square castle-looking building is a flour mill. This is the miller's home. In the lower picture, the round hump is the arch to the gate; inside is a large rectangle that used to be the courtyard. The living quarters are in the building to the right. I can imagine how the people felt to see a gang of "Chicago gangsters" rush into their courtyard, but they were very calm and we moved in without friction. The mill is running again, and a lot of the Poles and Russians and some more rabble tried to break in the mill and take all the wheat. The miller was in a bad fix, so I told him our soldiers were here to preserve law and order and for him to continue to conduct his business as before. He told us they had a ration system, and if they were looted or forced to sell without a ration book, the civilians would go hungry. Now that they see how we are, they told us they were sorry we had to go (we leave at 0400 tomorrow). The name of this town is Bad Kostritz. No harm in mentioning the name, as we'll be hundreds of miles from here by the time you get this. I don't know whether you can find it on the map or not—it's not too far from Weimar.

Be on the lookout for your package of perfume and your camera. A German officer led his men almost to our lines and fell pretty close to your little husband. As we couldn't get out of our holes, we reached out and pulled his pack inside to see what the Krauts carry around. The other guy took his pistol and gave me his camera, as the Kraut didn't need it, and if it were left it would be picked up by somebody else.

I'm sending you a knife to open your mail and a cup I picked up in Mettendorf.[20] After the fracas there, your little husband was sitting around in the rubble and found the cup. I stuck it in my pack and carried it hoping to find something else to send, but couldn't so I sent it before I broke it.

I received the snapshots and they are so nice—I could eat you up you look so good. Say, Betty is growing up isn't she? Getting to be a nice-looking girl.

Do you remember me telling you about the lady propaganda announcer that plays the records of American tunes and heckles us between pieces? Well, we captured her radio station and she's out of work. It's just as well as she has caused us a lot of trouble. The fellows in the Pacific say they get the same broadcast from Tokyo, and the woman calls herself Tokyo Rose.

Dear, it's time to hit the hay as we have a long march tomorrow— lots of love.[21]

Love

Your little husband

p.s. I love you, kid.

---

21 April 1945

Germany

My darling wife—

Well darling, here I am almost to Czechoslovakia, and really in a poor section of Germany. I think we landed in the "Dogpatch" of Germany.[22] We came rushing to this little village, as we usually do, and after we had established ourselves in the houses we had the people fry up eggs for us as our K-rations get pretty tiresome. They did—and we gobbled them up. Later we saw what they had for supper—black bread and weak German coffee—boy that got us down—we all slipped them our Ks, and they were tickled to death. They acted like a bunch of kids on Xmas morning. I've never seen such poor people since I've been in Germany.

They told us part of their crop has been turned over to the army and the ration system has been so tight they haven't been able to get new clothes for the past six years. They were neat and clean but poor as church mice. Today we had hot food at noon so we gave them a real meal. We had pork chops, mashed potatoes, gravy, green peas, bread, and jam. In this section, white bread is as scarce as cake. We haven't been running into so much resistance in this section, and the people here are sick and tired of the war. (I am too.)

We've been moving around so much I haven't heard from you for some time. Rumors are running wild here but I'm almost afraid to pin much hope on them. We captured a German radio and can hear music from England—sure makes me homesick.

I got the pictures, dear—they were so nice. I can't tell you how much I appreciated them—you look so good. Some of the men saw them and exclaimed how good-looking you were. They were telling me what a cute

Sergeant Smith
wears his new scarf.

little wife I had. They weren't telling me anything—I knew it all the time. You were a lucky catch for me, and I'm not going to let you get away.

Well dear heart, I've been doing a lot of traveling since I left you. Germany is beautiful—no doubt about it—the climate is cool and snappy and keeps the people healthy and full of pep. It's going to be hard to keep these people down—the people do everything precisely and plan everything carefully—the houses, the roads, and everything are made of stone or brick. I haven't seen a wooden house since I've been in Germany. Even this little house is made of stone—it's really old though. As peppy as these folks are, they don't have the modern conveniences that we have and do everything the hard way. I can't get over how hard they have to work in the fields. The country is mostly agricultural, and the people are dependent on the farmers. I wish you could see the pretty scenery here, as you would probably enjoy it more than I do.

We have a snappy addition to our uniform—we wear blue scarfs around our necks. They are pretty and give us a little "zip"—they are made of some soft material and are supposed to protect our necks from the itchy wool shirts.

Dear, I'm going to baby you for a long time when I get home—later maybe if we feel like it, we'll see about the "family." You'll probably have to domesticate me all over after the rough life I've been living. You'll have to get after me to shave, as I didn't shave for weeks at a time.

Darling—it's a madhouse here so I'll have to stop as I can hardly hear myself think, much less write. Good night darling.

>   Lots of love
>   Your little husband
p.s. I love you, angel wings.

---

23 April 1945
Germany
My darling wife—

Dear, it's cool and rainy here. I'm in Nuremberg at the present—one of the largest cities in Germany—it's beat nearly flat and the resistance is about over. One whole section is bombed and shelled flat. I've never seen anything like it—and I've seen a lot of beat-up towns. We came up from a

The back of the photo reads, "Nuremberg. We had just finished mopping up the last bit of resistance . . . our men and theirs were still laying in the streets."

Sam Cordon, Smith, and Robert McAllister in Nuremberg

little town about 40 miles from here that was very pitiful. We were the first Americans there and were quite a curiosity—that is, after the folks found out that we were harmless.

The city we are in now has that big stadium that we used to see in the newsreels where acres and acres of German soldiers used to drill and march for the Fuehrer—there's not too much to see here now as the place, as I mentioned before, is in a shambles.[23] Then it's not too safe to be wandering around looking at the scenery as the "party members" are still active in some sections of town, but they will be subdued shortly. They make a nuisance of themselves by sniping at us—several women were caught trying to shoot at us too. This war is foolish, and nobody wins in things like this. Hitler told his people to elect him Fuehrer and in ten years they wouldn't recognize the place—boy! He was right—you would never recognize these piles of junk as cities.

I had a nice long truck ride today—the country was beautiful as usual—green grassy hills and beautiful landscapes—Lombardy poplar trees and weeping willows—too bad there has to be a war here.

We have an apartment house for our billets while we are in Nuremberg—they were swell once before the Amerikaners came—now most of the plaster and windows are knocked out. Tonight we found some potatoes in the basement and made French fried potatoes, even with flour—remember? The fellows had never heard of such a thing, but they really went for them, as they were delicious. Made me think of you so much. I washed our dishes tonight, and as my assistant dried them, he was telling me that it must be fun to be married. Boy! I'll say—but it would be a lot more fun to be home with my angel wings though.

>   Lots of love dear
>   Your little husband
> p.s. I love you dear

------

24 April 1945
Germany
My darling wife—
Dearest little sweetheart—I'm so glad you received your little cup. I wondered what the writing said and happy to hear Mr. Berrig could trans-

Cup from Mettendorf, dated 1913: "Wake up happy every morning. Drink your coffee without a care."

"Far away, I stand in service to the Fatherland and cannot give you my hand today." These phrases also appeared on beer steins.

late it for you. I picked it up during a battle for the village of Mettendorf. While we were waiting for our artillery support to come up, I found it laying in a room in a tavern. The bullets were zinging all around and every time a shell crashed into the street, big sheets of plaster fell on us. I thought you would like it so I put it in my pack and when we were able, we attacked and pushed on to a village called Wissmannsdorf on the Prum River. While I was there, I found the paper and wrapped it up. I had to stuff one of my sox in it to keep it from breaking.

You'll have to tell Mr. Berrig that Germany is in a helluva shape right now, but I'm sure they will rebuild it in a jiffy, as the people are too progressive to let this get them down. I'm enclosing some photos that I found in the building that I'm using for my headquarters. I'll write on the back of them so you'll know that they are. I didn't make the snapshots myself. I'm in Nuremberg now and most of the scenes are of the city or nearby—the scenery is mostly what I want you to see, as it's so typical and so beautiful.

Dear, I note what you say about not letting the "smart-looking French women" get me. But I don't want them—you are the only one for me. I think no one would ever do for me except you. I don't know how the other men get along, but when I got married I took a vow that you would be the only one. And you will be. If I thought someone else had an affair with you, it would break my heart—and if I feel like that about you, it's no more fair for me to do something I shouldn't than you. As you say, it's a lot in your mind—and I keep my thoughts on nobody but you. It's a lot of manure about men having to do "it." Gee! I don't think I would know how to act with anybody else but you—and I don't want to find out. Don't worry dear—you are the one for me and I could never face you if I had an affair with another woman. I always thought it was hard for women—one of the keystones in the German propaganda setup was to make the American soldiers suspicious of their wives—it works too because I have to handle a lot of divorce procedures for my men and I've seen lots of them break down and have to be sent to the rear because they yielded to the suggestions of the radio programs and the other literature they find—it brings up memories, and the propaganda boys and girls really work on that.

Personally, I don't pay any attention to that crap as I trust my wife and want her to know that wherever I am or have to go, I'll always be true to her only—you are the sweetest wife in the world.

Yes, the war news looks good and we are getting along pretty good—the town of Nuremberg was still burning when we arrived. Part of the city was under control, but we could hear rattling machine gun fire in the distance—our men and the Germans were still laying in the streets—but the generals decided that we would take the town at all costs, and that was all there was to it. The mayor of Nuremberg was killed by the S.S. and Gestapo men when he tried to surrender the city. The last place to fall was the Gestapo headquarters, and some of the tunnels are still not cleared. But all and all, I think the end is near.

Today I needed some thumbtacks and office supplies, so I armed one of the privates with a crowbar and we invaded a big electrical factory—I picked up some of these pictures and a stapling machine and some paper and pencils. The factory is really a mess—incidentally, there isn't a house in Nuremberg that isn't hit—the apartment I have is beautiful but the walls are cracked and big hunks of plaster are missing—the electricity is out and the water is off. War is really hell.

The civilians have to stand in long lines to get water, food, and medical supplies—they have to carry their water in buckets to their homes, all the businesses and houses are ruined, and the people are eating potatoes mostly. In the country, the farmers have a better break, as they grow their own livestock and food while the people in big cities are dependent on the canned stuff and the vegetables the farmers bring in.

Nuremberg is one of the big cities of Germany and probably one of the

oldest—part of it has (or had) a wall around it that was erected hundreds
of years ago—when knights in armor had to defend it. It had ancient tow-
ers and battlements and made a beautiful picture—now the "gangsters"
from America came with a bunch of airplanes and tanks and artillery, and
all but smashed it flat. I cannot describe the destruction and do it justice.
It's terrible and personally I wish they (the enemy) would have declared it
an "open city" to save the historic buildings. When they declare it an "open
city," we and they promise not to fire on the city. If we are successful in
taking it, we respect the property rights and so forth—but they decided to
fight to the last man and house to house—they fought for nearly a week.
Lots of women were taken prisoner when they were discovered shooting at
us from the rear.

Yes, the coins are made with a cheap metal—all the brass and silver
coins were taken up and made into implements of war. They went all out
for the war—everything that could possibly be used against us was used.
Every house that I've been in has a chart or map for the people to use when
they observe our aeroplanes, and they report it to their air raid warden.

Darling, I hope and pray this foolishness will soon wind up so we can all
go home. Guess we'll have to start all over again—but I don't care as long as
I have you. Tell everybody else hello for me, as it looks like you are the only
one I'm writing to—my little wife comes first. Take it easy, darling, and
don't forget I love you so much.[24]

Lots of love dear heart,

Your little husband

p.s. you are an angel, kid.

---

28 April 1945

Germany

My darling wife—

I'll write you another "quickie" before some more business comes up
and interrupts my letter writing. It's drizzling rain and the sky is gray so
I guess we are in for a few days of bad weather—I'm really glad we are
indoors. It looks like we'll spend the rest of the war indoors as we are getting a little relief and they are letting the newer units get a "whack" at the
enemy. . . .

We have a time with our mail—the mail section works like the dickens to get our mail up, as we would rather have that than our food. But something always happens when we are on the move—I'm sorry to hear you didn't hear from me for three weeks once—that must have been when we first came into Germany. I try to write to you once a day when I can, then if I have to miss a few days it works out about right. I guess I'm getting to be quite a letter writer and will be sorta lost when I don't have to write any more. I won't be too lost, I'll be busy making love to you. I notice you mentioned in your letter that you loved me—Gee! that's so nice—I love you too, kid—sometimes I think too much 'cause I might squeeze you flat when I come rushing home to you.

You have another package on the way—a tapestry of Nuremberg (before the Americans came), a pair of German field glasses for football games, a couple of rolls of film for your camera. Every camera used in military operations against us, we grab and hold. So I got a couple before the mob in the rear comes up to take charge. I marked the package as a gas mask or something nobody wants—I think the "dizzys" in the rear help themselves to packages when it contains something they want. When I

The back of the photo reads, "Supermen waiting for our column to clear the road so they can continue back to the P. W. cage. This is just a few of thousands. All look alike. No pep. No goosestep. No nothing."

went to Nice, I found out I could have sold the flag I sent Betty Sue for two hundred bucks—I hope she gets it as it is really a nice one. I also sent her a little leather case that she can use for a beach bag or something. When I was in Easy Company, one of my messengers gave the case to me and said he took it from a prisoner. Later when we crossed the Rhine, the messenger was killed.

    Good night and lots of love

    Your little husband

p.s. I love you angel wings

---

29 April 1945

Germany

My Darling wife—

How is my "little angel" today? Maybe I'll have a chance to "talk" to you a little bit before it gets too dark. We had a nice long truck ride today and crossed the Danube River near Regansburg. It was a little disappointing, as it wasn't beautiful and blue as the song goes—it was greenish and a little muddy. It really isn't so wide either. On the other hand, maybe I didn't do it justice as I was tired and irritable by the time we reached the river, and no doubt it is more beautiful up or down the river from where I was.

We crossed on a pontoon bridge. Do you know what they are? They are like little rubber boats blown up like a sausage and put one next to the other and planks are laid on top and the bridge is all set. It's simple when you look at it, but the engineers make a big to-do over it and run around putting nails and stuff in the planks. It holds heavy trucks but things like tanks have to go over a bridge called a Bailey Bridge. Remember the erector sets the kids used to get? Well, a Bailey Bridge is like that—the engineers come up and take a look to see how wide it is and then get as many pieces as they need and put it up in a jiffy. When they come by on the truck they look like a lot of steel beams.

I mentioned a few days ago that we were very grateful to the field artillery—guess I better tip my hat to the engineers now while it's on my mind. One night we intended to sneak across a river in the dark—they actually built a bridge somewhere in the woods and brought the whole darn thing up on a truck and put it down. They are pretty proud of their work, and they always have a big sign by the bridge telling you who built it—or that you are crossing the river by courtesy of such and such engineer company. They are quick to rebuild the railroads too—all in all, they are pretty much on the ball and lean on their shovels as we march by and give us a good razzing.

Say, kid, the war news looks pretty good. We haven't had much fighting and taking a helluva lot of prisoners. We rolled by a line of three abreast about a mile long today—they were headed toward the PW enclosure. When we passed, there must have been three thousand waiting for our trucks to take them to our PW camps. They won't have to worry about the war now. I'm for having them all build houses for the veterans, so when we get home we can just walk in. I hope somebody mentions it to our Congressman—I'd rather have that than a bonus.

I guess I have gained a little weight—I weighed myself on a scale in France and the little card dropped out and had 63 on it. I said "Hell!" and threw it away. Later it dawned on me that in Europe they use the metric system and that was 63 kilograms or about 138 lbs. Wow! I'm getting to be a fatty—maybe the scales were wrong, I don't know. I feel pretty good but my trouble is mental and that won't take long to fix that up after the terrible shooting ceases. It will take a long time to forget the horrible battles I've been in but the best thing for me is my little wife—you'll have to be patient with me as I fly off the handle at little things—just don't get mad at me and I'll get straightened out in no time. Now don't get excited. I'm not whacky. It's just that "gol darned" indifferent attitude that I'll have to overcome.

Dear heart, it's time for your little husband to go to bed again so I'll have to tell you good night. Sure do love you kid—

Lots of love

Your little husband

p.s. you are an angel—

---

30 April 1945

Germany

My darling wife—

We are waiting in a village for our trucks to come up to move us to our next town. Resistance is pretty well cleared up, but it breaks out in little spurts now and then, so we have to go straighten out the bad boys. I'll be so glad when this thing is officially over.

There will be a reorganization before we go to the Pacific, and I'm in hopes that I'll be one of the lucky ones that won't have to serve over there. Of course, I'm getting ahead of myself, as this one isn't over yet. Quite a few soldiers will be discharged after we are through in Germany, and I'll try as hard as I can to be one of them.

Have you been getting the picture cards I've been sending you? This is a pretty place, isn't it? Too bad the joint is getting beat up like it is. Nuremberg was really a mess—I think I enclosed photos of some of the wreckage. I doubt if it will ever recover. Hitler really sold these folks out when he decided to fight to the end. I understand he is still in Berlin.[25]

Our air force and the Russians are on guard not to let a plane leave Berlin, so it will only be a matter of days now until he is located. I guess it will be too bad if the Russians catch him, as I don't think they like him. I never visited any of the prison camps where the Russians and Poles were kept and tortured, but some of the men did and said it was awful.

The wife of the commander of one of the prisons liked the tattooing on one of the prisoners' chests and had his skin made into a lampshade. That sounds incredulous, especially in a civilized country, but the lamp is still there, shade and all, and the authorities are requiring some of the German people to go through these prisons so they can see for themselves what sort of madmen they were supporting.

Some of the folks that were confined there and survived really tell some stories to our men that make your hair stand on end. One section of the prison was some sort of factory and employed several thousand Polish girls. The only articles of clothes they were allowed to wear were a pair of wooden shoes and a handkerchief around their head to keep their hair out of the machinery. The guards were all armed with whips that have about ten strands of leather and when one of them slowed down, she would get whipped. They also had to screw the garrison, at the discretion of the prison commander—the ones that didn't, they put into another prison—the ones who submitted were kept in the factory. When they became pregnant, if they were ordinary Poles they were given care, and when the baby was born it was sent to an orphanage where it could be raised as a "Hitler Baby"—the Polish girls who were part Jew and got "knocked up" were tossed into a vat of quick lime which ate their body up completely. The girls that didn't want to screw the supermen were put together in one part of the prison and tried before the matron—and we were told that generally they were beaten so soundly they begged to have an affair with one of them. A lot of them were tied down on their backs and their legs pulled apart, and a red hot iron was stuck in them. That generally killed them or made them insane, so they would toss them into the quick lime pit. The men were treated about as badly. They all must be crazy.[26]

We moved about twenty-five miles today and nearly froze—it was cold and raining—I don't think they even have any summer here. I'm writing you by candlelight—can you read it okay? The electricity is either out of whack or been turned off. Boy oh boy—am I glad you are where no war is going on. Hitler really terrified these folks with propaganda about how cruel we would be—but after we are around a while, they get wise. I don't think Americans can get tough for long at a time. There is one guy that works at Battalion HQ that is a German Jew—his parents and sister visited Germany before the war to try to get his grandparents out as the Germans were bothering the Jews and they were getting afraid. Well, to make a long story short, the grandparents, parents, and sister were all sent to prison or one of the work camps. It was just lately that he has officially heard that all are dead. They tell me he really handles the German people rough that he comes in contact with, and I really don't blame him. To me, the war has been hard and cruel enough without adding more misery to the world.

I guess we'll really have some talking to do when we get home to-gether—that is, after we do some loving. Eight months is a long time, and it will be a few months after the war before I get to come home. I guess everybody will be yelling to go home first. And the first time their wives give them hell for something they will be yelling to get back in the army again.

Maybe we can go somewhere by ourselves on another honeymoon when I get home. Here I am mooning over what we will do after the war, and it's still going on—I guess that's the only way I can keep up my spir-its—thinking of my little angel.

> Good night darling
> Lots of love
> Your little husband

p.s. I sure do love you, kid.

1 May 1945
Germany
My dear little wife—

Honey, you would never know that today was May Day—it actually snowed here—mostly it was sleet and rain. We moved by trucks and tanks to this little village across the Isar River—my Company piled on the back of the tanks and away we went clanking down the road. When we went into the town, the people told us that the war was over—that is, that's what they had heard over their radios. But all that stuff is still unconfirmed by us, so I guess there will be little groups of diehards to police up for several months to come.[27]

We are in another "Dogpatch" section of Germany, and the people are mostly refugees from the big cities that have come to these little places. They are really hard up here, as you can well imagine. Most of the civilians were completely terrified at first but soon caught on that we Americans are

1 May 1945

a bunch of "dumb fish." They are all scared of the [word was blacked out by Elizabeth, but it is the N-word] and the Russians. That's the first thing they want to know—if the Russians or the [N-word—again blacked out] are coming. I've never seen anything like it.

It snowed like the dickens last night and everything is white with snow. I slept nice and warm last night in one of these short beds with a big fluffy feather tick on top. I'm going to hunt around for some pictures of the inside of one of these houses to send you. It's really another world, everything just like grandmother used to have. The first time I slept in one of these beds I tried to sleep on top of the tick—it didn't work and I nearly froze. The next time I got underneath, and after I got to sleep and was completely covered up, some "Joe Blow" came in and said "ah ha! a bed" and tried to crawl in on top of me. It didn't take me long to get him out though.

Yesterday, part of my Company rode tanks into town, and that reminds me I haven't told you about them as yet. They are another screwy bunch—they are our "Prima Donnas." It's hard to imagine when you see how big and ugly a tank is. They, like the artillery, paint all kinds of names on their tanks. Yesterday one had an old alarm clock dangling on the end of the long gun poking out of the turret. I think I've seen everything hanging on them as they really go in for hanging crap on them.

They are very cautious with their tanks, and if they hit some opposition they remind me of big overgrown babies—they have to almost be pushed into the battle. Of course, when the enemy sees them they become the target, so you can't blame them too much. Once they get started, they rarely stop until they reach their objective. They like to have the Infantry with them for protection, and we always cross rivers first to clear a place for them to come over. Frequently, when the enemy tanks are waiting on the other side, we have to sneak bazooka teams around to knock them out. It looks funny to look back and see several miles of tanks all waiting for a couple of "Joes" with bazookas to knock out a German tank that has a good position before they move on. Once the tanks get going, they rush right through and we follow them and mop up the final bits of resistance.

We are all praying that the war will soon be officially over—the German people really can't understand why we ever entered the war. We bombed their cities and they are deathly afraid of us until we get there and then for the most part they find us friendly. The Americans are a race these people can't understand (neither can I).

Dear, I'll never get used to living without you, so I've quit trying. I'll just be homesick for you till I get home.

Lots of love,

Your little husband

p.s. you are the sweetest one, kid.

---

3 May 1945

Germany

My dear wife—

Good morning dear. I hear the trucks rumbling down the street so I don't know whether I'll be able to finish this letter now or if I'll have to stick it in my pocket and finish it later.

We hit the jackpot yesterday and I spent the night in a "scrumptious" apartment that we picked for our headquarters. We jump from "Dogpatch" one day to Xanadu the next.[28] This Kraut we moved in on owned a big department store and must have been a good party member 'cause he had everything. I guess I mentioned it before—there are only two classes in Europe—rich or poor. We jump from one extreme to the other—foxholes to mansion to hut and back—we rarely stop more than 24 hours at any one place.

The news on the radio (we even hit a place with electricity) is very good. We get the news from the British Broadcasting Company—and I hear our old adversary von Rundstedt has been captured. He's the old bastard that gave your little husband such a hard time in Luxembourg—he's the fellow that dressed his men up in American uniforms and murdered so many of our men. It's a good thing your little husband didn't catch him—I would have laid down my carbine and never would have laid a hand on him—I'd kick him to death. With every kick I could call the roster of the men in my Company that were killed in Luxembourg. On the other hand, you have to admire their tenacity about what they think is right as it takes more than courage to continue the fight when all is apparently lost. But this is the first time the news has really been encouraging—they really haven't quit though.

The tanks and T.D.s (Tank Destroyers) are clanking by, so I guess our trucks will be up in a few minutes and we will join the convoy and be off for another town. Thank goodness all we are doing is occupying these villages and policing up the last of the bad boys.

In spite of all the hardship and misery, funny or pathetic things happen—I just stopped writing a few minutes to listen to a discussion some of the men were having. One of the men had been in the hospital recovering from wounds. On the next cot was a paratrooper who was shot in the arm and couldn't write, and the man telling the story offered to write for him if he wanted him to. The guy said okay, and the other fellow wrote a little note to the man's wife telling him he was hurt but not too badly and not to worry if she didn't hear from him often as he couldn't use his arm. The paratrooper read it and scratched a few words with his left hand and they mailed it. Today the fellow that wrote the letter received a reply from the wife—boy it was a "lulu." She told him all her troubles, married and otherwise. It must have been one of those "marry-a-soldier-in-a-hurry-before-he-goes-overseas" marriages. In a way it was funny the way the letter was written, then on the other hand she must have been pretty lonesome—but so are all the men here. The lowest fine for speaking to a German, other than official business, is $65. The only good times the men have are writing to the folks they love and occasionally they liberate a wine cellar and have a party—or a bull session as it's all "sojers."

I've been trying to describe the things I do and see to you, but it's a hard job. I'll just have to talk to you—it is hard to describe the terrible empty feeling I have when I'm separated from you. You are part of me and I'm always thinking that I'm leaving something behind or that something is missing. Even when you used to go to Atlanta and leave me at home, I used to be so miserable I didn't know what to do. I used to open the closet door and just look at your things hanging there, and if somebody caught me, I would have had to pretend I was looking for my hat. I even spent a New Year's Eve waiting for your bus to come in. I don't think I'll let you go anywhere when I get home—so you better tell all your folks that when your husband gets home, you are going to disappear with him. We'll send the folks a photograph now and then—

Dear heart, I'll have to get ready to move now—so goodbye for now.

Lots of love

Your little husband

p.s. I sure do love you, angel wings

Kaufhaus J. Kreuzer - Dingolfing
Inhaber: Adolf Kreuzer u. Eugen Steiniger

Adolf-Hitler-Str. — Ritter-v.-Epp-Str.
Postscheck-Konto:
Amt München Nr. 9906
Bankkonto:
Kreis-Sparkasse Dingolfing, Gewerbe-
und Landwirtschafts-Bank Dingolfing
Fernsprecher Nr. 11

Dingolfing, 4 May 19 45

My Darling Wife —
Pretty fancy stationary ah kid? How do you like the name of the town? I almost laughed when I saw the name on the sign post. The place we are spending the night is really an up-to-date apartment — its in an outt old building that has been remodelled — and its elegant. Too Susaneto' place would be put to shame — the furniture is heavy and covered with thick tapestry — this is one fat little Nazi that didn't even know there was a war going on — we will only cause him a nights inconvenience and he can wire his congressman if he don't like it.

A portion of a letter written on department store stationery. Smith mentioned they were staying in the home of the proprietor.

5 May 1945
Austria
My dear wife—

Good morning dear. I'll write you a little note while we are waiting for the traffic jam to clear up so we can move along. We crossed into Austria yesterday, and I had my first look at the Bavarian Alps—the view was so magnificent that it nearly took my breath away. I don't think I've seen anything quite so beautiful as the snow-capped Alps from a distance. They looked like big dishes of vanilla ice cream on a green plate.[29]

The weather is cool though, and I doubt if it ever gets hot here—maybe except for a few weeks in the summer. The people are very friendly even though they have been thoroughly "Nazified." They were the first country to fall to the Fuehrer—as you remember—the Germans executed the Austrian Chancellor—Dollfuss, I believe was his name—and took over the government. However, they are glad the war is over for them. They tell us the German war effort took all their crops and they were sick and tired of giving everything up. We stopped for the night at a typical house and I took one of my men to arrange accommodations for the night. We generally put the civilians in one or two rooms so they won't be too uncomfortable as we rarely stay more than one night. These folks made us take the entire house and of all the hustling and bustling around—the mama and papa and kids were running all over the joint. They insisted on sleeping in the cellar. I guess these folks will be jabbering about our spending the night with them for some time to come.

Darling, I wish I could see you and will be so glad when we can all go home to our little wives—where I belong.

Well, dear it's time to move again.

Lots of love dear

Your little husband

p.s. I love you.

------

6 May 1945

Austria

My darling wife—

We came a long way to meet the Russians, but when we arrived at the place we were supposed to meet, they hadn't made it yet, so I actually haven't seen Russian soldiers as yet. We have released scads of Russian prisoners but we haven't actually seen any real Russian soldiers. I can't get over our entrance into Austria—the people lined the streets as we were quite a curiosity to them. Every town we go through they turn out in droves and wave—however they no doubt did the same when the German soldiers took charge of the place. I'm getting so I don't trust any of these people over here.

Yesterday, the truck I rode in the convoy broke down, and we had to wait about four hours for the mechanic to come by. After he fixed our truck, we had to try to find the route the convoy took—we missed it and went through several towns that American soldiers hadn't actually occupied yet. When we found out about it, we were really scared—we stopped for the night at a place that corresponds to an American U.S.O., but it was for the German army. It just happened that the only Germans going through the town were prisoners on the way to PW camps in the rear.

Recently, we occupied a Gestapo headquarters, and as I was looking around their elegant offices I found a couple of leather correspondence folders, so I confiscated them. While we were in Dingolfing, we guarded a department store and had to keep the liberated Poles and Russians from running wild in it, so the owner asked me if I would like a souvenir. I told him yes and picked out a pair of pigskin gloves for you.

I've been in France, Luxembourg, Germany and Austria, and I still say that America is the best place to live. The women in the old country have to work so hard it's really a shame—but I guess they don't know any different. Dear there's so much fuss that I can't concentrate so I'll hit the hay.

> Good night darling
> Lots of love
> Your little husband

p.s. I love you, angel wings

---

7 May 1945

Austria

My darling wife—

Hello dear heart—how is my little angel wings this morning? I sure will be glad to get home to you. I'm so tired of this silly war.

Now that we are in the enemy homeland we see that they have been having a hard time too. While I'm writing you our interpreter is talking to an old woman here where we stopped for a few hours—she has three sons—one in the Berlin sector—one in Italy—and the other she doesn't know where. The son in Italy has been missing since October, the one in Berlin hasn't been heard from since Easter—just about every place we stop it's the same way. Yesterday, the housewife said her husband had been in the army for six years—when he came home for his furlough he spent all but two days looking for his family, as they had moved to escape the bombings.

We have been riding trucks for the past four days, and the prisoners have been streaming by on the way to the rear. I'd heard of them, but yesterday was the first time I have seen any women German soldiers. They

The back of this photo reads, "This is me the day the war ended, 7 May. I had just stepped out of the column to arrange for our trucks when one of the men snapped it."

were all marching down the highway with their packs and equipment with the men prisoners. When the enemy gives up, we make them throw away their helmets so our men won't shoot them by mistake. The only way you could tell they were women was by their hair. One of the men on the truck couldn't believe his eyes—so he hollered, "Fraulein Soldaten?" The girl replied, "Ja!" The soldier in my truck said, "Boy oh boy, why can't I ever capture something like that—I wouldn't let her get in line with the prisoners. The girl grinned and said, "I also understand English." The soldier nearly fell through the bottom of the truck. It's a good thing the truck started moving again, as he was too embarrassed to stay anyway.

I think our army is the only one engaged at the present time, as the Germans in the other sectors have surrendered. I don't know why these birds don't call it quits so we can all go home. Of course, we are not running into too much opposition, but any at all is too much now.

Did you notice that I stopped writing for a few minutes? I was lying on the bench in the kitchen as I had become drowsy and had planned on finishing the letter to you later. As I was dozing I heard our radio call— "White six to George six"—"White six to George six." That meant the Battalion commander wanted to talk to our Company commander. Our Company commander was muttering to himself as he went over to the radio, "Why don't they let us alone—every time we stop we have to move again." He picked up the transmitter and reported, "George six to White six." White six replied, "As of 10 minutes past four the war in Europe is officially over." "Over." The transmitter clicked and Lt. Damkowitch stood dazed for a minute; then he said, "George six to White six—Roger" "Out."

He burst into the room hollering, "Smitty! Smitty! It's over, it's over"—I raised up to see if he was going nuts. When it dawned on me what he had told us, I had a strange feeling of exultation, and then I didn't feel like celebrating for some reason. I felt so sorry for my comrades that were killed and wounded and also for the enemy as they suffered the same as we did. I'm still a little dazed as it doesn't seem possible. I've been on the front eight months and that is almost a record as our average length of time on the front is less than two weeks. I gave a silent prayer—the Chaplain visited us and told us he was having a Thanksgiving service tomorrow—I think he will have a good attendance.

We are stuck in a little village of Hofern which is south of Wels, Austria—I doubt if you can find it on a map as it's really a "one horse" town as the expression goes. We just received an order for a 15 minute alert, so I guess we'll move again—this time I hope to a nice town as I don't want to inconvenience these people, and it's not so good anyhow.

Goodbye dear. I've got to eat my supper and pack and leave—all in 15 minutes.[30]

Lots of love Darling

Your little husband

p.s. I love you, kid.

5

POSTWAR OCCUPATION

I believe that every day that I fought I died a little.

Immediately after the German surrender on 7 May 1945, my father's regiment became part of postwar security enforcement, first in Austria until early June and then in southern Germany in several different locations until soldiers were slowly shipped home.

Now that he had more time to write and was no longer censored, Dad's letters became longer and more descriptive. Obviously, soldiers were eager to go home, but moving millions of American troops back to the United States created an immense logistical bottleneck. Many had to remain in Europe until the end of 1945 (even though their duties were light) due to the implementation of a ranking system that allotted points for a soldier's length of service, campaigns, and awards.

The letters here reflect the anxieties of soldiers waiting to go home, insights into what they were doing to pass the time, and reflections back on wartime details that my father had not previously shared. As hard as wartime service had been, waiting so long to go home added other burdens to the minds and hearts of soldiers.

8 May 1945

Austria

Dear Mother—

Just a little note to tell you that I am safe. Organized war is over—over here, but we have a lot of police work to do until these folks get organized.

I'm way up in the Alps—from my window I can look out over the snow-covered mountains. The parts that aren't covered with snow are covered with green trees. The mountain peaks are in the clouds. I went to a Thanksgiving service, and we held it in the yard of the church in the center of the village—it was a pretty place to hold it.

This is a mess—refugees, allies, Germans, all mixed up trying to get untangled. We direct traffic, putting all the Germans in one town—and starting the other folks on their way home. We also have to guard the banks and gold supply. The housing problem is fierce—we have as high as twenty soldiers in one room. Last night, one of the women in the house with some of our soldiers had a baby, and one of our soldiers had to get up and get the doctor.

I don't know when our job will be finished, but will be so glad to get home. The war lasted one day longer than two years since you wrote in my testament, 6 May 1943. I've lost everything except my wedding ring and testament—it's pretty well beat up but I still have it.[1]

Love, Jr.

8 May 1945

Austria

My darling wife—

Dear little sweetheart—here I am high in the Alps but wishing I was with you. We are occupying a little town in order to help maintain law and order until the Germans can get control of the situation. It's really sort of funny that we received orders that the war was over, but we have more work to do. We act as guides for lost Axis soldiers trying to rejoin their units so they can be formally surrendered.[2]

When we arrived at this little town, it was full of German soldiers trying to get to the next town where they are collecting—we had to take over guarding the Hungarian gold supply and direct the traffic of misplaced persons. You've never seen such a mess—people all mixed up and lost—how the hell they got up in these mountains beats me. The Alps are beautiful, though, and now I'm right in the middle of them—some of the tops of the mountains are actually above the clouds.[3]

I stopped writing to attend church service—it was held in the yard of the church downtown—it was such a lovely scene. All around were high, snowy mountains—the part that wasn't snow-covered had pretty green trees and grass growing on them. The grass is the type that doesn't grow out very long and always looks fresh clipped. We had a very nice church service, and after I came back to my office, I found that I had two letters from you—the first mail we've had in 10 days. We moved so fast the mail section couldn't keep up with us.

I got a big laugh when you asked where the damn British were—that's exactly what I used to ask all the time. When we heard some of the peace talks on the radio, the British were hogging all the credit as usual. After the war, I'll just say the British won it anyway—save a lot of time and argument.

You asked if I would like to go to the Pacific—heck no! I want to go home to my wife. I sure hope I get a discharge or get transferred to some job in the States where I can have you with me. Maybe the Japs will give up also—they always copy everything the Germans do.

You asked me what Division I'm in—it's the 80th—Blue Ridge Mountain Division—called that because it was raised and trained in the Blue Ridge mountains. Our insignia is three blue humps that look like three tits on a background of olive.

Before I forget it, I'm in Spital, Austria, at the present time, but expect to move up the road a few miles to the next town tomorrow to greet the Russians. The ones we've released have been "sad sacks"—looked like a bunch of Mortimer Snerds to me.[4]

The mountain air is nice, but I notice a lot of people with goiters—you know—big lumps on their necks. I asked a doctor about it and was told the water didn't contain enough minerals—iodine or something—and it caused goiters to grow on their necks. As usual, most of the people are farmers—they raise crops of vegetables in the day and crops of kids at night. For a nation that's always fighting, these folks manage to do all right. Every house has a bunch of kids and one on the way. As one guy said, "Maybe they don't out fight us but they sure out fuck us."

For the past week or so, I've been riding on the back of a truck and passing the remains of the finest army in the world—they are sad cases now. A few days before the surrender, they were going to the rear in droves—their uniforms dirty and ragged and they were certainly pitiful. While our truck was stopped for a brief rest, I called one of them over and asked the interpreter to ask him how old he was—"15" he replied. Can you beat that? There were men 65—men of all ages—girls and women too—I guess they felt that if they took her husband, she may as well go too. The women all had the regulation uniform.

Speaking of uniform, I still wear my wool suit and my long underwear, and here it is the 8th of May. It's not too cold here—just comfortable with wool clothing.

I hope I haven't changed while I've been away. After eight months on the front—where every minute seems like a month—it may have made me different, but I'll soon feel the same when I get home to you. I guess the big thing is to try not to jump up in the middle of the night and wonder where the hell you are and why you don't have your clothes on, and where your gun is. And the helmet—I've worn it so much, I think I'm really going to miss it.

Somebody wrote rules to observe when we return to civilian life—they said not to jump in a ditch when you hear an auto backfire and not to jump up and yell in a room that nobody leaves the damn room until the skunk that took your helmet gives it back. There were more but I don't remember them right now.

Oh! I do remember a little story I heard not long ago. A lady took a couple of pet monkeys that had died to a taxidermist to be stuffed—the clerk wanted to know if she wanted them mounted. "Oh dear, no," she said. "Just leave them holding hands."

Dear, will you excuse me a few minutes, it's time to heat my K-ration for supper—corned pork loaf, bouillon, crackers—same day in and day out. Just a minute, dear—..........

Here I am back again—it wasn't much of a supper, but it will have to do until our kitchen train catches up with us—I wonder how the people in Europe will make out, as the crops couldn't be planted very well as

the armies were running to and fro on the fields. The folks on farms are
in pretty good shape, but the people that live in towns will have it rather
rough. Maybe they should start a victory garden—remember my row of
beans? In the picture of me in the air raid warden's outfit I can see part of
it in the picture. I've had a lot of fun with that picture. The guys couldn't
believe that I used to be an air raid warden. It seems like a long time ago
that I used to rush off for air raid drill.

Things are really in a mess here—German soldiers going one way, refugees the other. Darling, I'll have to tell you goodbye for now.

> Good night darling
> Lots of love
> Your little husband

p.s. I love you—so much.

9 May 1945
Austria
My darling wife—

How is my sweet little wife tonight? I'm still way up in the Alps—maybe
I should learn to yodel while I'm here. You remember the pictures of men
in short pants and suspenders and short coats with embroidery on the
collars? This is the place they hang out. Their hats have a pretty feather in
them—quite fancy. I'm afraid the boys would whistle after a guy if he tried
to walk around in a rig like that in the States.

I told you in my letter yesterday that the Germans were collecting in a
town about 15 miles from here to formally surrender. Our forces have control of all the territory up to the Enns River. The Russian forces are to join
us there, but they have been delayed, so I guess it will be a couple of more
days before they can make it.

Lieutenant Damkowitch, our C.O., asked me if I would like to ride up to
the next town and look at the situation. I was busy and said I had already
seen all the Germans that I cared to, so he went on with somebody else. He
returned just a few minutes ago and said it was really a sight. All the people
on the Russian side are frantic to get on the American side, and he said
that men and women were stripping off their clothes and trying to swim to

Air Raid Warden Smith in 1942 at his home on Redwing Street in
Jacksonville, with his row of beans.

the American side. He said he never saw such a sight before—the river is
so swift that men, women, and children were drowning by the scores in the
swift mountain river.

The Germans are terrified of the Russians, and they have good reason to
be—as I told you in another letter about the horrible prison camp the Germans put Russians, Poles, and Jews in outside of Weimar. I didn't think the
Germans could be so cruel—of course, maybe there are some good ones.

For quite some time the Russians killed every person they encountered in Germany. They must be a bloodthirsty gang, too. But I guess I would be pretty "hot" too if my wife and children (if I had any) and my parents had been slaughtered or been taken into slavery to some godforsaken place. I often wonder how all this hate got started—but it's hell—and I thank God every day it's about to run its course and maybe then will really be "peace on earth and good will toward men." I can truthfully say our men are fierce fighters and fight to the last man if and when it is necessary, but I've never seen them mistreat an enemy soldier that throws down his gun and raises his hands in surrender. Before every operation, the enemy is always invited to give up. But when we start Oh! man—there is nothing like it.[5]

No matter where I go or where I've been, I think of you constantly—I haven't had my wedding ring off since I left you—sometimes it was covered with mud so thick I couldn't see it, but it was still there. Often when I've laid in the fields under the terrific artillery fire, I would lay with my hand in front of my face and peek under my helmet and see my wedding ring in the flash of the bursting shells—it made me feel calm when I should have been scared. Then, when I'm lonesome and blue, I look at it and it makes me feel so much better. I've lost just about everything I've brought overseas with me except my wedding ring, my pen you gave me and the little testament Mother gave me.

It would be hard for me to describe how much you mean to me—words big enough haven't been invented yet. To tell you the truth, I doubt if I could have endured the campaigns that we have fought if it hadn't been for you waiting for me. It's hard to say, but there were times a bullet to end our misery would have been welcome—but as I had you, you were my inspiration.

Dear—it's getting past my bedtime so I'll tell you goodnight.

    Lots of love

    Your little husband

p.s. you are the sweetest one—

10 May 1945
Austria
My dear little wife—

Hello honey—it sure is a pretty day here, and the mountains are beautiful—the snow glistening in the sunlight. I guess this is the best time of the year to be here—it's just cool enough to be pleasant. This would be a nice place to vacation and rest—that is, in a few years after all the commotion subsides.

We grabbed an apartment for our headquarters—two bedrooms, a kitchen, and a "johnny." There are five of us in it so we are really well off. The bathtub is in the laundry room downstairs. In order to take a bath, you have to heat the water in the laundry boiler and scoop it into the tub with a bucket. But first, you have to run the housewives and a bunch of kids out. They all congregate there and wash clothes all day, it seems.

We have a coal stove to cook on or heat stuff, and the kitchen finally caught up with us—the only thing is they didn't have anything to cook. So we still have to eat our K-rations. There is a little bitty sink by the stove, and the water that comes out of the faucet is ice cold. One of the men tried to bathe in the stream behind the house and got one big toe in and that was all—he said it nearly froze his toe off.

Rumors are flying again—some say we are going to be occupation troops—then we hear we are going to the Pacific—then again we hear we might come home. I'm afraid by the time my Division gets home, the war will be forgotten. It seems as though we get all the dirty work. Every time there was an emergency, we were rushed up to take care of it. We entered Germany and fought a campaign and then we were pulled all the way back to France and started another campaign into Germany. If the war hadn't ended, I hear we were scheduled to make another entrance into Germany via Norway.

We just received an alert to move—will tell you more about it later.

Love—your little husband

11 May 1945
Austria
My darling wife—

While I was writing yesterday's letter to you, we received a message to proceed south and guard bridges. The Russians were due any minute, and our general wanted us on these bridges to maintain law and order.

We went through the town where the Germans were congregating to be surrendered, and you never saw such a sight. The German officers were very helpful, and they are cooperating 100%—they are loading all the Germans on trucks and sending them back into Germany—it's hard to describe—vehicles of all descriptions—cars, busses, trucks, buggies, horses and wagons all jammed with all kinds of Germans—soldiers, men, women and children all trying to clear out before the Russians meet us. Miles of German ambulances loaded with wounded all jammed on a road that is hardly wide enough for two passenger cars to pass, and so high in the mountains—just like a ledge way up in the sky. The German trucks are so old they break down and slow the whole convoy down. We had to pass all this mess on the way to our positions last night. Do you remember in the picture "Gone with the Wind" how great areas were littered with rubbish and debris when Scarlett started back home in a wagon? That is exactly how it looks here—this train has been moving or trying to move for the past four days and we passed miles of debris, yet to move.

A few days ago, we selected some of our men to greet the Russians officially when they reached us at the Enns River. We were sent to the town of Landl to wait. As we moved through town, we met two Russian advance guards at 2220—they were dressed in light brown uniforms with red epaulets or red decorations on their collars. They had thrown away their helmets but wore a cap similar to the one I used to wear when I was home on furlough. They had their rifles slung over their shoulders, and if they hadn't been armed, I would have taken them for Hungarians. They jerked their weapons off and into the "ready" position and challenged us.

"Amerikansky?" they cried—"yeah! yeah!" we hollered back. "You Russky?" "yah! yah!" and all of the hand shaking and sign language—you never saw the like of it. We met the Russians before the official greeting. On down the road, there were lots more, towing their artillery with horses. They are a peculiar people—like grown kids—they are awfully hard-headed, and it's difficult to reason with them. They were on our side of the river, and to convince them they should move across to their side was more than an hour's job with sign language and pictures—"Roosky here" "Amerikansky here" kind of talk—and all during the conversation there was handshaking and cigarette passing around, and when everybody thought they understood one another—they just stood there looking dumbly at us.

I don't believe these Russians know the war is over, as they think nothing of sending patrols into these border towns to take anything they want—the slightest resistance and they "clean out" the town, and I don't mean maybe—they are bloodthirsty, and I hope we won't have too much trouble with them as we are here to preserve law and order. As rough as they are, you have to look at their side of the picture, too. The Germans were just as bad or worse, and they murdered and executed the Russians wholesale when they were in power.

The Germans are really thankful to see us now. Last night after we finished placing our guards on our bridges, we stopped at a little village and knocked on the door of a Gasthaus. We knocked and knocked—our interpreter yelled in German to open the door. In a few minutes, a head stuck out the window and in a scared voice said, "Roosky?" "Naw," we yelled. "American." The guy was so happy to see us, he nearly wept. He spoke some English and said, "Come in boys." They fixed us up for the night. They had seen the Russian patrol go through the town and were terrified. It doesn't take the people long to find out we are "dumb fish" and will protect them. Of course, I'm not mean—and I guess America will always be behind the 8-ball—but I like the way the Americans operate. I'm glad we are not raised to hate like the people over here.[6] Some of our newer men that haven't seen much of the horrors of war were scandalized that the Russians were so rough. I don't know what will come of all this, but I sure will be glad when it's cleared up.

Love
Little husband

The back of this photo reads, "Platoon of Russian soldiers. Tough bunch! Landl, Austria, 10 May 1945."

The back of this photo reads, "Here's your husband with a platoon of Russians. I'm standing by their captain. Some of our men are kneeling in front. Landl, Austria, 10 May 1945."

13 May 1945

Austria

My darling wife—

Hello honey—how is my little angel today? I'm still high up in the Alps—across the river the Russians are sitting, so we should wind up our business soon.

I'm not quite sure where I am in relation to borders and so forth but there are lots of refugees here from Vienna—also Hungarians—the name of this little village is St. Gallen. I doubt you can find it on the map. I have a room in a Gasthaus and as I'm writing you, I can look out of my windows at the beautiful hills and mountains. I really hope I can bring you over here someday to see them. I believe Luxembourg, Austria, and parts of Germany are the prettiest sections of all Europe.

Looking out of my windows to the left are the remains of a medieval castle—it's on a high hill and plants and vines are beginning to cover it. It's in ruins now, but it must have been a dilly in its day. The hill is covered with green trees. Across on the other mountain are rocks and snow. Today the air is warm and pleasant—almost like Florida, except the air is dry. The fields are pretty too, as the farmers only cultivate a section of their land at a time, and when you view it from a distance it looks like a huge checkerboard. Their idea is to let one field lie idle and cultivate it every other year—they think it makes the soil richer. Today is Sunday, and I noticed a huge procession of people walking down the street carrying some sort of religious banner before them. When I inquired what they were doing, somebody told me it was a religious ceremony to bless the land to make a bountiful crop.

The people here are potato eaters—it's their main source of food, but it'll make you fat if you don't watch out. Most of the women are big and strong as they have to work very hard. It's amazing that folks are busy all the time doing this and that. Over here you have to have a permit (or so they think) to do anything. Some German soldiers came to my headquarters the other day to give themselves up and wanted a paper to show that they had surrendered. They were dumbfounded when I told them to beat it, change clothes, and go home. We'll make Americans out of them yet. They are beginning to catch on to "Hokay."

I'm looking forward to the time I will be able to see you again—maybe it won't be too long, as the Russians tell us they expect to declare war on Japan soon. As it is, Japan is getting a sample of what went on here in Europe.

I've had so many adventures and seen so many things, good and bad, that I'll have to ask you what would you like to hear about—the countries and the scenery—the battles I've fought—the people—the Russians—the atrocities that the Germans and Russians committed or what—or what I'd do if I were home.

Dear—I think of you all the time—every night until I go to sleep I imagine I'm with you—maybe it sounds crazy, but I do anyway. It doesn't seem possible that we will soon be married 5 years, does it? I hope to goodness we can spend the rest of our lives together—not a husband in Austria and an angel wings wife in Florida, no sir, that's not the way to do it, and if I can't come home soon I'm going to start writing my Congressman.

Darling—it's time for me to go to bed again. Lots of love dear little wife—take care of yourself.

Lots of love

Your little husband

p.s. you are an angel—"angel."

A postcard from St. Gallen, Austria, sent to Elizabeth

15 May 1945
Austria
My darling wife—

Hello! darling—it's 8 o'clock here but just one o'clock where you are—
it's almost dark here but it's just about noon where you are—I like to imagine what you are doing each hour of the day, but as there is a seven hours
difference in time, it makes it kinda hard.

I'm awfully lonesome for you dear, and maybe by having a talk to you by
letter it will make me feel better. I haven't heard from you for almost three
weeks, and will really be ready to jump on the mailman if I don't get a
letter soon. But I guess it's an awful job to get the mail up into these mountains—it's hard enough to get our rations up here.

It will be wonderful to come home to you and try to forget that I was
ever in the army—to get away and try to forget those awful attacks, the
clattering of machine guns, the shriek of the shells, the screams of the
wounded and the horrible sights of men without arms and legs—to get
away from the flash of the rocket guns and the bursting mortar shells—to
get away from the vicious counterattacks that follow our attacks when the
enemy tried to regain ground that they lost—try to forget the awful lost
feeling you have when the enemy brings up tanks—to run us out of the
holes so he can mow us down. I believe that every day that I fought I died a
little. But now it's over, and I'm looking forward to forgetting about all that.

We saw more Russians. They are a different type from us—there is
something frightening about them—they are grim and determined. They
drove up to our headquarters in an American jeep and Ford truck (all
lend-lease stuff). The captain was dressed in khaki riding trousers, black
boots, and a blouse that buttoned up to the chin—the blouse was almost
as long as a smock. He wore a little cap like a streetcar conductor. On his
left breast he wore the Red Star, which is like our Infantry Badge. He was
extremely courteous—his truck had the American, Russian, and British
flags displayed—a very friendly gesture. The soldiers were very friendly
but reminded me of a bunch of goons, you know. They insisted that we
watch them drill—it was very impressive—after they started marching
they started singing—a very haunting melody—very similar to the folk
dance—the Weavers Song I believe they called it. Anyway it was hard to
forget the tune.

As I mentioned before, they are very primitive and I doubt if most of them believe the war is over. The Germans and the Austrians are terrified at the mention of the word "Russian." The people around here are breaking their necks to get across the river to the American side. The Russians have a good system. They take anything they want—no questions or arguments. What they don't want or can't understand, they smash up. Some of the refugees were complaining to me that they run them out of their homes and go to bed with their boots on. Our C.O. went to visit them on their side of the river, and he said they had cleared the room they were using for a headquarters—all the furniture was tossed out except a table and a couple of benches.

But, crude as they may be, I'm thankful they fought on our side. Maybe we should adopt the same attitude toward the Germans—after all, they did the same way when they were overrunning Russia and Europe. I guess we're a lot of "dumb fish."

Smith looks at a photo of Elizabeth.

Another thing that irritates the local Krauts is that the Russian soldiers quite often occupy a house and rape all the women. Of course, that's the Krauts' story—and I suppose they are doing all they can to turn us against the Russians.

We've already rubbed the Russians the wrong way. Their General came down to meet our General, but our General didn't show up—what the hell could be more important, I don't know—sometimes I think our higher officers are a bunch of dumb bastards—tricks like that confirm it. The Russians think a great deal of courtesy, and it looks like heck for just a Lieutenant and me, a First Sergeant, to entertain a group of high officials in the Red Army. Maybe somebody will wake up before we get in a scrap with our best ally. Let's hope so, anyway.[7]

It's a beautiful day here—this is a resort town and it's in a beautiful spot. One of the camera stores had film, and one of our men who has a camera made a few snapshots. Maybe he will give me a negative or two. It's hard to get the paper to develop them—most of it went to the army—as they photograph our positions daily—or used to—it's hard to get used to thinking the war here has ended.

I don't know when to hope for a discharge as the point system is a little rough on me. About the only men who are eligible now are the men with a lot of children. Don't do anything about it for me—please, I'll take care of that when I do get home.

Lots of love little angel wings

Your little husband

p.s. I sure do love you, kid.

------

18 May 1945

Austria

My darling wife—

Good morning dear—We are alerted to move again, so maybe I'll get to write you a few lines—then I'll stuff it in my pocket and finish it later.[8]

I told you about the Russians, and here's a little more. My Company occupied a little village and guarded its bridges. We were on one side of the river and the Russians on the other. The people were so afraid of the Russians that they rushed to our side, and it really caused a mess. The people were so glad to see us that they ran out with flowers and cheered as our trucks rolled into the village. The mayor or Burgermeister put me and my "staff" (ha! ha!) in the local hotel. The people took the other soldiers into their homes. They figured if they had American soldiers in their homes, it would be good protection from the Russians.

An ex-German soldier insisted on carrying my pack to the hotel, and they put flowers in the room. Boy! are these people scared of the Russians. After we got situated, the Russian officer called on us—and when they saw the stripes on my arm they ran over and gave me a big salute. I got right in the "swing" and said to myself, I may as well put on the dog with these birds as I couldn't lose anything. We really got along swell—they couldn't understand us, nor we them. The only way we could talk was through an interpreter who spoke German to their interpreter who spoke German— you can imagine how straight the messages were translated. I could tell by some of the blank looks on their faces they didn't get all we were trying to say. Their officers are all young men—most of the soldiers we've met are young also. They look pretty crude though. But the Infantry makes anybody look crude if you survive a couple of months of fighting. After the Russians had paid us a visit and after the handshaking and saluting all around, they departed and the civilians began to circulate again.

The next day a couple of elegantly dressed Hungarian officers called on us. They are a bunch of political acrobats and wanted to find out which way they should jump to get in the gravy. I told the "Fuehrer" (that's what we call our C.O., Mike) that since we were in complete power up here, he may as well put on the act—what the heck—those guys were shooting at us a few days before. Well, to make a long story short, we set the "Fuehrer" up as a sort of military dictator—somebody found him one of those leather riding crops. We saw a General or somebody with one and thought it would be the thing to do.

Those birds were bowing and scraping and clicking their heels and saluting all the time when we were near. Of course, they smoked up all our cigarettes, but it was a lot of fun. We managed to get a load of food from the German army for the Hungarian refugees and that put us in solid—more flowers, more heel-clicking and saluting—you know, dear, this place is just like the movies, the customs and stuff have been going on for years and years. One of these birds was an Austrian count and had a castle nearby, so he invited the "Fuehrer" to visit him. When Mike got warmed up to the game, he decided to give a return party. He invited me over and we went through the heel-clicking saluting routine again—I think all the stripes on my arms got those Austrians and Hungarians, as their colonel gave me a salute—by the time we were relieved I didn't feel like talking to anybody lower than a major.

The Hungarians were a little dismayed when we pulled out—somebody must have dropped a hint that we were going to stay a year and take over the government in this area. Oh well—we don't often have much fun, and this time we had a good time leading our ex-enemies around by the nose. Then we did them a good turn, as we kept the Russians off of them and had German food sent up to them. The only trouble is, we can't get the "Fuehrer" to come back to earth again.

Our C.O. is quite a character—you know I told you about him once before, how his wife started running around and finally got a divorce and he had to give away his home, furniture, and car when he came overseas. He has told me lots that he wished he would be hit and end it all—he used to volunteer for the most dangerous assignments and got himself promoted to First Lieutenant and a medal or two. In order to pep him up, we set him up as the "Fuehrer," and I think he's quite proud of his title and he's picked up and takes more interest in what's going on. Now he runs around in his jeep waving his riding crop and having a helluva good time—just like a kid. It's better to have him like that than like some of the officers we had in the States. In the States, most of the officers were a pain in the fanny—I had a letter from one of the men from training camp in Mississippi, and he told me that my old company commander turned yellow and ran away the first time he heard an enemy bullet. He was awful in the States and everybody hated him—he used to tell me he would shoot the first man that ran away when we went into combat. I guess a "barking dog doesn't bite" after all. That Division didn't get here until the war was nearly over—I wish I had come with them instead of having all the battles I did. Then, on the other hand, maybe I'm better off here.

We've all been wondering what's going to happen to us—we have so many rumors, we really don't know what to think or believe. All indications point that we will be reshuffled and a lot of us sent to the Pacific—some will remain as occupation troops and a few will be discharged. I don't have too many points so I don't know whether to start hoping or not. I hate to get steamed up and then be disappointed. We are still moving around in the mountains, and it looks as though we'll stay around here a few more weeks anyway. I wish we would stay still, though—this moving around every day or so looks like an awful waste of gasoline to me. Oh well, I've taken a lot more interest in the scenery, and the more we move around, the more I see.

The next time you send me a box, drop a book of two in it—a detective story or something.

Lots of love,
Your little husband

---

21 May 1945
Austria
My darling wife—

I'm in a village on the Enns River called Grossreifling, about 150 miles from Vienna. We're still up in the mountains, and it gives one a terrific

The back of this postcard reads, "This is where I'm staying, a village called Grossreifling in Austria. I'm staying in a house to the left-center. Not much doing here except to rest and look at the mountains."

appetite to live in these high altitudes. We have brought our kitchen up
with us but they don't seem to be able to get enough rations to fill us up.

Now before I go any further, let me re-read your letters to see if there
is anything you wanted to know—yes—8 May was some day for us too.
We heard the news on our field radio at 10 minutes 'till four on 7 May. But
somehow we didn't feel so much like celebrating either—I'll bet the stores
at home looked like something with their victory decorations. The reason
it took so long to sign the peace surrender was because there was nobody
to surrender for the German people—their units were so disorganized
and scattered that they were unable to tell them the war had ended. After
we heard the news, we helped the German soldiers find their town where
they were assembling. It seemed funny to let the German soldiers come
through our lines carrying their guns and ammunition—but we let them.

It's difficult to describe this country. The "old" world is quite a place—
take for instance where I'm staying. It belongs to a big lumber man. No
doubt the house has been here for years and years—several generations
have lived here. Judging by the antiques and general appearance of the
place, they are very well-to-do. But they have no bathtubs or running
water. I mentioned the fact that everywhere in America we have hot and
cold running water and build our homes for convenience. They were a little
aghast at that and told me they prefer it this way, as it's part of their tradi-
tion to live exactly as their father before them. Most of the beautiful homes
do not have steam heat and get their water from pumps and cook on coal
or wood stoves. It's not a question of money, as they are well-to-do. They
just want to keep things as their forefathers had it. At first, it seems a little
odd, doesn't it? Then, when you think about it, it gives you a sense of security that things won't change. I was talking to a Hungarian officer yesterday, and he told me his home hasn't been changed, except for the people,
in 500 years. They do not even have electric lights, as they prefer to use the
old-fashioned oil lamps. I'm happy to say these folks have electricity, as we
will probably be here a week or so.

The Old World traditions are nice but I think I would rather have a little
more comfort—but then I can see us arguing with our children when they
wanted to throw out our stuff and redecorate the place. We'd say it was
good enough for us and it's good enough for them.

It's been raining in the afternoons—on one mountain you can see rain
and the other sunshine—this climate makes me so hungry I could eat

The back of this photo reads, "This is me organizing my Company for retreat." Smith stands at the center, facing the Company, in Grossreifling, Austria.

a horse. I guess the food shortage is going to be a problem here shortly. Everybody seems to have gardens but I don't know how much damage was done to the crops as a whole. At the hotel I stayed in recently, they had a garden, and the guests had to work in the garden if they wanted to eat at the hotel—that's not a bad idea.

Darling, it's time to go to bed again, so I'll tell you good night and give yourself a big hug for me.

Lots of love
Your little husband

———

22 May 1945
Austria
My darling wife—

Dear, as I'm writing you I can look out of my window and see the cold rain pattering down, and I'm so thankful that I'm inside a nice house and not out in it. It's been raining almost all day and I had to wear my raincoat to church—I went to church in a room of the local inn here. The local church is Catholic so we just used a large room in the hotel—it used to be a dining room, I guess. The Enns River is very pretty—the water is ice cold and rushes down the mountain. I guess it's hard for you to imagine that it's cool here, as about this time of year it's scorching in Jax. It's so nice and quiet here, I've almost forgotten about the war.

Did you notice on the picture of me and the "Fuehrer" and Sam that my wedding ring is really shining? I got all the mud off at last—I never have taken it off, so there may be some mud under it. It must have been hidden under the mud for weeks at a time.

Before I forget—be sure and send me a box and put a photograph of you in it. I can carry one of the larger ones now in my correspondence folder. I'd like to set it up in front of me while I'm here—I've almost worn the snapshots out pulling them out of my pocketbook looking at them. And send some candy (if you can find it) and canned food, as this altitude gives me a terrific appetite. Might toss in a can of coffee, too, as ours is mostly German coffee. Say! I'm just asking for everything, aren't I? And of course, a book or two—the "two bit" kind as I'll pass them out to the other men when I finish with them. Send me one of the little pocket dictionaries, too—I'm teaching a few men to spell and having trouble myself (ha! ha!). If you root around in the desk, I think there are some instructions on the slide rule. I thought I'd work on it to occupy my mind until I find out what happens to me. I guess you are thinking—"What the heck does he think

Percy Smith, Mike Damkowitch, and Sam Cordon. "Did you notice in the picture that my wedding ring is really shining?"

this is? Christmas?" Well, send what you can, as I know it's tough to get things at home. And I'll be able to make use of anything you send.

Darling, you're an angel—and don't try to deny it 'cause I know. Every day I say a little prayer of thankfulness for bringing me through the war that I may soon return to you.

Lots of love

Your little husband

p.s. I love you dear

———————

24 May 1945

Austria

My darling wife—

I'm so glad to hear you have some boxes for me—send them on kid. I could eat a little horse. I'm enclosing some scenic photos of the place I'm staying—it's a beautiful spot and the mountain air is swell. The higher altitude gives you a good appetite, and the weather is cool and pleasant all summer. I used to think a trip to the mountains was about as uninteresting a place as one could go. Now that I'm here, I find it very nice. My administrative work is not so difficult, and I have lots of time to rest and just look at the mountains. I have a very good pair of field glasses, and can see the hills very well without having to go to all the trouble to climb the mountains.

This little village has a lumber mill and that's about all. As you can see from the snapshot, it's a "one horse" town. I doubt if the natives that live here have ever seen a picture show or ever came out of the hills. I guess the only amusement they have is scraping the mud off their shoes and raising kids.

The other day, the C.O. took me for a ride in his jeep—he had to do some business for the Hungarians and asked me to ride up to their place with him. They have an old castle on the side of a hill, and it is certainly picturesque—but not very comfortable. It belonged to one of the Hungarian officers' family, and they sent the women and children there when the war was getting close to them. The castle has a huge swimming pool in the yard and the water comes from the melting snow on the mountainside. I think you'd have to be a polar bear to get into the pool. Of course, the castle is pretty much run down now, but once upon a time it must have been quite a place.

A Hungarian officer posing with Smith

These Hungarians were in very dire circumstances when we took charge of this section of the country. They had eaten all their food and could not buy any more. They fought on the German side but the Germans apparently lost interest in them when the war was over. The local people had their hands full trying to take care of their own people and the refugees that fled from the Russians—so our C.O. forced the German commander to allow the Hungarians to have a couple of wagon loads of food. One of the Hungarian lieutenants speaks very good English. He visited us last night and played on the piano for us—he used to give concerts in Vienna. We have quite a place now—a huge living room with a grand piano and a radio—of course the C.O. seems to think it's his. I have a room and office combined and my assistant has a room and office—boy, this sure is a change from the foxholes.

    Goodbye for now dear,
    Lots of love
    Your little husband
p.s. I love you—kid.

26 May 1945
Austria
My Darling Wife—

The food is getting to be a problem over here—goodness knows how it will work out. After each meal there are quite a number of little children waiting around our mess tent for scraps of food that we do not eat. I've given instructions to divide up what we have left over as equally as possible—usually it isn't very much as we are feeling the food shortage, too. Recently, we've only been having two hot meals a day and one field K-ration for the third meal.

I'll be looking forward to a home-cooked meal—and a salad fixed by my little angel. I keep thinking about our cute little apartment in Mississippi—of course, it wasn't much to look at, but it had you in it, and you made it so homey. When I return home, we'll get us another place all to ourselves. It's so much more fun to have you fix my supper for me. Even if it were just a can of stuff opened—if you opened it, it would be swell.

Lots of love dear –

Your little husband

p.s. you are the sweetest one, kid.

---

29 May 1945
Austria
My darling wife—

I had a letter from you today that was postmarked in Jax just a week ago. How's that for service?

My points are very low, I'm sorry to say—37 at this time. I'm due to get a Bronze Star, and that will give me 5 more points—I'm also supposed to get two more campaign stars at 5 points apiece, and that will bring my total score up a little, but I'm still below the 85 mark. There is quite a dispute going on, as we who fought the war are trying to get more points than the men that loaded the rations on the trucks way back where there was no shelling and it was safe.

The way they have it figured for me now, I only get 5 points for fighting at the front in France, Luxembourg, Germany, and Austria—Boy oh Boy! I was so burned up, I was ready to throw away my ribbon and tell them what to do with their points. Then the *Stars and Stripes* says that we are entitled to more points. If it works out right according to the paper, then I'll have 15 points for combat duty. The thing is such a mess it burns me up to think about it.

I got a hold of a Red Cross or some kind of book—bound in paper for the armed forces—the name is *Dragonwyck* and very good. I haven't finished it yet but I like it very much. Gee! but I wish I were at home with my little wife. I'll be so glad when I can wake up in the morning and find my little "honeybun" beside me instead of a "smelly sojer." Oh! Boy will I be glad to take that ocean ride home to you.

Lots of love darling

Your little husband

p.s. I sure do love you, kid.

---

31 May 1945

Austria

My darling,

What will we talk about today—Oh! yes—what I've been doing. Well, usually not much. I get up at 0715 and eat my breakfast (two pancakes and a cup of coffee), then I fill out my reports and tidy up my room. I usually write you a letter in the morning and finish it in the evening.[9]

We are not the military government in this area, but are just a police force to maintain law and order—but all the civilians come to us with their problems. One lady was in this morning—her home is in Vienna. The Russians have control of that city now, so she slipped across the river and tried to go back to Vienna. That is strictly against orders as all people were supposed to stay right where they were when the war ended or the food situation will get so screwed up that a lot of civilians will actually starve. Well anyway, this woman took off and went across the Enns River and started for Vienna. She got raped three times by the Russian soldiers before she could get two miles, so she had to withdraw to our side of the river. Those Russians must be some characters. Some of the fugitives from Vienna that made it to our side said when the Russian soldiers arrived in Vienna, they collected all the women from 15 to 50 and raped them all—then put them to work repairing the city. All you have to do is say "Roosky" to these people, and they all hold their heads and holler oi! oi! In the American army the penalty for rape is death.

When a Russian visits us on business, the civilians all scat, and you don't see them again until the Russians leave. As I told you before, we have some bridges to guard—that is to see that the Russians don't come over to our side unless they have official business. At one bridge, part of the little village is on the Russian side—so our sergeant in charge of the bridge asked one of the civilians for a bottle of wine. Oh! no! no! the civilian replied, we haven't any—so the sergeant said, "Okay don't get excited—if you ain't got it you ain't."

"Well," the sergeant said. "In a little while the Russian guard came into the town, posted their guard on the bridge, and the Russian sergeant kicked the civilian out of his house, moved in, and took sixty bottles of wine out of the cellar." The Russian sergeant gave our men all of it they wanted, as they like us very much. But our sergeant couldn't get over it. "The lying so and so," he said. "All I wanted was one bottle. Maybe the Russians have the best system after all."

I've never seen the Russians in action, but they all seem very friendly toward us and have always conducted themselves like gentlemen when they were visiting us. I don't think we should mistreat the people, but I don't think we should pamper them either. The Germans were for the war 100% when they were winning—our government, I think, is too darn soft with them. When we came into town and saved them all from being looted and raped by the Russians, they tossed flowers on our trucks and soldiers. Now that we've been here a week or so and they see that we are really here to maintain law and order, they are beginning to demand their rights, etc. The other day one of the civilians tried to deny us the use of their bathroom to bathe in. We promised to leave the place as neat as we found it, but they tried to give us trouble so I told the civilians if we hear another peep out of them that we would move them out into the street until we had all finished washing. That's the only language they understand—now they are happy and everybody got a bath. Your husband is a meanie, isn't he?

Darling, it's time to go to bed again—lots of love dear, and I only wish I could hold you in my arms and tell you how much I love you.

    Lots of love dear

    Your little husband

p.s. I sure do love you dear.

2 June 1945

Austria

My darling wife—

The Colonel had all the First Sergeants down to his office for a meeting today. After the meeting, he told us that as far as he knew now, we would remain in our present positions until about 1st August—then we would move to the area we were to occupy and go to school until we were sent home. He also said that quite a few men would be sent to the Pacific, but indicated that they would be men that hadn't been here very long. He said as far as he knew, we would definitely be occupation troops.

That's good and bad. Good that we are out of the fight but bad that I can't see my little wife for a while yet. They say we just don't have enough transportation.

I'm writing you from a balcony just off my room and the view is just reversed on the card I sent you. Now I'm looking down the valley and watching the water rush by—it's pretty and peaceful—I guess this is just what I needed, so I'll be able to act like a normal person again. Sometimes it's hard to imagine that there ever was a war. Did I tell you that the people that own this house had a son that was in the German air force? He was shot down by the Americans and is in an American hospital. In the room I have, there are pictures of him since he was a little toddler until he has his army uniform on.

The people are having an awful time now, as the food shortage is very acute here. All of the discharged German soldiers are being put to work to grow crops, as it will be very serious this winter if some kind of program is not started. What hurts you is the little children—you never saw so many—looks like every house has seven or eight. Judging by the photographs edged in black in the houses we've occupied, the toll in life during this war must have been stupendous. Hitler sure screwed this country up good. I guess the farmers will save the country if all their crops come through—but if the crops should fail, it will be awful over here. We get all of our food from America—we eat canned stuff and dehydrated vegetables and we're not getting too much either. We give the civilians whatever we have left. Sometimes we have coffee left over, and they really go for it.

Speaking of coffee reminds me of something—back during the fighting, somebody got a Xmas box with a pound of coffee in it. We were in houses that were all beat up, but still had a stove and we used it to make coffee every morning. As we were drinking our coffee, we would look at the can and remark that we ought to write and tell the people how much we enjoyed it. So the guy that received the box wrote home and told them—and me and a couple of other guys wrote to the coffee company. We told them how good it was and laid it on thick—mailed it and forgot about it. Lo! and behold, the other day I received two pounds of coffee from the manufacturer. Now wasn't that nice? It comes in handy too as we don't always have coffee.

It's cool again now—I don't think it ever really gets hot here. I've been sleeping under a blanket and it feels pretty good. But as nice as all this is, I'd rather be home sleeping under a blanket with my little wife.

Darling, it's getting late, so I'll have to tell you good night—darling.

Lots of love, dear

Your little husband

p.s. I love you—kid.

3 June 1945

Austria

My dear little wife—

Here it is Sunday again, and I've just returned from church. There is usually not much doing in a small town, and even less on Sundays. The people are pestering us to death for passes and permits to go here and there, as they are not happy if their pocketbooks are not crammed full of permits and passes of some kind. It's got so bad we have to put a guy on duty at the door that speaks German to tell them to "beat it" and leave us alone.

Say, I had something nice happen to me today. The people that own the house invited the C.O. and me to Sunday dinner—it was so nice—these people are good cooks and they are the kind of people that really know their politics and manage to know the right people to get food and stuff. We had venison that tasted very much like roast beef, fried potatoes, rice and gravy, and a lettuce salad—the lettuce was grown in their garden and is real leafy and not firm like our lettuce. The people are middle-aged, and they have a brother or some kind of relation their same age living with them. One woman spoke English and tried to help them talk to us about some business or other. She turned out to be a Baroness of some kind in the old defunct monarchy. She knew Sinclair Lewis, Dorothy Thompson, and

William Bullitt very well. Mr. Bullitt is (or was) the American ambassador to Russia—Dorothy Thompson has a newspaper column in most of the newspapers, and Sinclair Lewis has written a lot of books. The Baroness's son has been captured by the Americans too, and she said she had received mail from him regularly until we upset the postal system. She says he's in a prison camp in America. I'm getting away from the dinner though, aren't I? We didn't have bread as it's hard to get over here. I supplied the coffee from my can that I got from the coffee company. It was the first meal I'd had cooked homestyle since I left you in August, and we sure did like it. Rumor is that we may get an allotment of Coca-Cola soon—Wow! Won't that be something?

The German soldiers are beginning to arrive home now, all discharged—makes me mad that I'm not home, too. The German soldiers are needed badly on the farms as the women have been running them all by themselves.

One day, we'll get us a place all by ourselves and "live happily ever after" just like they do in storybooks. You'll be my princess—huh?

    Lots of love dear

    Your little husband

p.s. I love you.

———— ————

7 Jun 1945

Austria

My darling wife—

We have another hot rumor that we'll move a hundred or so miles from here and live in pup tents. I guess that's why they call this a dog's life. "They say" we will stay until our whole regiment is assembled and then move to the area we are to occupy.

When we arrive in the area we are to occupy, we will all go to school, so at least our time won't be entirely wasted. I've signed up for a couple of subjects I've always wanted to know something about and would never do anything about it. This would be a good chance for me to learn German, but we are not allowed to talk to the civilians, so I don't guess I'll ever learn more than two or three words. It's a $65 fine for a soldier to talk to or associate with any Axis people other than transacting business.

Until the military government people get here, we have to take care of everything, and our C.O. is a sort of king around here. The mayor and businessmen are all trying to get on the new bandwagon, and every time I leave my room, I stumble over a bunch of them jabbering in broken English. I'm enclosing a snapshot of this burg, taken out of the window of the house we live in—you can see that it's really a one-horse affair. But the railroad makes it a pretty important spot for the whole community. The Germans had an English PW camp here until the Americans arrived.

The Austrian and German people are not too bad, and they try to cooperate with us 100%. I don't know whether they are sincere or scared. But at any rate, the only way we can help them is for them to cooperate. The discharged German soldiers are being organized for farm work. But the Hungarians are an entirely different type—they are parasites. The civilian police have already had the Hungarian officers before us for taking horses and food from the civilians by force. We had previously obtained food from the German army for the Hungarians, and they immediately took advantage of the situation and began to impose on us. It didn't take me long to catch on that they were a bunch of bums in fancy uniforms. To give you an example, neither our C.O. or myself smoke cigarettes, so when these Hungarians called on us, we would take out our cigarette ration and offer them a smoke. When they were ready to leave they would invariably empty all the cigarettes into their pockets and take them with them. Just that attitude burned me up, and I told the guards never to let them in our headquarters again.

Well, dear, it's time for me to get back to work. I've got some stuff to take care of so I'll say so long for a while, sweetheart.

> Lots of love dear
> Your little husband

p.s. I love you angel wings

---

11 June 1945

Austria

My darling wife—

Hello honey, I'm on the move again. We left Grossreifling yesterday morning at 0800 and loaded on trucks, then we rode about two hours in the rain to a railroad siding where we were loaded into boxcars and were hauled up to a little town of Wartberg. The boxcars we rode in were used before to haul cattle or horses and they smelled rather strong—both doors were open and the roof leaked—we were glad to get off when we arrived at this little village about 5 o'clock in the afternoon.

This trip reminded me of the time when I went up to join my regiment last September when we were fighting around Metz in France. Then we went up in boxcars that didn't even have a top on them—we were crammed into them with all of our baggage, and then several cases of C-rations were dumped in and we took off. We rode for three days and nights and nearly froze to death—when it wasn't freezing it was raining. We had 40 men in each boxcar and didn't have enough room to sit down and stretch our legs, so we had to take turns trying to sleep on the bottom of the jolting boxcar—I think one of the wheels was flat, too. Have you ever heard the men who were in the last war remark about "40 and 8"? The remark came from an inscription on French boxcars that reads in French "40 men or 8 horses" in each boxcar. In other words, the horses got more room than we did. There were no toilet facilities, and the only way we could relieve ourselves was when the train stopped. The men were pretty bashful at first, but after a day passed they didn't much care whether anybody saw them or not. We had a canteen of water which we were supposed to drink and wash with for three days—you can imagine how much washing we did. Then, why wash?

About twelve hours after we got on the train in France, we built a fire on the floor of the car—we were really messes when we arrived at our Replacement Depot. When our train was getting close to Metz, we could hear the big guns—like thunder. On the tracks next to us were miles of hospital cars, crammed full, and a steady stream of ambulances were coming up and discharging stretcher after stretcher into the waiting hospital train. On the next track was trainload after trainload of ammunition. That wasn't a very pleasant sight for a replacement to see—two coming up and one going back. From then on, till we actually joined our Companies, the roads were jammed bumper to bumper with ambulances going to the rear. Even the most boisterous were pretty calm and quiet after we saw what it was really like.

The next day, I was put on a truck with 29 other guys and sent up to my Company. I arrived about six o'clock, and it was just getting dark and we were brought up to the kitchen train that was about three miles from the front lines. We were afraid to pitch our tents, so we just wrapped up in our blankets and slept on the wet ground. Just as we were about to doze off, there was a terrific ear-splitting crash behind us—I yanked off my blanket and sat up wide-eyed. About that time, the other hill seemed to catch on fire as it was completely covered with flame, then another ear-splitting crash. By this time, every one of the new men were all but terrified—one of the men that worked at the kitchen came up to me and said, "Oh! I forgot to tell you we are just in front of an artillery battery, and they fire all night at different times." That's called interdicting fire, and the guns fire at targets the aeroplane spotted during the day, usually on roads, crossroads, or any place the enemy may be moving around at night. Well, this kept up all night—the next morning at daybreak we were all awakened and told to turn in all our stuff except half of a tent and one blanket. I stuck my razor and toothbrush in my pocket, and we moved up to the Company. When I arrived, they were trying to see who was left in the Company as they had been all but 24 killed or captured the day before and the 1st Sgt was among the missing. Well, I had my hands full straightening out that mess—then we had a break as the whole war seemed to slow down while both sides got reorganized for our push across the Seille River.[10]

Now how did I get off the subject? I was talking about my ride up here in a cattle car—we are living in tents until we move on to Munich tomorrow. I'm in my tent writing you now—and the rain is pattering on top of my tent.

The binoculars I sent to you were from a German who was an observer. He directed artillery fire on us, and the numbers in the glass when you look through them is a scale that you can estimate range with. They are only good for long distances—on short distances, they blur. The German observer couldn't get away fast enough, and we captured him before he could say "doodly."

Did you like the pictures of the little refugee children? They couldn't speak a word of English or me German—but I gave them some of my chocolate and they followed me around all the time. A guy can't get mad at a bunch of kids even if they are on the other side. One little girl was 10 (I found that out by sign language and holding up fingers) and reminded me so much of Shirley Temple that I got one of the men to snap a picture of me with her.

These are not the refugee children Smith mentioned in this letter. The photo was taken a few days later as his regiment moved back to Germany. Written on back, "This was taken out the side of our boxcar. We tossed candy to a couple of kids, and two seconds later the yard filled up. June 1945, Germany."

Oh! before I forget it, the Russians have a new order now for them to behave and leave the women alone, so they are all good boys now, and the people were beginning to venture home on the Russian side. I guess the women feel funny now walking near Russians and not having to run for the cellar before they got raped. They'd hang us for such foolishness.[11]

    Good night dear

    Your little husband

p.s. I sure do love you.

---

17 June 1945

Germany

My darling little wife—

No honey, I haven't forgotten to write my little wife—just been moving around again. I'm in a little town at the foot of the Alps near Switzerland. It's pretty and all that, but I'm ready to come home to my wife—did you know it honey? We left the little village of Obergunzburg the other afternoon on an hour's notice and you can imagine the swearing and confusion. Each time we move, we think that it will be permanent. This is some life— the army life is not for me kid, and I'm ready to come home any time now.

It will sure be a glad day for me when I can tell you I'm on the way home. But three million men is a lot to move at one time—so I don't guess

I'll be along any time soon. We've only sent one man home and only have about four others that have enough points to go home, and they are all men who were in England or Alaska or some other place. There is nobody left in the original Company—me and two more are the oldest serving members of the organization—that is, except Captain Damkowitch. He got promoted at last, and he is happy as a kid. You know I told you that his wife was caught spending the night somewhere with another man. Just as he got his divorce, he had to go overseas—it must have been a terrible blow to him, but now he is snapping out of it, and although he can't talk to these Germans, he takes notice of all the pretty girls.

While we were on the border, he helped some Hungarians and some Germans to get a supply of food, and they really gave him a big play—they visited him officially and brought their wives and gave him quite a party. All the officers were some kind of defunct nobility, and that really impressed him—he made eyes at some countess or other, and that was all he could talk about for days. You would hold your sides and roll around the floor with laughter if you could hear him tell of his experiences with the Hungarians. He always looks hurt when I laugh when he tells me about the Hungarians 'cause I think they are a bunch of no good parasites, and the country would have been better off if we would have killed them all—but I'll have to tell you about them in another letter.

Sure—it's okay to let the girls read your letters, but be careful which ones 'cause you might get embarrassed—huh? I just write down what I'm thinking and sometimes I get a little rambunctious.

Lots of love darling

Your little husband

p.s. I love you.

———————

21 June 1945

Rosshaupten, Germany

My darling wife—

Hello! dear—If I'm stuck here this winter, somebody will have a hard time getting me away from the stove—the house I'm staying in has double windows and huge porcelain stoves in every room—the one in my room is taller than I am and is made of yellow porcelain or something that looks like porcelain. I guess these people never got around to building furnaces yet. The mountains are beautiful—now that they are pretty and green, but most of them have snow on them all the year around. We made tables out in the open to eat our food on and at every meal I have a good opportunity to look at the scenery. Most of the day, I'm busy trying to reorganize my files and records that I had to neglect when I was fighting—it seems like there are always a hundred and one things to do that don't amount to a thing.

The two women who own the house we are occupying were quite upset at first, but now that they are allowed to come over in the daytime and fuss around with their garden and flowers they don't feel so badly—I promised them that we'd leave everything as we found it, and they seemed rather satisfied. They were a very well-to-do family, and this was their summer home.

They have a lot of oil paintings and things hanging around. A nice oil painting really sets off a room—I've seen some beauties around here and bought two from a local artist of the scenery around here and sent them

This is one of the paintings my father sent home. The artist's name is illegible.

to Mother as I hadn't sent her a thing—maybe I can get more. The trouble is, the artist doesn't want to part with all his works because he plans to open a studio someday and wants a few to hang around. Another thing is the lack of colors—you see, they can't buy art supplies in Germany now. The paintings cost me 5 packages of cigarettes, 5 chocolate bars and a bar of soap, and 70 marks. 70 marks is about 7 dollars. The cigarettes were rations I saved and the chocolate was issued to us some time ago to eat in an emergency—that is, if we couldn't get any food. It's the very strong type of chocolate and not too good to eat as a candy. But these people haven't had any chocolate for such a long time it is more valuable to them than money—which is hard to spend because there is nothing to buy with it.

I'm also sending you a little something in this letter. It's what I've been saving out of my pay each month in hopes that I might get a chance to go to one of the larger towns in France and buy you something really nice, but they don't have anything to sell but souvenir junk at terrific prices. I had hoped to buy you some nice lingerie—but what they have for sale is so limited and rationed so carefully I thought best not to buy it and you can use the money to buy yourself something nice.

I think you've done mighty well with your bank account and I always did say you were the smartest wife there ever was.

> Lots of love dear
> Your little husband

---

22 June 1945

Germany

Sweetheart—

Dear heart, I had two letters from you last night, and I enjoyed them so much. Yes, I can just close my eyes and imagine what you are doing when I read your letters. I'm starting your letter while I'm supposed to be on duty—my office is in what used to be the kitchen, and I've set it up as my headquarters. A kitchen is usually a bad place, but as I don't allow anyone to come in and cook and mess it up, that isn't too bad.

We are playing a ball game this afternoon with my old Company, Easy Co, and the clerk got so fidgety that I told him to go and watch. Then I noticed the orderly was looking forlorn, so I told him he might as well go too—both of them left like a shot out of a gun so I'm all alone. Somebody has to remain on duty all the time, so I told them I'd do it and they could go to the game.

The guard system is really funny. In the American army, somebody is always guarding something. Even in peacetime at a fort in the middle of the U.S., the guard is on 24 hours a day. They even guard the tomb of the unknown soldier. On the alert 24 hours a day—that's us. I guess we owe a great deal of our success to being able to slip around in the dark—the German soldiers used to like to sleep, and we took quite a few by surprise. They could rarely surprise us, as even when we were in foxholes, one stayed awake while the other slept. The only time I hated to guard anything was the Hungarian gold supply.

After we contacted the Russians, who should come up but a Hungarian captain—he opened his conversation by trying to give us something— some kind of dried beef or bologna I guess you'd call it. I told him (through his interpreter) that we were well supplied and thanked him, then he got down to the real business—he wanted us to transport them back to their homes in Hungary. As that was in Russian territory, I suggested he see the Russian commander. He left, and later our C.O. met another delegation of Hungarian officers, and he was so impressed by their fancy uniforms that before he knew it they had him "sucked in" and he actually invited them to dinner. That did it. From then on, they hounded us to death. One of the Hungarian officers was a concert pianist and played the concert version of the "Blue Danube." It was beautiful, and I thought of you—as you often said it was your favorite piece. They brought their wives, and it looked like a regular ball.

The Hungarian officers in their fancy uniforms put us to shame—when they were ready to go home, they cheerfully borrowed five gallons of gas from us and sped away to their castle. From then on, you could always count on them dropping in at mealtime. It took the C.O. a long time for it to soak in that they were giving him "the works." I finished with them when I missed some of my German cigars, and I strongly suspected one of them—then later the rest of our men began missing little articles. I refused to see them anymore and told the guard to shoot them if they tried to get in again.

They were continually trying to get us in an argument with the Russians and told us all kinds of tales that the Russians were on our side of the river.

They had me fooled for a while too and I was really glad we found them out—shiftless and no good. Our poor C.O. was hurt when they drank all his liquor, smoked all his cigarettes (or swiped them), and ate everything they could find. They smiled, clicked their heels and bowed from the waist and were off for a new sucker. It was almost like a play—if you could get a detached view of it. They were a type of people that are interesting, charming, and have no conscience at all—it makes me think of the rich people that used to travel abroad and marry some of this defunct nobility. They aren't for me.

Darling, I guess I better go back to work. I sure do love you kid—you are the most wonderful wife in the world.

> Lots of love dear
> Your little husband

p.s. I sure do love you, kid.

---

26 June 1945
Germany
My darling wife—

Rumors are running wild again and the latest one is that the 80th is due to land in New York on 2nd of October. Some guy picked that one up back at Division Headquarters. The army practically lives on rumors, and everybody believes them all. There may be something to it as we haven't started the education program they were "blowing off" about so much.

All we've been doing is taking exercise, drilling, and playing ball. Last night I went to a ball game and nearly hollered myself hoarse. It stays light here until ten o'clock and gets daylight about 0330. Sure seems funny to have to go to bed just at dark.

There are a lot of kids and civilians around with nothing. We felt awfully sorry for them and shared our rations with them. That's one thing about Americans—they sympathize with the people that are down. But we are hard when we are fighting. That's what fools the Germans—they can't understand such goings-on. Well, it's hard to learn to hate in a short time, and our Sunday schools and churches have taught us a much better way of life than hate. But we always rise to the occasion.

I'm sorry I couldn't get more of the scenery in the snapshots. Every time I look around at the scenery, I think how much you would like it if you could see it.

Lots of love

Your little husband

p.s. I love you.

———————

2 July 1945

Pfronten, Germany

My darling wife—

Dear, it's been awfully cool here for the past few days. I only hope we get back somewhere warm before winter really starts—if it's cool in the summertime, I know it will be rough when winter starts.

I had quite an experience today. I had to stand and review my entire Battalion. It was quite an impressive ceremony, and I was awarded my Purple Heart, then the Battalion marched by and each Company saluted me by turning their heads to the right as they marched by. I'll mail my medal home tomorrow, but I'll keep the ribbon to wear on my blouse when I come home (wish I knew it was soon).

The Purple Heart is one of the prettiest medals I've ever seen. It was originated by General Washington and has been awarded in our army ever since the Revolution. It has a picture of General Washington on a background of a Purple Heart. It's awarded for military merit but there's one catch to it. You either have to be wounded or killed to get it. I got wounded in action during the Battle in Luxembourg, but it wasn't so bad, so don't get excited. It was mostly concussion and shell fragments—I was wearing so many clothes at the time that I didn't get hit too badly and I wouldn't tell you about it before so as not to cause you any worry. I'm perfectly well and you can't even see the places that I was injured. I was following a tank during an attack and the Germans fired a cannon directly at the tank and blew it up. I was right behind it and got hit on the arm and in the face—it was a close shave but I made it and that's all that counts, they tell me.

Mike Damkowitch leading Company G of the 317th Infantry Regiment in Pfronten, Germany, July 1945

Smith receiving a decoration

I had a letter from Betty Sue the other day, and she was at the camp at High Springs. Maybe the camp will be good for her—teach her a little self-reliance. I'll send her a little money order when I send yours, and you can help her pick out a coat or something she needs. Teach her how to select clothes, dear—and don't let her dress goony—tell her it's best to have one good outfit than two not so good. You know bud 'cause you've got good taste. That's another thing I've always admired in my little wife—such good taste. I was always so proud to be with you 'cause you always looked so good. You could see the envious stares of the other women as you swept past. And then you are always doing things for people—visiting your friends when they are sick and things like that. And never fussed at your husband, and I know I must have gotten in your hair sometimes, but you never hollered and yelled at me. I look back on our marriage as the happiest moments of my whole life—you are just wonderful dear—I'm so lucky to get you for my little wife, I don't know what to do.

Now, when I should be home making love to you—here I am thousands of miles away in a strange country—I get so homesick for you sometimes I don't know what to do. Maybe it won't be too long before I can come home to you—I hope and pray that it won't be too long.

Dear, it's getting pretty late and 0530 comes very soon so I'll tell you good night dear.

Lots of love

Your little husband

p.s. I love you, dear.

---

3 July 1945

My darling wife—

Just received the letter you wrote the 24th of June. I'm so sorry that you were down in the dumps, and I was glad if my letter of 24 April cheered you up. The latest rumor seems to have us leave for the United States about July or August—it would be wonderful to be in the States when the Pacific war ended. But anyway, I hope if we come home, I'll get a job in the United States and you'll be right with me kid. Darling—from the minute I return to you 'till "death do us part," I'll devote myself to trying to make you happy. I know now I must have made some mistakes

Articles like this about soldiers appeared in hometown newspapers across the nation. The *Florida Times-Union*, undated clipping.

Wins Award for Heroism. In an impressive ceremony in Pfronten, Germany, First Sgt. Percy M. Smith, Jacksonville veteran of three important European battle campaigns, was awarded the Bronze Star for gallantry in action against an enemy of the United States.

Assigned to an Infantry Company in October, 1944, Sergeant Smith took part in some of the fiercest action of the Western Front. He was in the Rhineland, Ardennes and Central European campaigns. His citation states that on November 29, 1944, when his company engaged the crack SS troops in the Saar Basin and the situation looked hopeless for his men, "he called for and directed artillery fire on the enemy tanks and enabled his men to reorganize are repulse the enemy with numerous losses."

Sergeant Smith again was cited for distinguished service during the intense fighting in the Ardennes campaign. His regiment was ordered from St. Avold, France, to Luxembourg to halt General von Rundstedt's drive. "After riding for 48 hours in open trucks in freezing weather, Sergeant Smith's company arrived in the Duchy of Luxembourg and, without hot food or drink for 48 hours, immediately launched an attack to halt the German advance. During an all night battle on Christmas Eve, Sergeant Smith was wounded by a German artillery shell, but despite his wounds he remained with his company and in the absence of the company commander, he reorganized the company and successfully captured their objective."

A third time he distinguished himself by heroic action when he led his company across the Rhine River at Mainz, Germany. The crossing was made in the middle of the night under intense fire from fanatical SS troops defending the bridgehead. Under the sergeant's direction, his company won the bridgehead and captured over 450 towns and villages in spearheading the Third Army's successful drive into Germany.

Sergeant Smith also won the Combat Infantryman's Badge, the Purple Heart, Good Conduct Medal and the Silver Star for gallantry.

His wife, the former Miss Elizabeth Camp of Atlanta, lives with her mother, Mrs. Nina Camp, at 3340 Brentwood Avenue. He is the son of Mrs. B. C. Willis of 1321 Market Street. Before entering the service, he worked for Southern News Company.

and hurt you unintentionally, but I was just a dumb little husband—I'll try extra very hard to make you happy when I come home.

It's pretty awful not to have anybody but a bunch of soldiers to talk to. I guess I'd get like a guy in a penitentiary if I had to stay around a couple of years. Then it must be bad for you too, so I try to keep busy and think about the fun we've had in the past and plan for the future. I'm sure looking forward to our home when I get back to you. We can have such fun fixing it up. If we buy a place, we can get one large enough that your mother can live with us any time she wants to or all the time. You'll be the boss of our house.

When the government started a program to feed all of Europe, they cut our rations all out of proportion. For several weeks we were really hungry, but now it's gradually getting adjusted. I told the men if things didn't get better, I would line them all up and give them a piece of paper and make them all write to their Congressman before they could leave the formation. But I guess the dummy that engineered this brilliant cut in the food must have awakened to the fact we weren't getting enough. And it wasn't any too soon either. Sometimes I think our army officials are the most stupid nincompoops there ever were.

We are supposed to have a parade through our little village tomorrow—4th of July—but I'm afraid it's going to be a terrible flop. A parade isn't so good in the rain. I've been out in the rain so much when I had to, that I think it's a lot of foolishness to parade around in the rain when you don't have to. All through France and Luxembourg, it rained practically all the time, and it was something to be dry. Many a time, I've had to march 30 miles a day with everything I owned in my pack or in my pockets plus my carbine and a belt full of ammunition. As I sloshed along, I said to myself if I ever made it through the war safely, it would be a hard job to get me out of a dry place when I ever got to one—and sure enough I'm really hard to get out of a house now.

Really, I guess in a way this visit to the Alps was a good thing for us 'cause it gives us a chance to live like people instead of animals—But I would rather be part animal and home with my little wife. I guess I'll be a little wild anyway.

Dear, it's time for your little husband to go to bed, but I sure wish I was with you—or anywhere as long as it is with my little wife. Darling, I'll be dreaming of you.

Lots of love

Your little husband

p.s. I sure do love you, kid

From MIA to KIA

A memory in story form written circa 1979–82

In July we had moved to the village of Pfronten, Germany. Life was easy, and athletic games were the order of the day for our soldiers. Routine Company affairs were relegated to Corporal Redfern and his buddy Corporal Roberts. I poured a cup of coffee and looked at the pile of Morning

Reports on my field desk. I picked them up and idly flipped the pages. I stopped on 23 December 1944. The terse entry included, "Forced march, under attack, weather freezing." Those few words told volumes. On Christmas Day, we had limped into the village of Niederfuelen. As First Sergeant, I had prepared the draft worksheet of the Morning Report in a room crowded with disheveled exhausted soldiers. All men not present or accounted for were listed as MIA. A clerk at the Regimental level would make adjustments from the reports received from Field Hospitals and Graves Registration.

My eyes scanned the list of missing men with the terse notion "from MIA to KIA." Anuskiewicz's name caught my eye. I thought of the skinny platoon sergeant rallying the men of the first platoon in his shrill voice. Then I saw the name of Joseph A. Moors. I felt a pang. He had been dropped as missing in action, but I had hoped that he was in a field hospital. Then I saw the notation "from MIA to KIA."[12]

My thoughts turned to the mild-mannered, shy soldier with a ready smile and to a girl he told me about one night in a dripping dugout. And to his happiness as he told me how her letters made him feel. My reverie evaporated when the mail orderly handed me two letters from Elizabeth.

After the war, I was struggling to make a go of a small business. My partner, Mr. Greer, was vexed. He had misplaced the address of a supply firm. Mr. Greer, an elderly man, impatiently exclaimed, "I can't imagine what I did with that address. I thought it was here on the desk."

"What are you looking for?" I asked.

"Oh, that supply company in Philadelphia. Now what did I do with it?" he mumbled.

I said, "This afternoon when I go to town, I can stop by the telephone company office and ask if they have directories for other cities. If they have Philadelphia, I can look it up."

"Good boy," he beamed.

That afternoon, in the office of the telephone company, I thumbed through the Philadelphia directory and jotted down the address. Then I remembered that Sergeant Moors was from Philadelphia. On impulse, I flipped the pages until I found the name of Moors. Several were listed, and one was a J. Moors. I made a note of the address and tucked it in my coat pocket.

Sometime later, I was preparing to take my suit to the cleaners, and Elizabeth reminded me to check the pockets first. There was the address. While it was on my mind, I penned a letter saying that I had served in the army with a buddy named Joseph Moors. I asked if he was a relative.

Like a boomerang, a reply came back quickly. It was from Joe's mother, Agnes. Mrs. Moors told me that she'd prayed that she would hear from a comrade that had been with Joe. She said that all she had was a telegram from the War Department announcing her son's death. She begged for any information I had.

I wrote her and told her about the night Joe perished. However, I played down the hardships. I can't remember what I wrote, but Mrs. Moors thanked me over and over, saying that to her, it was a memorial to Joe. We continued to exchange letters from time to time over the years.

Once, I mentioned that Joe had told me about a girl he admired, and I thought he had told his folks about her. Mrs. Moors said that Joe hadn't mentioned a girl, but she was glad that I told her. Then Mrs. Moors related the following episode, as I recall.

About two months after the telegram from the War Department, a young woman came to our front door. I heard the chimes, and my daughter answered the door. Moments later, the girl left. She was dabbing her eyes with a handkerchief as she hurried to a taxi. The door closed, and the taxi sped away.

I asked my daughter, Anna, "Who was that?"

"I don't know," she replied. "Somebody that knew Joe. When I opened the door, she asked if this was the residence of Joe Moors, and I said yes. She said that she had met Joe when he was on furlough. When I told her about the telegram, she turned pale and ran back to the taxi before I had time to ask her name."

Sometime later—it was 1955, I think—I received a note from Mrs. Moors's daughter, advising that her mother had passed away.

---

9 July 1945
Germany
My darling—
Yesterday, Sam and I climbed the big hill and looked at the scenery. It was really beautiful but it's so far from home—that's what I don't like. We

didn't climb all the way to the top 'cause it was too high. We just went up to an old ski jump. In the winter, the locals used to climb up and slide down on skis. Gosh, I hope I'm not here this winter—I'll freeze, kid.

We have our kitchen in a tent beside a house nearby—the cooks, supply, and a few others live in the house. A few days ago, a Kraut soldier came home with his pack on his back and his discharge in his pocket. I was standing by the kitchen when he arrived—he threw down his pack and rushed into the house expecting to find his wife and children. In a couple of seconds, he came flying out again and took a good look at the house again to see if he was in the right one, then he tried again. This time a soldier came out with him and explained that the place was under "new management" but his wife and children were down the street.

I guess we'll be having all kinds of confusion from now on, as they are releasing around 1,000 German prisoners a day in this vicinity.

Most of the Germans that are released that live in the area controlled by the French and Russians refuse to go back home. They say the French and Russians tear up their discharge papers and put them to work in France and Russia (what a shame). I wish America would pull out of Europe—all it does is cause confusion and headaches. One of the locals who speaks a little English tried to get me into a political discussion one time—so I told him that the difference between the French, Russian and American economic system could be illustrated by a cow. The Russians milk the cow and take the milk to a market and everybody that needs milk comes and gets it. The French milk the cow and take the milk around to the people, and if they want it, they buy it. But in America, I said, "If we have a cow, hell, we sell it and buy a bull." They don't try to get me started on any discussions anymore.

Darling, it's getting late again so I'll have to say good night for now.

Lots of love

Your little husband

p.s. I love you, dear.

you are an angel—

6

FOUR-STAR VISITOR

He has a nice fat ass, though, and it was all I could do to
keep from kicking it as he walked away.

In the early summer of 1945, General Patton returned to the United States,
apparently seeking a leadership post in the Pacific War. Instead, he was sent
back to Germany to oversee the military occupation of Bavaria. As part of

The back of this photo reads, "Pfronten, July 1945."

that job, the general toured the region and visited the troops. In mid-July, he reviewed the 317th Infantry Regiment in Pfronten. My father was there with his camera.

Patton's visit brought back battlefront memories and feelings of anger, and afterwards my father's letters speak of disillusion and sadness—even depression—and a growing anguish about the long wait to go home.

---

10 July 1945
Germany
My darling wife—

I'm enclosing some photo cards of the little village that I'm staying in. As you can see, this little village wasn't even touched by the war, and it's just like it's been for years.

During the fighting, I didn't know where I was going and didn't find out anything about it until after I left. In other words, I didn't know what to look at or appreciate until after I left. Not far from here is where Hitler and Goering had their castles, so needless to say, this is the most beautiful part of Germany.

A postcard from Phronten, Germany, sent by Percy to Elizabeth

Dear, when you send me another box please, drop a small jar of "Mum" in it—I'm wearing wool suits now and they get rather smelly before they get dirty—I remember my sweet little wife sent me a jar during one of the biggest battles, and I had to leave it in a broken-down house where we stopped for a few hours. At the time, I had to smile through my whiskers and dirt—my thoughtful little wife—and the poor little husband hadn't had a bath for a couple of months. But, it's pretty nice here. I have a private room and right across the hall is a tub—a real tub and a hot water heater. All I have to do is haul up some wood and build a fire—it's a wood burner. I've been taking a bath every day and it's wonderful. Sometimes the misery of the past months seems like a dream.

General Patton will visit us soon—isn't that something? I never saw him next to me on the front lines, so I'm not much impressed.

Darling, I love you so much. Just remember we've got a date just as soon as I get home to you.

> Goodnight darling
> Lots of love
> Your little husband

p.s. I love you

16 July 1945
Germany
My darling—

Maybe us being separated has helped us appreciate each other more, and when I return maybe our married life will be more happy—however, I don't see how I could love you any more, as I love you so much now I can hardly wait to hold you in my arms.

I'm so proud of my wedding ring—I like it more and more every day—once when it looked like I was going to get captured, the guy in the hole with me said we may as well throw away anything we had valuable, as there was no use letting the Krauts get it. I told him I didn't mind destroying my watch or anything else I had, but if they took my wedding ring I'd be dead 'cause they would have to kill me to get it. The thought of them taking my ring made me so damn mad I stuck another clip of ammunition in my carbine and raise up out of my hole and sprayed them good. Then I jumped out and fired while I was running and jumped into a ditch that led back through a draw and got away from them, and then I turned around and sprayed the Krauts while my buddy ran for the ditch. I guess they never expected us to do anything as daring as that—in fact, when we were safe again, I nearly passed out from fright. I told the other guy if he hadn't told me that the Krauts would take my ring, I wouldn't have dared try to get away. I haven't had my ring off since you gave it to me—of course it doesn't shine like it used to but it's more valuable than diamonds to me.

Dear, I've just received notice that I have to leave at 0730 in the morning to go back to some town in France for a court-martial. The officer going with me said we may be able to get a day off and visit Paris—wouldn't that be something? I don't care for the French at all, but it would be nice to say in later years that I had at least been there. The men that have been there say they hold you up something terrible for the smallest souvenir, and I can imagine it's so. Come to think of it, Paris is about the only city in Europe that hasn't been bombed flat. It was declared an open city by the French, then the Germans and the Americans. But then we may not even be able to make it—transportation is an awful problem.

It's raining again, and cloudy when it isn't raining. I never saw such a country—all I do is my work and read and write to you. I like to think and dream of the fun we'll have when I get the hell out of this blooming country—as far as I'm concerned, the "Supermen" can have it, scenery and all. I guess we'll do our traveling in the U.S., as it will be a long time before these folks can accommodate tourists. I've been ready to come home since last August.

    Lots of love darling
    Your little husband
p.s. I love you.

———————

18 July 1945
Germany
My darling—
Hello dear, here I am looking at your snapshot and nibbling the mints you sent me and writing at the same time. If you can find the hair oil, send it—if not send some other kind. I'll try to get my hair fixed up again—it's a

terrible mess now and if I'm coming home soon I'll have to look like something. It's hard to get straightened out after living eight months like a wild animal.

Don't you let those fresh soldiers scare you, kid. No, they weren't shell-shocked. I've seen plenty of those cases and they never smile—they just get off to themselves and crouch in the corner like a wild frightened animal. After the shelling, they can't walk or talk, just blubber like a baby, and when you get them into a house they crawl on the floor under the table and cry. You never see anybody that's really gone through a real shelling act like the guys you saw at the beach. They were probably from some Northern town and didn't give a damn.

General Patton was out at the Company today and honored us with a fifteen-minute visit to watch a demonstration we put on for him. Your little husband was about five feet from him—his face is old and thin and he looks like a tired old man. He spoke very quietly and didn't have much to say. I used to imagine he was fat but he isn't, that is, his chest and arms seem slim, he has a nice fat ass though, and it was all I could do to keep from kicking it as he walked away. He doesn't inspire me to want to die for my country. I was rather bored with the whole affair.[1]

Dear, don't work too hard and take care of your sweet self 'cause your husband is coming home before long and he's going to need a lot of loving.

> Good night darling
> Lots of love
> Your little husband

p.s. I love you, dear.

General George S. Patton

A memory in story form written circa 1979–82

General Patton and I were on the opposite ends of the military spectrum. While I knew of him, he didn't know that I existed. A flamboyant, controversial troop leader, General Patton was frequently at odds with other high-level commanders. He was a tank commander and troop leader with strong abilities, and he drove his troops to the point of exhaustion and then demanded more. His nickname was "Old Blood and Guts," but his weary soldiers grumbled and swore, "Damnit to hell! His guts 'n our blood."

In October 1944 when I arrived as a replacement, Company G command post was in a hole with telephone wires scattered across the ground and into the underbrush. A soldier with a scraggly beard was hooking wires to a field telephone. He looked at me. "I'm Sergeant McAllister," he said. "I'm the Communication Sergeant."

"I'm Sergeant Smith," I replied. "What's going on?"

"Nothing much right now," he said. "I just finished stringing wire to the platoons. Hey, how many replacements did you bring with you?"

"One hundred and forty," I answered.

"We took a beating the day before yesterday," he said. "That won't bring us up to full strength, but it's better'n trying to hold with twenty-seven."

My eyes widened. "You mean there's only twenty-seven men left?"

"Yeah," he grunted. "It was a little village called Sivry. It was a hot engagement, but maybe we'll be in a holding position for a while."

"You think so?" I asked.

"Yep," he grunted again as he fastened a wire to the field telephone. "The rumor is that the tanks ran out of fuel and can't get more until the British catch up."

Two days later, our dream of holding operations evaporated when orders came to "saddle up" and prepare to entruck.

"Hey," I called to a truck driver. "I thought we were in a holding position. What's up?"

"We thought we were stalled, too," he said, "but we got gas from somewhere."

"Didn't you hear?" chimed in another truck driver. "Somebody found a German fuel depot behind the lines, and Patton ordered a task force to attack it. In a jiffy, our guys captured the fuel and took their gasoline."

Whether the rumor was true or not, the trucks arrived and the infantry and tanks were on the move.

In the back of the bouncing truck, we sat facing each other. Field packs were stacked at our feet between us, and each soldier clutched his rifle between his knees. Bodies jostled and loose talk flowed as the heavy truck swayed to and fro. Laughter followed some outrageous anecdote, then a shout from a soldier in the front, "Hey fellas, all together now," and in unison everyone thundered, "SOME CRAP!" As the truck gears made a grinding noise, soldiers' heads bobbled, and the faint rumbling of artillery in the distance could be heard between snatches of conversation.

Months later, 21 January to be exact, the 2nd Battalion of the 317th Infantry suffered a severe mauling by German artillery. Terrified would be an understatement—I was rendered incoherent with fear. The bursting shells and exposure to the elements profoundly affected me. Me, a tractable, easy-going amiable soldier, suddenly turned bitter and malevolent. My feelings of bitter resentment festered, and during the next rest stop, I penned a letter to General Patton.

What the hell, why not? What else could happen? I was already condemned and in hell—a frozen hell. Frankly, I had no idea he'd see or read the letter, so I vented my feelings. I can't remember if I called him a "dumb son-of-a-bitch" or not, but I intended to. In retrospect, I realized that the letter was ridiculous. Me, a lowly sergeant giving advice to a general, a three-star general noted for taking advice from nobody, hardly from an enlisted man. Well, it was done, and I felt better after unburdening myself.

Some weeks later as we paused at a small village, the mail caught up with us. Among several letters was one with a return address "Headquarters Third Army." I ripped open the envelope and read a letter that exposed another aspect of General Patton. I fully intended to mail the letter home, but alas it was lost along with my gear at a disputed river crossing.

In substance, as I recall, he praised the 2nd Battalion for their splendid battle record. He agreed the rigors and hardships of combat were hell. He said there could be no enduring peace without the unconditional surrender of the Axis forces, and victory could not be achieved until the infantry controlled the ground. He said that tanks, planes, artillery, and other sophisticated armaments helped—however, until the infantry controlled the ground, there was no victory.

This was a switch. Here was a man that drove his troops to the point of exhaustion, was given to sulfurous language, and was generally irreverent, writing a letter that was almost compassionate. It was unfortunate that I was unable to preserve that letter.[2]

The war was intervals of sheer terror interspersed with periods of dull boredom. During a lull, the Company was dug in on the side of a snow-covered hill. It was midafternoon, and I idly watched a jeep roll to a stop at the foot of our hill. The driver made his way to a foxhole. I couldn't hear what he said, but the soldier in the foxhole pointed in my direction. The driver trudged through the snow towards my foxhole that was covered with a frozen shelter half to keep out the snow.

"You Sergeant Smith?" he asked as wispy vapor trails swirled from his mouth.

"Yeah," I responded. "What's up?"

"Sergeant Smith, I'm Corporal Kline from Battalion. Sergeant Major Purvis sent me to fetch you."

"How come?" I asked.

"Beats me," he answered, pointing down the hill. "The jeep is down there."

The headquarters of the 2nd Battalion was housed in a former schoolhouse on the outskirts of a village. Messenger jeeps scurried to and fro, and telephone wires hung from the windows. The sergeant major, swathed in a muffler and field jacket, glanced up as I entered. "Hi, Sergeant Smith," he greeted me. "Damn, it's cold." As he spoke, frosty vapor floated around his ragged mustache.

"This is real luxury," I lied. "You ought to be out there on the side of a hill with me."

"No thanks," he said, rubbing his hands together.

I asked, "Say, Sarge, what's this all about?"

He dug around in some papers. "Oh, here it is," he said, holding up a piece of paper. "You've been ordered to take the mail truck back to Division. From there, you'll be trucked to Nancy in France for a three-day rest and recreation leave."

"Sounds great," I grinned. "But why me?"

"I don't know. The order came from Division."

"But look at me," I said, pointing to my disheveled uniform.

"Don't worry," he replied. "You'll be issued a clean uniform at Division and toilet articles. If you'll sign this voucher, payroll will authorize a fifty-dollar advance."

"Show me where to sign," I cried. "And point me toward the mail truck."

As the truck sped back toward Division, I had ample time to think about my leave. Was it my letter to General Patton? Was it possible that he authorized my leave? Or was my name selected at random? I'll never know.

———————

In mid-February, a few days before my mother's birthday, the 2nd Battalion was quartered in the town of Diekirch, on the Sauer River and a short distance from the German border. Our engineers were doggedly attempting to repair a bridge over the river, while German artillery was equally determined they wouldn't. It was an impasse. Apparently the original plan was to repair the bridge, then move tanks and armor across the river. But the timetable was upset and the troops were held up at Diekirch.

It was late afternoon, and I was checking the guards. Each doorway held a soldier covering the sentry posted across the street. I paused to stare at the battered hotel that served as company headquarters. As I stood in the empty street, I felt nature call. So I stepped over to the side of the scarred hotel building that served as our company headquarters and faced the wall. At the first trickle, I heard the roar of a vehicle approaching at high speed. The tires screamed as a jeep rounded the corner on two wheels in a cloud of dust. The jeep surged forward and then skidded sideways as the driver applied the brakes. There was a squealing noise, and the dust swirled as the jeep thundered backward and screeched to a halt opposite where I stood.

A red flag with gold stars fluttered on the jeep. A soldier stood with his hands on the windshield bar. His helmet with three gold stars obscured the upper part of his face. At his hips dangled pearl-handled pistols. The yelling soldier with his mouth open was General George S. Patton, Commander of the Third Army. What an ignominious predicament. I changed hands and attempted an awkward salute while twisting away from the wall.

"Hey, soldier," bawled the general. "Where's that damn, son-of-a-bitching bridge?"

"That way, sir," I replied, pointing down the road.

"Let's go," cried General Patton, and the jeep leaped forward with a roar.

My fleeting encounter with General Patton lasted seconds. "What an undignified way to greet a general," I mused as I hitched breeches.

Back at company headquarters, I called to Sergeant Sumskis, "Hey, Sumskis, and you too, Bailey, listen, General Patton just barreled through headed for the Sauer River. After chow, we'd better get saddled up, 'cause I bet we're crossing that river tonight."[3]

"You think so?" asked Sergeant Bailey, "The bridge isn't . . ."

I jumped in. "Somebody has to cross the river and push the Krauts back so the engineers can reconstruct the bridge for the tanks to cross."

Sergeant Sumskis and I were talking in the chow line when the thundering jeep roared back through Diekirch.

At nightfall, there was a rumbling noise in the street. "What's that?" asked Sergeant Bailey.

Sergeant Sumskis peered out the window. "It's a convoy of trucks. They're running without lights."

"Hey," cried Sergeant Bailey. "They're filled with rubber boats all stacked in the back."

The buzzing field telephone interrupted his conversation. Sergeant Sumskis hefted the phone, listened, and then said, "Yes—yes—yes—Roger—out." He shoved the transmitter into the case and said, "Company Commanders conference in ten minutes. I'll tell Lieutenant McDonell."

"Yep," I said. "Those rubber boats are for us. Let's get our gear together. We're crossing the Sauer River tonight."

The next time I saw General Patton, the war was over. Following the surrender, we were shunted from place to place guarding bridges, directing displaced persons, maintaining law and order, and preserving the peace. Once those tasks were complete, the entire 2nd Battalion was moved by trucks to a mountainous region of southern Germany. Company G was quartered in the quaint village of Pfronten. Here, life was easy, and only a minimum amount of military discipline was maintained. Athletics and games were the order of the day.

In July of 1945, Captain Damkowitch returned from a Company commanders' conference and plopped his helmet liner on the table. "Smitty, General Patton is going to inspect the 2nd Battalion, maybe next week."

"Yes, sir," I replied. "We'll alert the platoons to get ready."

"Good," responded Captain Damkowitch. "Colonel Williams will let us know when he's due in Pfronten." He paused, "Oh, another thing—the colonel wants us to put on a field exercise or demonstration as part of the program."

"Yes, sir," I said, "What do you suggest?"

Mike waved his hand, "Oh, anything. Get together with the platoon sergeants and put something together."

"Very well," I said. "Shall we turn out for a company parade?"

"No," responded Captain Damkowitch. "The colonel suggested that we have the troops line up a short distance from the viewing site on each side of the road at five-foot intervals. After the general passes, the troops can fall out and watch the demonstration. Okay?"

"Yes, sir."

The troops received the news with enthusiasm. They had been inactive long enough to want some kind of action. There was hustle and bustle as the men cleaned their uniforms, and women of the village were pressed to help with the washing. Boots were brushed. Blue neck scarves and colorful campaign ribbons spruced up and added verve to the uniforms.

A squad of infantrymen was chosen to demonstrate an assault on a pillbox, and we selected an elevated viewing site on the side of a hill. Two Germans recently discharged from their army loaned us their uniforms.

After breakfast on the big day, Company G turned out in full dress uniforms to greet General Patton, but he didn't arrive until long after the noon hour. "Hurry up and wait," somebody grumbled. At 1500 the telephone orderly handed me a message. I scanned the slip of paper and called to Sergeant McAllister, "Hey, Mac, alert the platoons. General Patton is en route from Pfronten."

Spick-and-span, the troops lined the street at five-foot intervals. Soldiers stood ramrod straight, arms presented and eyes on the rifle stacking swivel as the staff cars whisked General Patton and his entourage to the viewing site. Folding chairs were provided for the dignitaries. On signal, the troops broke rank and swarmed to see the famous general and find a spot to watch the demonstration. I snatched my camera and hurried to join them. When I arrived, the troops were milling around and seating themselves on the ground downhill from the viewing site.

General Patton, clutching binoculars, was seated in the midst of his staff and attending officers. I heard him speak in a quiet tone as I stepped over soldiers and sidled close to snap a photograph.

The general quietly asked a question, and Colonel Williams gave a prompt reply. One of General Patton's aides whipped out a pocket notebook, but the general frowned and gestured toward the aide, "Don't bother, it really doesn't matter. I was just making conversation."

Surrounded by larger officers, General Patton looked small, almost frail. A tired, pensive expression was reflected on his face. I was staring at a weary elderly man.

Photo taken by Smith during General Patton's visit. Here Patton is flanked by his entourage. Mike Damkowitch is in the far back center, looking over his shoulder. Phronten, Germany, 18 July 1945.

My camera clicked, and General George S. Patton looked directly at me. In a fraction of a second, his eyes flitted from my helmet liner to my boots. His piercing glance embraced the left breast on my blouse and the green stripe under the chevrons on my arm. Several soldiers squiggled over and made room for me to sit with them. General Patton said something and Colonel Williams snapped, "Company G, sir."

A voice called, "Sir, the field exercise is ready to commence."

Colonel Williams waved his hand, and a series of rapid explosions proclaimed that the demonstration had begun. The general observed through binoculars as soldiers, holding their rifles at high port, darted toward the mock fortification. Some flopped and fired blanks as others wormed their way forward. The sound of German automatic weapons was interspersed with several loud explosions. Heavy smoke wafted in the breeze.

During the hubbub and clatter of exploding guns, my mind wandered. Did General Patton recall a letter from a Sergeant Smith in this battalion, a letter that could be classified as impertinent? The fraction of a second that our eyes met, I thought he might recall—but, then, why should he?

A light machine gun chattered as the cloud of smoke from explosions drifted away from the mock fortification. My mind flitted. The sounds of mock warfare engendered thoughts—bitter thoughts.

I resented being uprooted and sent over three thousand miles from home. I resented being shunted from one unit to another. I never got to be with the fellows long enough to know them. I was an outsider, and I couldn't share with them. The unending paperwork and lack of sleep. On forced marches, I'd drop off into a fitful doze every time the column halted. And now my resentment for the man seated so close to me festered. In my disenchanted state, Sergeant Bailey's remark came to mind: "If we don't freeze to death or die of fright, Patton will hike us to death."

My brooding evaporated with two louder explosions that made the earth tremble. That was the signal for the two soldiers clad in borrowed German uniforms to scramble out of the smoking fortification. Helmetless, they clasped their hands behind their heads and shuffled toward the viewing site, followed closely by the attackers.

The field exercise concluded, General Patton rose and spoke briefly with Colonel Williams, who stood stiffly at attention and rattled a series of "Yes sirs." The general turned and nodded to the group of officers who followed him to the waiting staff cars. I glanced at my wrist. The visitation had lasted fifteen minutes.

As the staff cars wended their way through Pfronten, the soldiers meandered down the hill amid catcalls and laughter. The men were in high spirits as they shouted obscenities back and forth at one another. A number of the men had formed lasting friendships. Nobody paid attention to the salty language because everybody knew they didn't mean it. But I didn't fit in. There was no way I could share the camaraderie and fellowship. War had been horrifying and alienating.

A voice called out, "Hey, fellas, how about that visit from ole blood 'n guts?" Then a reply rang out, "Forty-eight." That was the cue and other voices picked up the count, "FORTY-NINE." Then the entire group shouted, "FIFTY!" followed in unison by a thunderous "SOOOOOOOOOME CRAP!"

Looking back, I'm convinced that the rigors of warfare and the sudden transition to peace brought on an emotional reaction. For days afterward, I remained in my room in the chateau. I was moody and cross, and spoke sharply at any friendly attempt at conversation. What company business there was could be done by McAllister, Cordon, and Redfern. Several times, Captain Damkowitch asked if I was "crackin' up." His concern grew so great that he presented me with a bottle from his supply of "Halb und Halb," a sickeningly sweet concoction of ginger liqueur and brandy.

It was almost five more months before I finally came home. On 7 December 1945, I trekked down the gangplank in Boston harbor. My eyes were spilling tears as I offered a prayer of thanksgiving. Later that month, I completed my separation at Camp Blanding and was home in Jacksonville, an unemployed ex-serviceman.

The Friday, 21 December 1945, edition of the newspaper carried the news of General Patton's death following an automobile accident in Luxembourg. Back home, my feelings of resentment had subsided, and I felt a twinge as I read the news. I had to admit that General Patton's battle tactics, although harsh, were more effective than had he been less ruthless.

I thought of that day in Diekirch when General Patton roared through in his jeep to see firsthand what was causing the holdup at the Sauer River. Funny, I thought—he raced his jeep like mad back and forth on the battlefield during the war, only to perish in a car accident during peacetime.

He was laid to rest in Luxembourg.

---

21 July 1945
Germany
My dear little angel—

Everything is quiet and peaceful here. I've been pretty busy recently with the men that are going home and those that are being transferred— it's really a mess. The latest rumor is that after we're shipped home we will stay in the States and not go to the Pacific. Let's hope the war will end just as the boat docks or sooner.

Another of my men came to me yesterday with a letter from his folks back home that his wife had left with another man. She left their two children and sold all their furniture—it's too bad and there wasn't much I could do but change his insurance from his wife to his children. That was the second this week—so far I've had about ten cases. I run into a lot of things in my job, but I sure hate to hear things like that.

I really think they should pass a law that all husbands should live at their homes with their wives. This separation isn't so good. Oh, I don't mind being separated for an hour or so during the day, but I think I should be at home with my wife at night. I know my little wife gets lonesome too.

Yes, your husband is going to have another birthday soon. Gee, I'll be an old man when you get me back. The boxes you send arrive in good shape—you really know how to pack them. I come up to my room when I'm lonesome and nibble on snacks and think of you. At night I make coffee on the stove and have a little snack—I guess I'm getting like "Dagwood."

A day or so ago one of our planes crashed in the mountains, and they brought us the papers found on the bodies. We sent some men to bury them. There were two nurses in the group also, all killed and partly burned. Sure was too bad. They went all through the war no doubt, and then got killed by accident.

Well, darling, the mail truck's about to leave.

> Good night dear
> Lots of love
> Your little husband

p.s. I love you, dear.

---

27 July 1945
Germany
My dear little wife—

Yesterday, we had to see a training film—a series of orientation films like the "March of Time" about why we fight, etc. The film yesterday was "The War Comes to America" and showed all the different kinds of people that make up America.[4] It sure did make me homesick to see the familiar scenes of America—hot dog and Coca-Cola signs, automobiles and people on the streets. Boy oh boy, will I be glad to get home. You don't appreciate America 'til you leave it.

I'm so glad your sisters and their children could come down to see you. I know you had a swell time at the beach. Did you get a cottage? The men here all think it's wonderful to be able to go to the seashore, and a couple of them told me that after the war they are coming to visit us. Ha! Ha! They don't know we don't even have a tent, much less a house.

I guess it will seem strange to have your little husband home again, won't it? Some dope wrote in one of our papers that since he's been away so long, he wanted to know if he could have another wedding ceremony performed. One was good enough for me—all I want to do is get home to my little wife. If I could get home to my angel wife I would be happy to ride in the cattle car with the cows.

    Lots of love

    Your little husband

p.s. I love you, dear.

---

29 July 1945

Germany

My dear wife—

    Good morning, dear—how is my little wife today? Sure wish I could tell you good morning with a kiss.

    I'm disgusted with the army—seems like a lot of foolishness is happening all day. At least if I was in prison I would be learning a trade, but here you don't get anything but a lot of crap. I'll have to learn to control myself when I get out of the army, I guess, or I'll be punching some of these old bastards in the face. You never see the bureaucrats when you are fighting— that's what burns me up. But now that we have a chance to relax, up they pop and send out orders to get up at 0530 and train all day. Well, I guess I shouldn't kick too much—at least I'm getting paid for it—that is, if you can reimburse anybody for the fighting I've had. From now on, I'm doing as little as I can get away with.

    Did you ever get your paintings? I hope they don't get ruined in transit. After they are mounted and framed, they will look real nice. I guess we'll have to get busy with our home when I get back so we can start enjoying it. But I'll have to find a job first. By the time I finally get out of the army, jobs will be hard to find. Oh well, I'll worry about it when the time comes. In the meantime, I'll save all I can and send it to you to put in our bank account. You have really done well, dear, with our savings, and I'm certainly proud of you. You are really a smart little wife, and I thank God for you every night in my prayers.

    Lots of love dear

    Your little husband

p.s. I love you, dear.

Private Shima

A memory in story form written circa 1979–82

In July, we were quartered in the quaint little German village of Pfronten. The men were anxious to get home, but were content to rest in the Bavarian town. Rumors were rampant about shipping out to the Pacific and the war with Japan, another that we would return to the States, another that we would remain in Europe as a police force. Endless rumors.

The occupation of the village of Pfronten was a relief after wartime and combat. The troops were quartered in houses with the civilians, most of whom were women, children, and the aged. A minimum training schedule was kept up. Recreational facilities were constructed. Baseball teams were formed, and other sports flourished. As the astounded citizens watched, men handy with tools repaired buildings and broken furniture. The plumbing in the chateau was unclogged, and several men who had been raised on farms helped German families harvest hay for the winter. The men enjoyed constructive work, and the citizens were overwhelmed that we were not the savages their propaganda said we were.

During formation one day, Captain Damkowitch announced, "Men, I don't know what's going to happen to us, but for the time being we've got it nice. Let's keep it that way, no squabbling or fighting among ourselves. Understand? Don't mistreat civilians, they've had it tough, too. Above all, don't bother me, I'm tired, too."

For a while, all was peaceful. That is, until replacements arrived. New men, officers and enlisted men, filled the ranks after hostilities ceased, and the company was at full strength for the first time since meeting the enemy in August of 1944. The new officers, not accustomed to the informal relationship of combat troops and officers, were dismayed that certain social barriers had been erased via mutual suffering and hardship.

Captain Damkowitch, highly respected by the troops, was startled when one of the new officers objected to the men calling him Mike. "Damnit, that's my name," I overheard Captain Damkowitch tell the officer. "For the time being, go easy on military courtesy. We're relaxing and will tighten up on regulations before we move out."

One day the mail truck stopped at company headquarters, and a soldier climbed out of the rear. It was Private George L. Shima.

"Look who's here," beamed Sergeant Corden. These two had known each other since training camp. Shima had been gone since mid-December, when he had left to report to the hospital for a case of possible appendicitis. Now, seven months later, he was picked up on the Morning Report as "returned to duty."[5]

Back with the company again, Private Shima caused an incident that would unravel his story. One evening, a dozen soldiers were relaxing in a farmhouse. They pushed the furniture aside, and Sergeant Adam Heiser played a spirited tune on a concertina. A bottle of schnapps was passed around. Inspired by the schnapps and Heiser's tunes, Shima and another soldier attempted a Russian dance called the hopak. The men folded their arms across their chests and squatted on their ankles then attempted to kick their legs in time with the music. Their antics drew gales of laughter and applause as they stumbled and struggled to keep their balance.

Shima tried, without success, to coax the bashful women to join in the dance. The room vibrated with laughter, hand clapping, and whoops. At this point, one of the newly arrived officers, Lieutenant Julius Borys, entered the room. An argument erupted when the Borys attempted to quell the uproar of the merrymakers. Several uncomplimentary remarks were made about "smart aleck" officers. Shima waxed excited and offered to punch the officer in the nose. Then he did.[6]

The startled officer stumbled back, clutching his nose. Someone had the presence of mind to douse the lights before he could retaliate. In Stygian darkness, the officer was lifted from his feet by several soldiers. Squirming and protesting, he was carried out and unceremoniously flung on a stack of manure by the barn.

Humiliated and spattered with manure, Lieutenant Borys fled to Captain Damkowitch and reported the incident. Damkowitch rolled his eyes and held his head with both hands as the lieutenant wailed that nothing like that ever happened in Officer Candidate School.

Private Shima was placed under house arrest and ordered to stand court-martial for striking an officer.

The next day, Shima's old friend Sergeant Corden plopped down beside me in the Company Mess area. "Say, Sarge," he began. "Can I talk to you?" Corden fidgeted. "It's about Shima."

"What about him?" I asked.

"Shima asked me to ask you—I mean—he wants you to ask Mike to change the Court Martial to Company punishment. He said he'd apologize—anything, you know—to get out of the court-martial."

"Aw, Cordon," I said, "a court-martial will get all the facts. It may cause Lieutenant Borys more trouble than Shima."

"No," said Corden. "If Shima stands trial at a court-martial, he's headed for trouble, real trouble. He's afraid a court-martial will turn up something besides the flap with Lieutenant Borys."

"Are you telling me that Shima got into trouble while he was in the hospital?"

Corden squirmed and studied his hands, "Say, how about talking with him. Let him explain the jam he's in."

It was a short stroll in the village to the farmhouse where Shima was held under house arrest. He was seated on an empty ammunition box and looking through an old copy of *Stars and Stripes*. He looked up as we entered the room.

"Hi, Shima," I said as I ripped the cellophane from a cigar. "Corden tells me that you're in some kind of trouble if you're court-martialed."

"Yeah," agreed Shima. "It sure could be trouble." Shima cleared his throat, "Remember back in December when the medics thought maybe I had appendicitis, and I got sent to a Field Hospital?"

"Did you have appendicitis?" I asked.

"No."

"Shima, you must have had something for them to keep you." A sudden thought flashed through my mind, and I asked, "Hey, you were in the hospital, weren't you?"[7]

He didn't answer right away. He averted his eyes, "Well, not exactly, I mean, I did go to the hospital, but . . ."

"Shima, Shima," I moaned. "I should have known."

He glanced up and then hung his head. "The truck hauled us to a Field Hospital in France—I don't know where. Casualties were pouring in when we got there. Ambulances were bumper to bumper on the road. When we got inside, the corridors were filled with hospital beds and bloody stretchers. It was bedlam. Doctors and nurses could barely cope—it was pure hell. There was so much confusion that they didn't even notice us. I felt somebody tug on my arm—one of the soldiers that was on the truck. He said, 'Let's get the hell out of here. They'll never miss us. C'mon, let's go.' I asked him where, and he said, 'Come on—follow me.'"

Before I could say anything, Shima went on.

"And I did. We just walked out of the hospital. We climbed over a wall and headed for the village. We saw a service unit and got in their chow line. The guy I was with told the mess sergeant that we were on detached duty with a special unit, and he just nodded. Heck—if we lied with confidence, we could get into any chow line and get other things like clean uniforms and supplies. We lied and nobody asked questions."

"But Shima," I interrupted. "Where did you sleep? Did you bed down with the service units?"

"No," replied Shima. "After chow, we walked to a house, knocked, and explained we were arranging quarters for an officer that was arriving soon. 'Officer' was the magic word. The old man who answered the door got excited and started yelling for the womenfolk. We stood there looking very military and dignified while the family ran around getting a guest room ready for us. They brought in firewood, lit the stove, and heated up water for us. My buddy mentioned wine and here they came with a bottle for us. We swore 'em to secrecy, and then we occupied the room. We did that day after day."

"Well," I interrupted. "You and this guy just wandered around France?"

"Yes," replied Shima, "that's about it."

"How come you bothered to return to George Company?" I asked.

"We blew it," he sighed. Shima studied his hands a moment. "One afternoon we made the usual arrangement for our 'officer'—then we went to a local bistro. While we were gone, a real officer knocked on our host's door, looking for accommodations. Our host told the officer that two of his men had already been there and made arrangements for his quarters, and he then showed the officer into the room. When we got there at dusk, we found the officer's valpack and duffle bag in our room. The smart thing to do would have been to leave quietly and get the hell out."

Shima took a breath, "But, no, we had been getting away with our tricks for so long, so we just threw the officer's gear out of the room. Hell, let the sonofabitch find his own room! And just then a lieutenant walked in and demanded to know what we were doing. My friend didn't bat an eye. He said, 'We're clearing this stuff out for Captain Adams, sir.' But the officer took out a notebook. 'Give me your names, serial numbers, and unit.'"

"I said, 'Sir, Captain Adams is in his jeep across the street. I'll fetch him and he'll vouch for us.' I said that with confidence, and the officer and my companion just stared at me while I left the house. I got on the first truck leaving that town, and eventually found one going to the 317th and asked if I could get a ride to George Company. The driver said, 'Sure, hop in.' Turned out he was bringing mail up to the units."

Shima shrugged his shoulders and said, "And here I am."

I looked at my cigar, "Shima, now I understand why you don't want to be tried by a court-martial. All this will come out."

He nodded his head unhappily.

"Yeah," added Corden. "Sarge, talk to Mike and try to persuade him to change the court-martial to company punishment."

"How about it?" pleaded Shima. "Will you talk to Mike?"

I relit my cigar and puffed several times. "Shima," I said. "You're a lousy, good-for-nothing excuse for a soldier, and I'm crazy to intercede. But let me see what I can do."

His voice was contrite, "Gee, thanks Sarge."

I glanced at Sergeant Corden, "C'mon Sam, let's get back to Headquarters."

As we entered the Company Headquarters, Captain Damkowitch looked up from a cup of coffee. He saw me and said, "Hey, Smitty, I want to talk to you."

"Sure, Mike," and I poured a cup of coffee and pulled off my helmet, looking expectant.

"It's about the charges Lieutenant Borys filed against Shima." He commenced, "After he calmed down and thought it over, he decided to drop the charges. Frankly, I'm glad." He chuckled, "Lieutenant Borys is a little stuffy and probably brought the trouble on himself." He became solemn. "Nevertheless, Shima's action was inexcusable and must be punished."

I breathed a sigh of relief, but wondered if I should report Shima's other escapade. What about my responsibility? What good would it do to expose him? I decided to keep my mouth shut. Why cause any more suffering for anybody? "Sure, Mike, I agree."

"Got anything in mind?"

"Well, Mike, you can order Company punishment," I answered. "How about the woodpile? If we're here during the winter, we'll need all the firewood we can chop."

Mike agreed and I sent Sergeant Corden to fetch Shima. I followed Corden to the door and whispered, "Tell Shima to keep his mouth shut. Okay?"

When Shima arrived, he stood with a sheepish expression on his face. "Shima," said Captain Damkowitch, "Lieutenant Borys has decided to withdraw changes."

"Thank you, sir," replied Shima. "And I'll apologize to Lieutenant Borys, yes sir, I will."

"But Shima," interjected Captain Damkowitch, "I don't condone your conduct. It was inexcusable." Shima stood silent. "I'm sentencing you to company punishment. The woodpile. You're to chop firewood for a week."

"Sir," I intervened, "make it three weeks." Shima winced but kept quiet while I explained, "Sir, I've a feeling that Shima has done something that hasn't come out yet."

Captain Damkowitch stared at Shima, "You got anything to say?"

"No sir."

Damkowitch looked back at me, and I added, "Knowing Shima, he deserves any punishment he gets."

"Maybe you're right. Shima, I sentence you to three weeks chopping firewood. Each day, after breakfast, report to Corporal Redfern, understand?"

"Yes, sir."

"Dismissed."

The back of this photo reads, "These were bad boys, so I had to give them something to do." Private Shima may be in the photo. Phronten, Germany.

1 August 1945

Germany

My darling wife—

Here are some pictures I had made, and as you can see, the war hasn't made me any younger.

Civilians are frozen to their villages and cannot go more than about 8 miles in any direction. Our work is to pick up anybody without proper identification. Most former German soldiers are falling in line and are properly discharged—we release about 1,000 a day in our district—as they are desperately needed to harvest the crops before the winter season. I had to laugh when I read what you said about the German girls. No honey, don't you worry. If you could see the German women—you or none of your girlfriends need worry about us even talking to them.

Two of them clean our house every other day, and they are typical of the German women in our section—big and sloppy and work like horses. They clean the whole house (three stories) and mop all the rooms in about three hours. We give them their noon meal and that's all. Other than "good morning" and "good-bye," that's all we say to them. The men in my company have seen too much hardship at the hands of the Germans to feel friendly toward them. My company lost hundreds of men, so you can easily understand my attitude. On the other hand, most of them have lost their brothers, husbands, or sweethearts, and you can imagine what they think of us.[8]

Percy Smith, not looking any younger

Just imagine how friendly you would feel if the Germans had killed your little husband and were stationed in Jacksonville. There can't be too much friendly feeling, and where the magazines and papers get such crap beats me. Maybe that's why so many of our men have been having trouble at home—the papers tell everybody this is like a big U.S.O. show, and the girls at home get the wrong idea.

What's burning them up now is an article in our paper about a certain state allowing wives that have had babies by other men to put them into a state orphans home before the husbands return from overseas. A guy gets to reading stuff like that and the first thing he knows, he's hurt his wife or girlfriend's feelings and a big row starts. I've had fifteen or more men come to me with letters from a relative or friend saying their wife left with some other man—and they can't do a damn thing but sit—most of them have had such a miserable time over here anyway, they can't even cry. [Letter ends with no closing or signature.]

------

6 August 1945
Germany
My darling wife—

It's quiet here in my office today. The Red Cross donut wagon has just come up, and I let all the fellows go down to get donuts and coffee. They play American records, and the guys can look at a couple of American girls for a change. The Red Cross girls deserve a lot of credit, as even when we were fighting they used to come as close as they could to bring us coffee and donuts and chewing gum, etc. Each Company would rotate back from the front to take advantage of the little entertainment they had to offer. Lots of times they were caught in artillery fire the same as us. They used to look pretty cute in their combat suits with muddy shoes and a steel helmet (weighs about three pounds) cocked on the back of their heads—hollering out of their trucks, "C'mon Joe—shake a leg!" Most of the time, you couldn't tell them from any other Joe Blow unless you happened to see some of their hair stuck out from under their helmets. Believe me, out of my eight months on the front line, they were the only people that came up to entertain us at all. The U.S.O. shows must have been good, but we never saw any.

The back of this photo reads, "Red Cross girls bring us donuts and coffee. Note the names on the truck and the states."

Once back in France, the mud was so deep the Red Cross truck couldn't get through, so they put their coffee pots and a box of donuts on one of the army trucks and came on up to our positions. One of the boxes of donuts turned over in the truck and got all muddy. The donut girls didn't want to give them away, as they were dirty and some of them had been stomped on—but if you could have seen those men grab for them you would have thought they were from the finest bakery in the world.

Darling, I think of you all the time. I don't know what I would do without you. Good night sweetheart.

Lots of love

Your little husband

p.s. I love you, angel wings

———————

9 August 1945

Germany

My darling wife—

Our fifth wedding anniversary is just around the corner. Why, it doesn't seem more than a few months ago I was a brand new dumb husband.

I could never tell you how happy I've been. These years that I've been married to you—you are everything a man could ask for, and I'm mighty proud that you are my little wife.

The wind is howling around the corners of the house tonight—one of those pitch-black nights, and there is a slow drizzling rain—you know, a really miserable night. We are sending several hundred men into a large town nearby tonight to search every building—just in case. These Krauts don't give us too much credit for having any brains. Oh well—I guess they will have to learn the hard way.

Everybody here is glad to see that Russia is taking a hand in the Japanese war. It looks bad for them, but if it will shorten the war, I'm all for it. They don't seem to like the new bomb we are dropping on them, but we didn't like the Pearl Harbor attack either. The only word of consolation I can give them is that "it's tough all over."

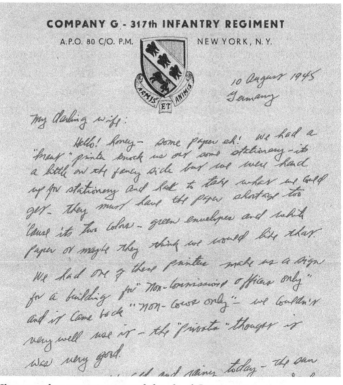

Short anecdote on stationery made by a local German printer

Well dear, I have the water hot in the bathroom so I better grab the water before some of my buddies use it all. We have a hot water heater that uses wood, so I usually build a fire every night and have a good hot bath. Maybe I'll get caught up on my baths before I get home.

Lots of love dear

Your little husband

p.s. I sure do love you, angel wings

---

12 August 1945

Germany

My darling wife—

How is my little wife today? I slept late this morning then I cleaned my room. The captain came in and he was restless too, so we went out in the yard and pitched a couple of games of horseshoes—I'm getting to be a regular "rube."

It looks like the peace or surrender [of Japan] is really a fact after all. We had heard so many rumors and reports and contradictions that nobody knew what to believe. We all hope that the war has really ended and we can live peacefully.

I'm reading the book you sent me—*The Maltese Falcon*—remember the picture with Humphrey Bogart and Sidney Greenstreet? I think we saw it at the Capitol Theater together before I was sent to the army.

Dear, I guess I'll take this letter down to the mailroom and mail it and hang around and see if I get any mail from you today. The mail goes out and comes in at 4 o'clock each day, so I'll sit around 'till it comes in.

Lots of love

Your little husband

p.s. I love you, angel wings

---

14 August 1945

Germany

My darling Sweetheart—

Gee! But I wish I was home with you dear. Maybe it won't be too long now that the Japanese have officially surrendered. I'll be so glad to be with you again.

I had my overcoat issued to me today, and from the looks of things, we'll soon need them. The civilians tell us it gets awful cold here in the winter. Our men were out cutting wood today for the coming cold weather. I just hope we sail soon for America.

This afternoon Walter (our interpreter) went to see a man who was a press correspondent for the German army and looked at some of his photographs. He is coming around in a few days to take some photos of your little husband—I'll send them to you when they are finished.

> Lots of love
> Your little husband

p.s. I love you, dear angel wings

Photos taken by a former German Army photographer. Perhaps this was the photographer's dog.

Smith pals around with a German pooch.

18 August 1945

Germany

My darling wife—

Just got your letter dated 11 August—the one with the photos and you sure look cute—sweet enough to bite, honey. The baby is darling—but my baby is the sweetest.

We officially celebrated the end of the "wah" today—had a band and a parade and a twenty-one-gun salute—quite a rumpus, but I feel like you do, instead of celebrating we should offer a prayer that such a war will never come again, and I can't help thinking of the men who won't return with us.

I'm glad to hear our paintings are worth something. I'll try to get some more if I can—maybe you can send me a few tubes of paint to swap for them. I'll let you know, kid. I wish you could see the place where I'm living. It has four very fine oil paintings on the stairs leading up to my room, and the hall is covered with nice paintings. Everything is worn and used, but

Elizabeth holding a friend's child. Her high school friend Vivian Brown is in the background.

you don't notice it—kinda like a nice coat—even though you've worn it several seasons, it still looks good.

Glad you liked the Purple Heart and I hope to have a few more awards to send you soon. I'm supposed to get a Bronze Star and a Silver Star too—but it takes a lot of time as each award has to be checked and signed by all the commanding officers from my Company to our General. But I hope to get them soon—5 points apiece too, that's what I like about it.

Take care of your sweet self.

Lots of love

Your little husband

p.s. I love you, dear.

Oh! If you want the sewing machine, buy it. You'll save the difference on the things you make, huh?

———————

21 August 1945

Germany

My darling—

Today I went down with our interpreter and purchased three more oil paintings. The artist asked me if I could have some paint sent over, and I said I'd try. Take the enclosed list to an art shop and see if you can get any of this stuff—the ones marked in red are the ones worst needed—and a small camel hair brush and a large hard brush. Just try to get what you can, and mail them to me—first-class mail—rush—etc. Maybe I can get the whole gallery. Oh well, I may as well start furnishing our place now and they look pretty snazzy in a frame, but don't pay too much. We'll hold them till the next depression, then we can get them framed cheap (maybe).

Gee! Here I was staring at your photograph and daydreaming. In four more days, we'll be married 5 whole years. I hope you received your little card I made—Boy oh Boy! I sure hope we can celebrate our anniversary together next year.

Dear—I love you so much—I just don't have the words to tell you how much.

Lots of love

Your little husband

p.s. I love you, angel wings

This is a list of paints and supplies in the artist's handwriting.

29 August 1945

Germany

My darling—

The days are really slipping by so maybe it won't be too long before I am with you again.

Did I tell you about "Bed Check Charley?" Well! Charley is the name we gave to a German pilot who used to fly over us just after nightfall—and as he came about bedtime, we called him "Bed Check Charley." Well, old Charley wasn't such a bad egg, but it is an awful nuisance to have him shoot at us and bother us, so one fine night, we up and shoots his ole aeroplane and I got a clock from the dashboard that I carried around in one of the jeeps for a long time. The other day, I happened to think about it, so I pulled it out and it still would run, so I took it over to a shop nearby and had a stand made for it. I'll mail it to you as soon as I can get a box for it. It keeps good time, but it's a little noisy. Just the thing for our mahogany desk.

Yes, dear, I think after a few days at home, it will seem as though I've never been away. To tell you the truth, the war is beginning to be a memory now, especially since we've been up here in the mountains.

Darling, you are always with me in my dreams.

Lots of love

Your little husband

p.s. I sure do love you, angel wings

---

31 August 1945

Germany

My darling—

We were alerted to pack up to go to Czechoslovakia, but when we got ready we received another order that we wouldn't go. So we unpacked again—isn't that just like the army?

We are still planning to come home on schedule and may even beat the schedule by a few weeks—some rumor has it that we'll even fly home. You never heard so many rumors as you do in the army. You would think that's all we do is make up rumors.

Oh! I almost forgot to tell you—I bought two more oil paintings for our house. They are much prettier than the others, I think. I found another artist down in the other end of town—but they all cry the blues when you come around, that they haven't any paint or stuff to paint with. Oh well! We have eight—two at home, four on the way, and I just got two more—it cost me ten bucks, a pound of coffee, a pound of sugar, and a couple of packages of cigarettes. I'll send them very soon, and I'll also send your little clock.

Lots of love, "Honeybun"

Your little husband

p.s. I sure do love you, dear.

5 September 1945

Germany

My darling little wife—

Hello! honey—I love you, dear. Oh! Ever so much. Here I am all packed and ready to move again—this time to a camp to guard political prisoners until their trial. We expect to be there about 5 weeks and then start for home.

Dear—I don't think I'll be able to meet you at the boat when I come in—they tell me they won't let us out of sight 'till we are on our way to the camp nearest our homes. So I'll be marched from the boat to a train for Camp Blanding. But, if I find out I can get away, I'll let you know, honey.

I will mail you another big box today—the aeroplane clock I had made into a desk clock—two paintings and the mounts for them, a couple of pocketbooks (to put in your purse), a piece of Hitler china, and a couple of my medals—hope you get them before I get home.

> Good night darling
> Lots of love
> Your little husband

p.s. I love you, dear.

Life in Pfronten

A memory written in 1947

Many of the men of Company G were beginning to think of Pfronten as home when the order came to pull out.

"Where are we going?" queried a soldier.

"It beats the hell outta me," replied his buddy.

The day we left, throngs of villagers bid us farewell. Our arrival, after a tour of police duty elsewhere, had been greeted with sullen silence. The civilians had feared that we were "Chicago gangsters" and "devils in baggy pants." They relaxed when they saw the chow line allowed the children to fill their pails. The cooks supervised to ensure that all received an equal share. Any leftover coffee and even the coffee grounds were highly prized.

Throughout the village, the troops were billeted in homes with civilians. They were crowded, but villagers relaxed when they discovered that the men were not destructive—just the opposite—men handy with tools did any necessary repair work. Company headquarters occupied the chateau of an elderly baroness, her daughter, and daughter-in-law. Corporal Bauder, the company translator, talked to the baroness; then he turned to Mike and said, "She said they own other property in the village and could move out with a minimum of inconvenience."

"Good," said Captain Damkowitch. "Tell them they can take anything they need, and we'll take good care of the place while we're here." Corporal Bauder relayed the message to the baroness, who smiled and spoke to Bauder. "She said—about the garden—could they work in it for their food supply? Right now their garden is important."

"Oh sure, sure," replied Captain Damkowitch. "Tell them they can work in the garden anytime that they want." The daughter and daughter-in-law were garbed in rough peasant clothing and wore no makeup, obviously to discourage unwanted advances from soldiers.

Company headquarters moved into the chateau to discover that the plumbing was broken. Several soldiers obtained tools and wrenches from supply and started to work on the plumbing. Next, they unclogged the wood-burning hot water heater in the bathroom. As the water began to flow, at first it was dark and rusty but cleared after a few moments. The water supply was gravity flow from nearby mountain streams, and it was ice cold. The overhead flush box gurgled and filled, and the water cleared after a few flushes.

"Now, that's what I call luxury," exclaimed a soldier, "an indoor johnny that works."

"Let's get some wood and fire up the water heater," another cried.

Meanwhile, the men quartered in other dwellings were making repairs too. The military training schedule was minimal, and the men welcomed jobs to putter. Several soldiers formerly from farms in the Midwest volunteered to help the Germans cut and stack hay. "If they don't get it cut and stacked and out of the weather, they'll lose it," one told us.

Gradually, the local citizens became less suspicious of us and smiled at some of our antics. For instance, every evening the cows were driven from pastures through the village to their barns. This inspired a soldier to mount a street sign, "Cow Shit Alley." The natives were hesitant to use the street until someone translated for them—then they went into gales of laughter.

The chateau in Pfronten

Smith on the right

About two weeks after our arrival in Pfronten, I was standing in front of the chateau, gazing at a picture of the sun that was drawn on the chateau. The daughter-in-law of the baroness was working in the garden. She arose from her knees, brushed off the dirt, and approached me.

"Sergeant Smith," she spoke.

I whirled around and said, "Yes?" I was startled. "You speak English?"

"Yes, may I ask you—that is, the baroness wants to know—well, her son was captured by Americans and taken prisoner. He is a major in the German Army. She is worried about him. He is diabetic, and she fears that he will not get treatment for his disease."

"Don't worry," I lied. "If he's diabetic, he'll be sent to a hospital and given a special diet." I didn't have the slightest idea what would happen to him, but I told her this to save them from worrying.

"Do you think so?" she asked.

"Sure—and unless he's wanted as a war criminal he'll be released soon."

"No, no, he was in the regular army—he was not an elite trooper."

"Good," I said. "Just tell the baroness he'll be all right."

She thanked me and went back to her gardening.

Soldiers built picnic tables for an outdoor mess and laid out baseball diamonds in a meadow. Almost every afternoon, the air was filled with yells and catcalls as two teams vied for the company championship. Those desiring a less strenuous sport pitched horseshoes.

Sometime later, I returned from a ball game to find the daughter-in-law waiting for me. "The baroness's son came home today," she said. "And like you said, he was sent to a hospital. He was treated for his diabetes and released. They told him he was free to return home."

I breathed a sigh of relief, "Well, good," I said. "I'm glad."

———

6 September 1945

Germany

My darling—

Well—your little husband is all packed and ready to move again. We are going to move Sunday, up to a little town, or near a little town to guard some political prisoners. From the looks of things, it's going to be a "pain in the neck" as we will have to sleep on the floor of an old German

barracks—dirty with windows broken out—not much to look forward
to after having a private room in a country villa. But I guess the "dumb
bastards" that are planning all of this have to do something to keep busy.
I hope we will be on our way home before long, and then we can forget all
about this foolishness.

Darling, I guess I'm the one that's mean tonight—I guess I shouldn't be
fussing about moving and should be glad that I'm alive.

Dear, I received my box tonight—the one with the pecan candy and the
chili—oh boy! We'll have a little feast. Most of the guys don't like chili,
though, as they are from the north and hardly know what it is—so that's all
the more for me. They look at me like I'm not all there when I tell them that
me and my little wife used to go to the Pig Stand and eat bowls full before
we went home after gallivanting around on Saturday nights.

Just think dear, it's been over 12 months now since I've seen my little
wife.

Good night dearest
Your little husband
p.s. I love you, "honeybun."

10 September 1945
Germany
My darling wife—

One year ago today, I set sail for Europe. Sometimes it doesn't seem
long, then sometimes it seems like eternity. A lot of things have happened
to me in the last year, but the best one that could possibly happen now is to
get a boat for America and my little wife.

We arrived at our new home yesterday, and it sure is a mess. It was originally an anti-aircraft school but has been used to house prisoners, and now
it's used for us. It looks a lot like Camp Shelby, but it has heavy barbed wire
all around it. This is a miserable dreary place, and all the men are on guard
as we have several thousand civilian prisoners to guard and care for. They
are awaiting trial—men and women.

I don't think I could take this kind of life permanently. A couple of
times, I could have taken a commission but didn't want to fool with it—I
would rather be home with my little wife.

About Mrs. Mills—tell her to write to the "Personnel Section" of the unit to which her son was attached. They should have the information by now if he was repatriated or picked up by some other unit if he was released by our men when our forces took possession of the German prisons. Of course, he may have crashed and burned before anybody could get him out, and they may never be able to trace what happened. But, anyway, tell her to write—also to the chaplain of his unit. She doesn't need the chaplain's name—just address the letter to the chaplain of his unit, and give his name, rank, and serial number, and the unit to which he was attached. Generally, the chaplain writes to all the nearest relations when he possibly can, and has access to all the records and available information. In our case, we had thousands killed or missing in my Regiment and we have accounted for all of them except about three. Tell her to just hope for the best.

Honey, you have a date with your husband to go dancing as soon as I get home to you.

Take care of your sweet self.

Lots of love

Your little husband

p.s. I love you, angel wings

---

18 September 1945

Schongau, Germany

My darling wife—

Boy oh Boy! You should see my new home—it's a "doozy." I live in a walled city at least eight hundred years old—just like St. Augustine only older. It's near Oberammergau, where the passion players live. I'll have to try to visit there someday soon.

Guess what? I saw my first U.S.O. show overseas last night. (I never saw one in the U.S. either.) After supper last night, Mike said what about taking the jeep and running over to Garmisch and seeing a U.S.O. show that was supposed to be there. So we jumped in the jeep and drove 50 miles to see the "Radio City Music Hall Review." It was the Rockettes and was really good. They had a ventriloquist that was as good as Charlie

McCarthy, I think. The girls danced beautifully—mostly ballet and tricky dances. It lasted for over two hours and was worth the trouble to go that far. I sure wish you could have been with me. The scenery was beautiful driving over—beautiful hills and most of them have a crumbling castle on the peak. Everything is so quiet and peaceful now.

We are busy as the dickens now, men going and coming—they are taking men out of our Division down to 62 points and sending them home ahead of the Division—I still have 57 and may have 62 soon as I have some more battle credit coming.

The mail leaves pretty soon, so I'll rush to get this one in. Dear—I love you more than anything in the world.

Lots of love

Your little husband

p.s. I love you, dear.

---

25 September 1945

Schongau, Germany

My darling wife—

So my little wife is getting plump around the waist—good—that'll be more for me to love. Dear, if we ever have any children, it will be up to you to decide, for as far as I'm concerned you'll be my baby. But we will have plenty of time to think about that later.

This sure is a stinky little town. The people are all hicks too. They leave us strictly alone, but occasionally I notice them staring out the windows in wide-eyed wonder as four or five guys start dancing across the street, singing, "Are you from Schongau? Are you from Schongau? Well, I'm from Schongau, too," to the tune of "Are You from Dixie?" All this must be confusing to the Krauts, as some of the men are always horsing around doing something dumb.

Take, for instance, one of the locals will try to get friendly enough to get the cigarette butts from the ashtrays in our mess hall. He will try to engage one of the G.I.s in a conversation, telling him that he was never a Nazi and how much he likes democracy etc., etc.—the G. I. listens carefully, and then looks all around like he is going to tell a big secret and pulls out a souvenir flag with a swastika on it and says he's a spy and that the Fuehrer is going to free the German people again. The Krauts don't know what the hell to believe, but we give him the cigarette butts anyway. They don't seem to be able to understand us, so I guess they'd be glad to see us go. And I'll be glad to go, too.

> Good night dear
> Lots of love
> Your little husband

p.s. I love you, dear.

---

29 September 1945
Schongau
My dear wife—

Well, dear, I'm getting ready to go to Switzerland for a week. The army arranged a trip, and we will be gone about ten days. I don't know if I can call you on the telephone, as I'm not sure if it will be possible, and then I don't know about the phone connections, but I sure would like to hear your voice—oh boy!

Here are some snapshots of our little German friend. He is quite a character, as you can see, but I think the men spoiled him beyond redemption.

Honey, when I get home I don't know where I'll work or anything else right now. It depends on how much unemployment there is when I get home. I may be damn glad to get a job for 20 bucks a week—but I'm sure going to try for more. I've worked all my life for "chicken feed" so I better start trying to earn a little.

Don't worry if you don't hear from me for a few days, and I'll be thinking of you every minute. Don't forget our date to go dancing when I get home.

> Lots of love
> Your little husband

p.s. you are the sweetest one, angel wings

"Our little German friend" in Schongau

4 October 1945
Meiringen, Switzerland
Darling—

Hello honey, just a note to tell you that I'm really in Switzerland. A thousand soldiers came with us, but the tour is divided up in five routes so the place won't be too crowded.

You should see the trains here—all electric—fast and quiet. If the buildings weren't so old, I'd say it was more modern than America. Of course, I haven't had a chance to visit around much, but I'll take a walk with the other guys after lunch today and see what's what.

We left Lucerne this morning at 0930 and arrived in Meiringen about 1100—it was a beautiful ride. We went on the electric train and seemed to go right up the mountains. The trains run like the Swiss watches. Right on the minute. The Swiss are not breaking their backs to be friendly. They give me the impression that they don't feel like taking any "crap" from us, but they are nice. And if a lot of our soldiers don't mess it up, it will be a nice vacation for them. Of course, the men that expect a wild time and stay

On tour in Switzerland: The DuPont Hotel in Lucerne

drunk half of the time are in for a disappointment, as this trip is just for relaxation and looking at the scenery. We are only allowed to bring $40.00 along to spend, and it takes nearly all of it, as the tours and excursions are not free.

Remember me telling you how screwy the American soldiers are? Well, in Lucerne, me and a couple of more soldiers were out walking. Right down in the main part of town, the Swiss Boy Scouts were putting on some sort of demonstration and had a rope bridge across the street, and they were climbing across the street and the Swiss people were looking up and watching so we stopped and watched too. I touched one of the guys on the arm and said, "I wonder why some of the soldiers aren't trying that." I had no more than got the words out of my mouth when a soldier came walking across the rope ladder. It looks like they are into everything.

Now, dear, it's time for me to tell you that I think you are the sweetest little angelwife in the world—and I wish I was with you to kiss you good-night.

Lots of love

Your little husband

p.s. I love you, honey

Meiringen, Switzerland

12 October 1945

Schongau, Germany

My darling wife—

There were too many guys ahead of me on the telephone call, but I sure tried. The men that did get to call home said it was just like talking across the street, so sharp and clear.

What did you think of your watercolor portrait? I hope it didn't get squashed. I thought it was swell. The other one is your little husband. The artist painted me so I would be looking toward you when we hang them up.

I'm mighty proud that my little wife got her promotion and raise. I guess they will be harder to get now that the war is over—huh?

Dear, we are supposed to move to Czechoslovakia Sunday to maintain order during their elections, but it shouldn't delay my coming home.

Lots of love

Your little husband

p.s. I sure love you—

Dinner with the Nurses

A memory in story form written circa 1979–82

Comparing our occupation of Pfronten to Shongau is like day and night.
In 1945, Pfronten was a quaint country village with a view of mountains in
the background, and Shongau was an ancient town with gloomy old buildings reeking of damp, smelly plaster.

As trucks bearing Company G rolled to a stop in the main square, the
civilians coolly stared at the soldiers, then hurried on. Soldiers from other
units had been quartered in the town, and Company G moved in when
they pulled out. Our headquarters occupied an old hotel. The balance
of the company quartered in nearby buildings. The hotel faced the town
square, and across the street, in a dry goods store, was company headquarters. For the first time, we had an office and desks—but not much business.

Then an incident occurred that profoundly moved us. A jeep stopped in
front of our building, and an army nurse came into the orderly room. On
her collar were the bars of a lieutenant. The moment I recognized that she
was an officer, I sprang to my feet and yelled, "Attention!" As the lieutenant
returned my salute, I noted that she was very attractive.

"Where's your commanding officer?" she asked.

"We'll notify him right away, sir—I mean, ma'am," I stuttered. "Hey," I

Sergeant Smith at his desk in Shongau

called to a gaping soldier. "Go get Mike, I mean Captain Damkowitch—he's in his quarters across the street."

"Right away," the runner replied, pulling on his helmet liner.

"Would you care to be seated, ma'am?" I said, indicating to a desk chair.

"Oh, no thank you," she said. "We've been driving and it feels good to walk around." To the delight of the spectators, she walked to and fro. Other than a Red Cross girl dressed in a G.I. suit and boots and wearing a steel helmet, this was our first glimpse of an American woman in over a year. I peered out the door and saw two more women in khaki uniforms in the jeep. The lieutenant walked to the door and called, "Come on in—I'm sure this is the place." As the other two traipsed in, I noticed that they were also lieutenants. "We're from the Field Hospital," one said with a smile.

"This is Company G, 317th Infantry, ma'am," I replied.

"Yes, we know," replied the lieutenant. "We saw the tactical marker in front of the building." After listening to swearing soldiers for so long, these voices were like music.

Mike entered the orderly room with his captain's bars gleaming. Most of the time we were informal—in fact, Mike preferred it that way—but today we snapped to attention. The nurses in their uniforms of skirt and blouse stood erect and saluted.

"I'm Captain Damkowitch," he said, returning the salutes. "Mike Damkowitch from Scranton—any of you from around there?"

They laughed and murmured something about California. The feminine laughter was like a breath of spring. They told Mike they were from a Field Hospital headquartered in a nearby village, and they had heard there might be a stable of riding horses in Shongau. They wanted to know if we could arrange for them to do some horseback riding.

Mike looked at me. "Smith, you know anything about a stable of horses here in Schongau?"

"No sir," I replied. "We can inquire."

"I know where it is," interrupted a runner. "It's near the edge of town." The runner explained the location, and Mike agreed to make arrangements for three riding horses for the nurses. Mike walked with the nurses to their jeep, and they drove away.

The next day, Captain Damkowitch and the company officers accompanied the nurses to the riding stable. Sometime in the afternoon, about 1500 or so, Mike and the nurses entered the orderly room. Mike was in rare form and clowned around. He accompanied the nurses to their jeep, and the presence of females—American females—drew soldiers, crowding into the square.

Mike said something, but I was too far away to hear. At first, the nurses' heads wagged in a negative gesture—Mike said something else, then he exclaimed, "Okay, it's a date. You'll be our guests Saturday evening." They laughed and waved as the jeep drove away.

Mike burst into the orderly room, shouting, "Hey, they accepted! They'll be our guests for chow next Saturday." He was excited as a kid, "Say, get Pierorazio over here."

The mess sergeant, in a white apron and rolled sleeves, crossed the street and entered the orderly room. "What's up?" he asked me. I looked toward Mike, who blurted, "Say, Pierorazio, those three nurses, the ones that came over to ride the horses."

"Yes sir," replied Sergeant Pierorazio.

"They will be our guests for chow on Saturday evening. Can you put together somethin' special?"

Sergeant Pierorazio looked thoughtful. "Well sir, all we got is canned stew, hash, dried carrots, and peas. Regular rations, sir."

"This is Tuesday," said Mike. "Reckon you can work out a little something extra by Saturday?"

"Yes sir. Say, we're set up in the local hotel restaurant. We could fire up their range if I can scrounge some coal. We could bake pies." And then, "Oh!" he exclaimed. "We can use the hotel china and silverware. Yes sir, we can work out something. How big is the party, how many?"

"The entire Company," said Mike. "I'm sure we can all fit into the dining room. Saturday evening we'll do away with the chow line and have a sit-down dinner."

"Yes sir!" said Sergeant Pierorazio. "We can even get table waiters, I'm sure we can. Let me talk it over with the cooks—yes sir—I'll keep you posted."

News spread like wildfire, and the bored soldiers were electrified. Women—real American women—it seemed like a dream. Of course, they were officers in uniform, but their skirts and blouses were more feminine than the Red Cross girls.

Everybody got in the act. Uniforms were cleaned and boots polished. The kitchen crew bustled, baking and making the dishes, and getting

Captain Mike
Damkowitch,
"To my fox hole
buddy, your pal,
Mike."

silverware ready. Civilian hotel staff redoubled their cleaning efforts. The
dining room sparkled. Captain Damkowitch summoned Corporal Bauder,
the company interpreter, and between them they persuaded the owner of
the dry goods store to sell them gifts for our guests. It was pitiful. All that
was available were a comb and brush, a hand mirror, and a scarf. Gift wrap-
pings were out of the question, but the cooks found some clean paper sacks
for the presents. A trio of musicians was engaged to play dinner music.

Saturday arrived. Somebody gathered enough wildflowers to make a
crude centerpiece and a flower for each table. Everywhere platoon sergeants were bawling, "Aw right you sons-a-bitches, watch your friggin'
language—these are ladies." The dining room had two tiers, probably for
musicians in the past. It was decided to seat the guests and the officers at
a table on the top tier so they would be visible to the soldiers. The non-
commissioned officers were seated next to the guests and officers, and the
balance of the company were to take their places anywhere they could
sit. Hotel staff covered tables with white tablecloths with place settings
of silver and white napkins. It was the soldiers' first civilized meal in at
least a year. "Damn," muttered one soldier, "I forgot what knives and forks
looked like."

One of the officers volunteered to give the invocation, and Mike prepared a welcome address. By 1500 the troops were ready and eagerly awaiting the guests. The planned line of march was that the platoons would assemble in front of their billets and march to the square in time to assemble by 1600. The guests were expected at approximately 1630, and as they arrived the company would be standing at "Present Arms." In presence of the guests, Captain Damkowitch would bawl, "Order Arms."

Next, there would be a company formation and reports taken. At the conclusion of my report, I would salute and take my post in the rear of 2nd Platoon. Captain Damkowitch would then give the order to "Stack Arms." When rifles were stacked, the troops would be dismissed while the officers escorted our guests to the dining room, followed by the troops. All would remain standing until the guests were seated. The routine had been rehearsed over and over, and all was in readiness.

The troops waited in the square. 1630 and no guests. 1645 and still no guests. "I did tell them we'd have dinner at 1700, didn't I?" Captain Damkowitch asked. "Yes sir," responded an officer, "I heard you, and I heard them say they'd be here." 1700 and no guests. "Damn," muttered Mike, "I wonder what happened?"

He bawled, "Smith," and I trotted up. "Something may have happened—let's call the Field Hospital." We went to the orderly room, and I cranked the field telephone. Battalion answered and transferred me to Regiment. Regiment relayed me to Division. Division transferred the call to the Field Hospital. The operator at the Field Hospital referred the call to a colonel, a female colonel in charge of the hospital nurses.

As her crisp, no-nonsense voice crackled, I said, "One moment for Captain Damkowitch," and handed the phone to Mike. Mike explained that three nurses from her command had visited Shongau to ride at the stable and that they had accepted a dinner invitation with Company G. Since they had not arrived, he feared something might have happened.

"Yes ma'am," I heard Mike say. "Yes, ma'am, Company G, 317th Infantry." He was silent and then replied, "Yes ma'am" several more times and then hung up. He stared at the phone for a moment and blurted, "Damnation!"

"What's up?" I asked.

"They're not coming," he said.

"Not coming? What's wrong?"

"I don't know—we're just outcasts. When they asked for a pass and explained it was to have dinner with an Infantry unit, the request was flatly refused."

"I don't get it," I said.

"The colonel used the word 'uncouth' several times—so that's that. Let's just have chow."

The men were silent when Mike explained that the nurses were unable to attend. He didn't say anything else, and maybe it was just as well.

On command, rifles were stacked and we filed into the dining room. The table waiters served the food. I stared at the head table, at the three vacant places, the makeshift centerpiece, and the three bags containing the presents. The trio played soft music. Mike, usually a hearty eater, stared at his plate. Presently, he arose and stalked out. The next day the Charge of Quarters said, "Mike sure got drunk last night—sounded like a herd of elephants stumbling around—boy oh boy, he really hung one on."

---

12 October 1945

Schongau, Germany

Darling—

At last I'm writing the note I've wanted to for over a year. Tomorrow I leave my Company to join a Division that is scheduled to leave for the U.S. this month. I don't know all the details, but I should be with you before next month this time if nothing goes wrong. I'll write more later.

Lots of love

Your little husband

p.s. I love you, kid. Don't write any more kid. Save it and tell me.

---

22 October 1945

Amberg, Germany

My darling wife—

The place where I'm stationed was a big German military school, so they have a school auditorium. Friday night, a U.S.O. cast put on a play called "Blithe Spirit" by Noel Coward. It was very good. I think stage plays are better than the movies.

Dear, things look pretty good here. I have a new Company—200 men and the other Companies are full too so it shouldn't be too long now before we are alerted to proceed to the coast (by boxcar). We also hear that the navy (hooray) will haul some of us on their battleships.

Darling, I don't care if I have to come home by rowboat, as long as I get home to you.

Lots of love

Your little husband

p.s. I love you, "Honeybun"

---

23 October 1945

Amberg, Germany

My darling wife—

I'm downtown in the Red Cross Club, as you can see by the stationery. It's an old, old inn. I notice that there is a slab of stone inscribed 1817 in the main dining hall where we eat our donuts and drink coffee. In the rear, they have a room with soft chairs and a radio, and if you are lucky you can get a table and write a letter.

Last night, I saw an awfully good movie, "Week-End at the Waldorf." The only amusement we have is the picture show—and the Red Cross club. The town is quite picturesque but it's been raining every day since I've been here, so I haven't had a chance to walk around and look at it. Amberg used to be quite a military town, and there are several huge stone barracks around the city. I live in one. It's quite a place and it reminds me of a jail, but I don't mind any place, now that I know we are nearly ready to come home.

Although I've been away 15 months or more, I feel as though I just left yesterday—I don't think I've changed any, but I guess I wouldn't be able to notice it if I had.

Don't forget we've got a date to go dancing when I get home—I probably need plenty of practice but the spirit is willing—

Good night, dear—

Lots of love

Your little husband

p.s. I love you, dear.

24 October 1945
Amberg, Germany
My darling wife—

Me and another guy walked to town tonight to go to the movies—"Here Come the Waves"—and now we're back at the Red Cross Club writing our wives.

As I told you before, this was a military town with several large camps, of which my Battalion occupies one. Well, the people have been getting pretty sassy recently—almost to the point where they try to shove you off the sidewalks. Most of the soldiers seem to be on their good behavior and try to stay out of fights with the civilians. Things seemed to be getting out of hand so I've been going to the movies with my buddies and was thinking about getting out my pistol 'cause this bunch aren't supermen to me. Last night, we received orders to arrest everybody that was causing trouble—this morning at 0400 we arrested every suspect. Tonight things were very much under control.

This is one country that doesn't understand anything but harsh measures. I guess it's hard for them to understand us. First, they are acting pretty "bigitty" and getting away with it—then swish—before they can get their eyes open good, they find their ass in the "Hoosegow." Thank goodness I'll soon be out of here.

Dear, I get to thinking sometime that love must be like a web a spider weaves—it stretches across the ocean and binds me to you stronger than any steel cable man can make, yet it's so frail and tiny—Oh! I just hope it never, never breaks and I come home to you soon.

Goodnight
    Lots of love
    Your little husband
p.s. I love you, dear—angel wings

---

26 October 1945
Amberg, Germany
My darling—

It will be a happy day for me when we can settle down and be Mr. & Mrs. Smith again. I'm afraid I'll be awfully fresh though—fifteen months is a long time not to have any loving, but I'll try to make up when I do get home. Since I've been married to you, the only things that stand out in my memory are the times we've been together.

Speaking of memories, the war already seems like a bad dream and soon will be forgotten by everybody. I'm just sorry for the men who were needlessly killed and mortally wounded on both sides. I'm not too fond of the Germans, but when I see their soldiers leaving the hospitals with no legs or arms (and there are plenty), I can't help but feel sorry for them. That was one thing that used to worry me—the loss of a leg or eyes—as far as getting killed, I never thought about it.

Gee! but I love you dearest. I think I was mighty lucky when you said "yes" when I proposed.

Lots of love

Your little husband

p.s. I love you, angel wings

---

1 Nov 1945

Amberg, Germany

My darling wife—

I had quite an experience today. Since we've been in the German Camp, there've been numerous cases of men breaking out with bites, just like bed bugs—maybe it's a German variety—I began to get "itchy" so I went to the Aid Station and got "sprayed." I had to go in a small room and take off my clothes and covered my eyes with gauze patches, and a man took a mosquito spray and sprayed disinfectant on me. This is a helluva time to pick up bed bug bites.

I went to see a pretty good movie, "The Clock." The trouble was that there were too many soldiers there and there's always a "smart aleck" in the crowd that keeps making smart cracks during the show. There's really a lot of crummy characters in uniform.

We saw a pretty good German vaudeville show that was put on at our camp the other day—they spoiled it by trying to sing American songs in English. You never heard such a mess—but the other acts were good. There are two American songs their orchestras play a lot, "You are my sunshine" and "My dreams are getting better all the time." Incidentally, I always thought the "Sunshine" piece was rather "gooney," but I've sung it so much both marching and in the barracks so that I'm getting to like it quite a bit. I imagine I'm singing it to you.

Good night dear
    Lots of love
    Your little husband
p.s. I love you, dear.

---

9 November 1945
Vicinity of Lohr
My darling—

Dear, for now I'm living in a village near Lohr. I guess you could call it a village; it's a cluster of houses around an old feudal castle—you guessed it, we live in the castle.[9] The place must be hundreds of years old, but it had been remodeled and used for a German military hospital. Now we have a Company of 200 men quartered there. I live in one of the tower rooms and have to wind around and around three floors to get there—it's a beautiful view as the castle sits high on the hill commanding all the ground nearby, but the weather is cold and misty, almost a cold rain. When I was a little boy I used to wish I could live in a castle—and here I am.

Yesterday I was standing in the courtyard looking around, and a guy came over to me and said, "Hello! remember me?" It was one of the men from Camp Shelby. He said he recognized me the minute he saw me— "you haven't changed a bit," he said. He's the only guy I've met in Europe that I'd known before.

Lots of love, dear
    Your little husband

While moving around prior to departure, Dad sent the following note to his former company.

11 November 1945
To Personnel Clerk
Co "G" 317th Inf—80th Div

Please send a copy of the General Order and a copy of the citation for the O.L.C. to my Bronze Star.[10] I left the 80th about the 12th or 13th of October, and the General Order was published about that time. Send it to my home address.

    Percy M. Smith
    3340 Brentwood Avenue
    Jacksonville (6) Florida

Incidentally, if Sergeant Wolff is still around, give him my regards. I've been trying to get home for a month now—this return process is a pain in the ass for all—

    P.

———————

14 November 1945
Vicinity Lohr
My darling—

We've been alerted to move tomorrow morning to a tent city encampment and spend the night there then proceed to Marseille to catch our boat. The trip from the tent city to the coast isn't supposed to take but four days, so we should be on our way soon.

We spent most of the day getting ready for the trip, packing and getting out money ready to be changed to U.S. currency—I had $84.00, but I haven't been paid for October yet. I sure don't need any money here. There just isn't anything to buy.

Last night, I rode about 15 miles in the foggy rain to see a movie, "Pillow to Post," a little on the screwy side but better than nothing.

Dear, from the looks of things you'll have a husband before many more weeks roll around. I was hoping I'd be home in time to help celebrate your birthday—but I am really hopeful of being able to spend Xmas with you, and it will really be one of thanksgiving for me too, kid.

Goodbye for now

Lots of love

Your little husband

———————

22 November 1945

Vicinity of Marseille

My darling wife—

I just finished my second Thanksgiving dinner overseas. It was much better than last year. We had turkey, dressing, asparagus, fruit cake, cranberry sauce, coffee, and a cigar. The news looks as though we will embark this Sunday, and it shouldn't take more than 8 or 9 days to cross the ocean.

Yesterday I received my influenza shot, so I'm all ready to sail. All we do is hang around in this huge camp. We are restricted to the area, so I don't guess I'll get to see the City of Marseille. I saw a couple of movies on the Post, "Murder He Says" and "The Bell Boy and the Princess." We have a huge open-air movie—so we huddle up in our overcoats and gloves and take it in. We sit on the side of a hill and watch the show.

I sure miss hearing from you, but soon we'll be face to face, and I'll try to spend the rest of my life making you happy.

Good night darling

Lots of love

Your little husband

p.s. Sure do love you, angel wings

WESTERN UNION

BAL3 NL PD CAMP MILES STANDISH MASS DEC 8

MRS PERCY M SMITH

3340 BRENTWOOD

ARRIVED BOSTON SAFELY STOP EXPECT TO LEAVE CAMP STANDISH FOR BLANDING

WITHIN 48 HOURS STOP WILL WIRE FROM BLANDING WHEN TO EXPECT ME STOP

WITH ALL MY LOVE

PERCY.

This is the telegram Dad sent to my mother on 8 December. He traveled by train to Camp Blanding, Florida, where he was discharged on 15 December 1945.

Five years later, my parents welcomed their first and only child.

EPILOGUE

At the end of 1945, my father returned home to mom and became a civilian once again. Dad now had a chance to live out his hopes for the future as he had written in so many of his wartime letters. Certainly, he was relieved and joyous to come home, find work, and start a family, but the war left my father with indelible memories and painful emotional wounds.

In his later years, Dad wrote stories about the rigors and comic aspects of training camp—too much to include in this book—the tedium of military bureaucracy, the carnage, the terror, and the pathos of battle. He only shared them with me and a few 80th Division veterans. All those decades later, Dad still recalled the words he exchanged with the dying soldier who thought that my father was his mother. In remembering and writing the words of comfort Dad spoke to him, I hope my father found some healing as well.

My father's account of that day under severe artillery bombardment 21 January 1945, moved me to search for the names of men who perished on that day. I found addresses for family members of about half a dozen of those soldiers. I composed a simple letter, saying that my father had served with their relative and that he wrote a story about what happened the day their loved one died. If they wanted to know more, I offered to send a copy of the story.

Some responded and wanted to read the story; others did not. For example, the sister of one of these soldiers told me that her brother did not enlist until someone in the neighborhood painted a yellow stripe down the middle of his car. He was so upset by the insinuation of cowardice that he joined up right away. She wrote a letter to her brother every day, and it was still hard for her when she remembered him.

My letter had a very different response from another family. Before the war, Eloise and John Turman and their three daughters lived on a Virginia farm. Like my father, John was drafted and became a replacement assigned to the 80th Division. Long lists of replacements in the official reports attest to the rate of casualties. By the end of the war, the 80th Division had accrued more casualties than it had men at full strength and had sustained more than seventeen thousand casualties. John Turman had been on the front lines for four months at the time of his death on 21 January.

When my letter arrived, Mrs. Turman's daughter called me right away and then put her mother on the phone. In a voice accented by a lifetime in the rolling hills of western Virginia, Eloise told me that she had prayed for all these years that someone would contact her with information about her husband. It had been fifty years since the official notice arrived in 1945, but she had never heard from anyone who knew more personal information or who had served with him. At her request, I sent her my father's story about the day her husband died. In this prewar photo, handsome, tall John Turman stands proudly with Eloise Turman and their daughters, Glenna, Nellie, and Lena.

The family of John Turman at home in Indian Valley, Virginia. He stands with his wife Eloise and their children, Glenna, Nellie, and Lena. Eloise Turman died in 2012 at age ninety-three. John and Eloise's daughters still live in the area and have thriving families.

This is the 80th Division shoulder patch from my father's uniform. The "Blue Ridge Division" was first organized in World War I, with soldiers from western Virginia, and the insignia evokes the Blue Ridge Mountains. In World War II, the Division originally included soldiers drafted from Pennsylvania and West Virginia, but replacements came from everywhere.

Fifty years after her husband's death in Luxembourg, Mrs. Turman still lived in the same area and had never remarried. In the mid-1990s, my family traveled to visit her home, and Eloise's children and grandchildren gathered with us for a meal and to honor John's memory. Later in the evening, Eloise brought out a small box containing her husband's few personal effects sent to her by the army after his death, and showed us a letter of condolence signed by President Franklin Roosevelt. John Turman's grandchildren had not seen these things, and they eagerly gathered around.

After dark, we followed Mrs. Turman outdoors. Looking up together, three generations of Turmans and my family and I gloried in the sight of the Milky Way sprawling above the darkened foothills of the Blue Ridge Mountains.

APPENDIX
Record of Events
October 1944–December 1945

During his time in the European Theater, Sergeant Smith's Morning Reports each ended with a brief "record of events" that described the action and movements of that day, including the location of the company command post. Company first sergeants gathered basic information and sent it along to higher levels of command, where these daily reports were augmented by hospital and grave registration details. The following appendix is a simplified version of Sergeant Smith's record of events while he was engaged. Missing dates indicate the company remained in place, usually reorganizing and receiving replacements, resting, and training, and sometimes seeking cover from artillery fire. The phrases and descriptions below are mostly verbatim, with only occasional minor adjustments for clarity. The official reports end in May 1945. Locations and dates during the months of occupation are derived from Smith's letters.

1944

3 October	Sergeant Smith arrived in Sivry, France, assigned to Company G of the 317th Infantry Regiment of the 80th Division
4 October	Defending Sivry under constant artillery and mortar fire
5 October	Still in Sivry receiving heavy artillery and mortar fire
6 October	Reorganizing and assigning replacements at Sivry
7 October	Hiked to Bezaumont
8 October	Moved by foot to Ville au Val
13 October	Marched to three miles northeast of Atton, near La Salle River
16 October	Moved from reserve to defensive position half mile west of Morville-sur-Seille

19 October	Returned to three miles northeast of Atton
20 October	Hiked to one half mile northwest of Morville-sur-Seille
22 October	In reserve three miles northeast of Atton
26 October	Moved to Pont-a-Mousson, reorganizing and training
2 November	Marched five miles, command post is two miles northeast of Atton
8 November	Attacked across Seille River, occupied high ground near Eply, expecting counterattacks
9 November	Moved to position east of Eply, under artillery fire
10 November	On foot through Raucourt to Secourt
11 November	Occupying hill north of Han-Sur-Nied
12 November	Under heavy artillery and mortar fire
13 November	Moved two miles to town of Many
14 November	Occupying high ground, under heavy artillery fire east of Many
15 November	Artillery fire continues to fall on position
17 November	Hiked one mile back to reserve position in Herny, reorganizing
21 November	Traveled by truck through Arraincourt to Many
23 November	Men fed turkey dinner and held Thanksgiving service, resting and reorganizing
25 November	From Falquemont attacked Teting Camp near Teting-sur-Nied, marching through woods under heavy artillery fire
26 November	Occupied town of Folschviller, mopping up continuing
27 November	Departed Folschviller on foot through Petite Ebersviller to east of Macheren
28 November	Left Macheren, advanced southwest, resistance moderate
29 November	Repulsed two tank attacks under terrific artillery fire, withdrew to Guenviller
30 November	Command post is located in Guenviller, reorganizing
7 December	Left Guenviller, marched to St. Avold, training and reorganizing
16 December	German offensive that began the Battle of the Bulge
18 December	Moved to Kirviller
19 December	Company in trucks, destination unknown
20 December	Detrucked in Junglingster, Luxembourg, thence two miles by foot to northeast
21 December	Moved by truck and foot to the town of Steinsel
22 December	By foot from Steinsel to Mullendorf, alerted and awaiting orders

23 December	From Mullendorf marched five miles to high ground northeast of Feulen, went into the attack at 1530, moved forward without opposition, stopped by enemy small arms fire after our four tanks were trapped, presently one mile northeast of Feulen
24 December	Occupying high ground in defensive position, enemy snipers active
25 December	In town of Feulen, enjoyed turkey dinner
26 December	Remaining in Feulen, roadblocks to prevent possible counterattacks
29 December	Marched approximately four miles to forward defensive area on high ground
31 December	Company in defensive positions two and a half miles north of Feulen

1945

1 January	Maintaining defensive positions, scouting and patrolling
3 January	Left defensive position in forest to forward position, sending patrols into enemy territory, snipers active
5 January	Sending patrols at night, receiving enemy artillery fire
6 January	Our patrols keep contact with the company on our left, heard enemy tanks
10 January	By foot and motor to Heiderschied, reorganizing and cleaning equipment
16 January	Michael Damkowitch assumes command, preparing to move forward
17 January	Marched from Heiderscheid to Tadler, in defensive position maintaining outposts and sending out contact patrols
18 January	Night march from Tadler to Heiderscheid
19 January	On alert, roads covered with snow and virtually impassable, visibility low
20 January	By foot at night two and one half miles northeast of Heiderscheid, receiving artillery and mortar fire
21 January	Went into attack 0600 toward Dirbach, distance marched approximately two and one half miles over treacherous and steep hills under terrific artillery fire, withdrew to Tadler at 1930, worked thirteen hours removing many wounded to aid station
22 January	In defensive positions at Tadler

23 January	Marched from Tadler, command post now one mile northeast of Wiltz
25 January	Left vicinity of Wiltz by foot at 2400, mission to cross and hold railroad bridges, attacked town of Lellingen, enemy occupied high ground, entered town at 0330 next day
26 January	Departed from Lellingen at 0530 hours by foot traveling northeast across mountainous terrain, discovered German ammunition dumps, repulsed three enemy attacks under heavy artillery and mortar fire, ammunition dumps destroyed by enemy
27 January	Left by foot at 0400, mission to take Schmitzbierg, superior fire-power of enemy automatic weapons and snipers held company in protective draw until at 2200 we attacked through snow two feet deep, one platoon reached edge of town but forced to withdraw, occupied and organized high ground one half mile west of Parc Hoingen
28 January	Moved by foot to Lellingen, had hot breakfast, then by truck to Oberglabach, billeted in houses, reorganizing and reequipping
5 February	Marched from Oberglabach to Diekirch, busy with care and cleaning weapons and training
8 February	In Diekirch, Smith assigned to Company E to help rebuild after 21 January losses
10 February	Left Diekirch via motor, set up temporary position in Beaufort, on alert
11 February	In reserve but on 30 minute alert order
12 February	Departed Beaufort on foot at 1700, at Dillinger Stuf crossed Sauer River in boats into Germany at 1930
13 February	Moved to high ground vicinity Bollendorf, Germany, maintaining contact patrols with adjacent units
14 February	Moved under cover of darkness one and a half miles north of Bollendorf, engaged the enemy on high ground, twenty prisoners taken
15 February	In woods on high ground above Rohrbach River [near Kruchten], moved from former position at 1730, set up perimeter defense, were attacked three times by enemy, each repulsed
16 February	Enemy attempting to infiltrate our lines, sharp encounters after dark, heavy artillery and mortar fire
17 February	Platoons deploying to attack, resistance moderate, patrols encountering minefields

18 February	Receiving heavy enemy artillery and mortar fire in Nusbaumhohe
19 February	Hiked one thousand yards to attack Nusbaum under cover of darkness, sustained direct fire from three enemy tanks, platoons are engaged in clearing houses, forty-one prisoners taken
20 February	Receiving direct fire from enemy tanks in Nusbaum
21 February	Maintaining roadblocks in Nusbaum, receiving enemy small arms and artillery fire
22 February	Moved one mile north of Nusbaum to clear woods north of town, set up roadblocks, dug in to prevent counterattack, resistance moderate, taking artillery and mortar fire
23 February	Exchanging small arms fire with enemy, hot food served to troops
24 February	Deployed in forward defensive position, artillery and mortar fire falling on our positions, small arms fire being encountered, sending out patrols
25 February	Left bivouac north of Nussbaum by foot at 1900 two miles to Freilingerhohe, slept, then to Mettendorf, on alert
26 February	Hiked from Mettendorf to Berg to Mulbach to Wissmansdorf, twelve miles, no enemy resistance
27 February	At 0700 crossed Prum River at Wissmansdorf
1 March	Departed Wissmannsdorf at 2300, went in to attack at 0200, took high ground northwest of Schleid, moderate resistance
2 March	Attacked town of Heilenbach, met no opposition, 70 prisoners taken, moved toward Ehlenz and swapped positions with Company F after dark
3 March	Marched one mile to billets in Ehlenz, care and cleaning of equipment
4 March	Resting and reorganizing, movies and Protestant church services held
11 March	Left Ehlenz in trucks to Gandren, France, distance traveled 70 miles
12 March	Via truck to Beurig, Germany, then hiked two miles to position one mile east of Irsch, deployed and dug in
13 March	Left bivouac area 0630 on foot, marched to one and a half miles west of Oberzerf, deployed and dug in
14 March	Moved from Oberzerf to one and a half miles south of Greimerath, dug in to repulse possible counterattack, receiving artillery fire, resistance moderate but determined

15 March	Heavy concentrations of artillery and Nebelwerfer fell on our positions causing some casualties
16 March	Departed bivouac area vicinity of Gerimerath at 1700, marched all night to Mitlosheim
17 March	On foot to Lochweiler, clearing houses and mopping up
18 March	Left Lochweiler 0300, marched ten miles to Neunkirchen [Nohfelden], resistance light
19 March	Via truck from Neunkirchen at 0300, traveled forty miles to Kusel, on alert, no physical contact with enemy
21 March	From Kusel by truck to Enkenbach, on alert, no physical contact with enemy
22 March	Left Enkenbach on foot Fishbach, entrucked to Bad Durkheim, marched to Niederkirchen, no resistance
23 March	At 1900 left Niederkirchen by truck to Gundersheim, occupying billets in defensive position, no physical contact with enemy
25 March	Departed Gundersheim via motor en route to Oberndorf, reorganizing and cleaning weapons, church services in the morning, ate hot chow and played ball in afternoon
27 March	Via motor from Oberndorf to Ober Saulheim, then to Mainz
28 March	At 2230 on the 27th hiked three miles to Rhine River, crossed in assault boats at 0200, intense opposition from machine gun fire caused heavy casualties, landed on east bank of Rhine and advanced, clearing houses in Kastel, rations and ammunition issued, hiked to Biebrich, arrived 2100, in billets with security posted
29 March	Company in Biebrich engaged in care and cleaning of equipment, hot meal served
30 March	Resting in billets, new clothing issued to men, hot meals served for breakfast and dinner, Percy Smith issued 7-day furlough to Nice, France
1 April	Smith arrived in Nice at United States Riviera Recreational Area
6 April	Sergeant Smith returned to Company G which had moved through Kassel and was now in Tungeda, Germany
7 April	Left Tungeda, on attack to Bufleben, met no resistance
9 April	At 0530, left Bufleben on attack to the town of Gierstadt, met slight resistance

10 April	Moved from Gierstadt through Bienstadt to Tottlestadt, no opposition met, then to Tiefthal, took small arms fire, 89 prisoners taken
11 April	From Tiefthal attacked Gispersleben, met stiff opposition on hill west of town, enemy used small arms, machine gun and direct fire weapons, attack continued, town cleared and outposted by 2200, repulsed counterattack by three German tanks and about 200 infantry, took about 80 prisoners
12 April	Marched two miles from Giespersleben to Schwefor, then by truck to Niederzimmern, left at 1130 and hiked about five miles to Weimar Germany, no physical contact with enemy
13 April	Company E was also in Weimar and reported: moved out via truck at 1015 to prison camp [Buchenwald] 4 miles northeast of Weimar for purpose of keeping order among the civilians and soldiers interned in the prison, relieved at 1900 and returned to Weimar
15 April	Company G left Weimar by truck, arrived at Hermsdorf Germany at 1200, attacked east and cleared woods to village of Reichardtsdorf taking 40 prisoners, then advanced to Bad Kostritz, resistance light
19 April	Located at Bad Kostritz, conducting unit training, attended presidential memorial service
20 April	Left Bad Kostritz by truck to Burglesau
23 April	Departed Berglesau by truck to Nuremberg, moved into billets
24 April	Maintaining security guard, took hot showers and had hot meals
29 April	Left Nuremberg via truck to Alteglofsheim, no physical contact with enemy
1 May	From Alteglofsheim by truck to Mengkofen, then south and crossed Isar River in assault boats, hiked three miles to Brunn, left one platoon, then walked ½ mile northeast to Dingolfing
4 May	Departed Dingolfing at 0500, crossed Inn River, to Timelkam, Austria, no physical contact with enemy
5 May	Left Timelkam by truck to one and a half miles southeast of Grunburg, no physical contact with enemy, prisoners surrendering by scores
6 May	Command post in town of Grunburg

7 May	Departed Grunburg at 0700 by truck to Hofern [one half mile north of Dorff]
8 May	Company received message of cessation of hostilities 1550 hours 7 May 1945, after a short prayer of thanksgiving, company entrucked at Hofern and rode approximately 30 miles to Spital [am Pyhrm], arrived at 2130 and went into billets, mission to guard & protect property and direct traffic of Axis prisoners to proper destination, weather mild, morale excellent
10 May	Left Spital by truck to Landl, contacted Russian army on Inn River at 2210 hours
11 May	Departed Landl 1400 by truck to St. Gallen, guarding bridges, keeping roads clear
17 May	Left St. Gallen by truck to Spital, conducting unit training and medical examinations
20 May	From Spital by truck to Gross Reifling, maintaining security and guarding bridges
30 May	Company went on hike and overnight bivouac
31 May	Company in Gross Reifling, guarding bridges
11 June	Moved to Wartburgasse, occupation duties
12 June	Munich, Germany
16 June	Obergunzburg
21 June	Rosshaupten
1 August	The regiment moved to Pfronten for its longest stable occupation location. General Patton visited the regiment here on 18 July. On 31 August the regiment was on alert to move to Czechoslovakia, but the alert was canceled
9 September	Company moved briefly to Altenstadt
12 September	In Schongau for the company's second-longest occupation position
1 October	Smith joined a G.I. tour of Switzerland, leaving Schongau to Mulhause, France, by truck and train, then by train to Basle, Switzerland, Lucerne, Meringen, Geneva, and Vevey

12 October	Returned to Schongau, Germany, where once again the 317th regiment was on alert to move to Czechoslovakia. Sister regiments 318th and 319th were transferred to the Czech border with the Soviets until December 1945, but the 317th did not go with them
15 October	Under the point system, as his eligibility to return home drew nearer, Smith left his company and was assigned to the 90th Division in Amberg
8 November	Lohr am Main, where Smith stayed in the Lohr Castle with other GIs
20 November	Moved to an encampment near Marseille, France, assigned to 79th Division in transit to the United States, once again on the USS *Mount Vernon*
8 December	Sergeant Smith arrived in Boston, Massachusetts
14 December	Smith traveled by train to Camp Blanding, Florida, to be discharged from the military service
15 December	By bus to Jacksonville, Florida, where Elizabeth was waiting

NOTES

Preface

1. V-Mail, or Victory-Mail, a microfilm process that delivered miniature versions of correspondence, was free to service members. Airmail postage stamps for regular mail cost six cents. The vast majority of letters in this collection were sent via airmail, and the originals are in the possession of the editor. See Thomas H. Boyle Jr., *Airmail Operations during World War II*, American Airmail Society, 1988.

2. Steven Spielberg, Robert Rodat, Ian Bryce, Mark Gordon, Gary Levinsohn, Tom Hanks, et al., *Saving Private Ryan* (motion picture), DreamWorks Home Entertainment, Universal City, CA, 1999.

3. Erich Maria Remarque, *All Quiet on the Western Front*, trans. A. W. Wheen, Little, Brown, and Company, Boston, 1929, p. 215.

4. These reports plus After Action reports and many other documents are public information, and I am grateful to Andrew Z. Adkins III, who organized and presented them on https://www.80thdivision.com/WebArchives/index.htm. Adkins also manages the veterans' association website for the 80th Division.

Chapter 1

1. An infantry division in World War II had three regiments, and each regiment had twelve companies, lettered A through L. There were four companies in each battalion, A–D, E–H, I–L. Therefore a company M was an outlier, a special unit for an unusual purpose. Also, each division had many supporting and attached units, such as artillery, anti-tank, armored, medical, engineering, and behind them a vast network of supply and intelligence units.

2. At full strength, an infantry company was about two hundred soldiers. At the time of this story, the company had been in action for two months.

3. War correspondent A. J. Liebling observed, "Among troops actively engaged, a K ration beat nothing to eat, but it was a photo finish." *Liebling Abroad*, Playboy Press, New York, 1981, p. 542.

4. Ernie Pyle described the scene at Omaha Beach on the day after the invasion. "I walked for a mile and a half along water's edge of our many-miled invasion beach. I walked slowly, for the detail on that beach was infinite. The wreckage was vast and startling. The awful waste and destruction of war, even aside from the loss of human life, has always

been one of its outstanding features to those who are in it. Anything and everything is expendable." *Brave Men*, Henry Holt & Co., New York, 1944, p. 366.

5. The incident is described later in a letter dated 28 February 1945. In the Wehrmacht, the equivalent rank was *Hauptfeldwebel*, which was often informally referred to as *Mutter der Kompanie*.

6. St. Augustine is forty miles south of Jacksonville. Although founded in 1565, the oldest structures in its town center date from much later.

Chapter 2

1. Winborn Stockton Catherwood, 1920–85, was a Jacksonville artist and writer who was part of a prominent local family. Smith had worked with Catherwood at the Southern News Company before the war. Catherwood later wrote two novels and short stories under the name David Telfair. Perhaps a shared love of the written word in this formative early adult friendship contributed to Dad's desire to record his wartime experiences in letters and later in stories.

2. By this time, my father had assessed the situation following the destruction of Company G at Sivry. In the coming days, the After Action Reports describe gradual advances and captures of towns west of the Seille River, which was the line between American and German forces. During the remainder of October, artillery and mortar fire were constantly exchanged, and nighttime patrols on both sides gathered intelligence.

3. His sister Betty Sue was fourteen years old at this time.

4. The Battalion After Action report for 8 November 1944 states, "Our attack surprised the Germans who did not believe we would attack in such unfavorable weather. The Seille River rose quickly during the morning and forced our troops to wade through water for about 200 yards. Regiment attacked at 0600 with mission of seizing bridgehead east of Seille River and advancing to the northeast."

5. In the days following crossing the Seille River, the 317th Regiment moved steadily to the northeast and then crossed the Nied River. Company G was in the village of Herny on the date of this letter. Every day there were reports of German resistance with artillery, mortar, machine gun, and small arms fire.

6. Robert M. McAllister was from Shamokin, Pennsylvania. He served with Dad throughout the war.

7. Joseph Moors from Philadelphia was a replacement assigned to Company G on 14 October 1944.

8. This is part of a longer single story originally titled "Staff Sergeant Joseph A. Moors" that has been segmented into four parts to place events in chronological order.

9. At this time, the company was in the village of Many, France.

10. Michael P. Damkowitch Jr. was from Scranton, Pennsylvania. His parents immigrated from the Ukrainian part of what had been Austria-Hungary. He was assigned to Company G on 24 September 1944 as a 2nd Lieutenant. On 16 January 1945, he became the company commanding officer. In a postwar letter to another veteran, my father wrote, "Of our commanding officers, Lieutenant Damkowitch was everybody's

favorite, known as 'Mike' to all the guys. He was a brave and resourceful troop leader. Many nights we shared a hole in the ground, and under the circumstances, I came to know him well."

11. G-2 refers to military intelligence.

12. Rudolph Decker's father immigrated from Austria. Decker was from Allentown, Pennsylvania.

13. Morning Report for 25 November 1944. "Company launched attack from Faulquemont France at 0800. Mission to take and secure Teting Camp [Teting-sur-Nied]. Company moved through forest under heavy artillery fire and took objective at 1530. Weather cool."

14. The Division G-2 Report, one of the After Action reports, for December 1944 noted that four time bombs were detonated while the Division occupied St. Avold.

15. After Action and Morning Reports for 29 November indicated that Smith's unit was under artillery fire all day and repulsed two counterattacks by five tanks and infantry of the German 17th SS Panzergrenadier Division. This happened east of Théding and north of Farébersviller, France. When Smith wrote this letter, Company G was in Guenviller, France, about two miles east of St. Avold.

16. Jesse Moon and Albert Rohrig were my father's brothers-in-law, married to Elizabeth's sisters, Frances and Vivian.

17. According to the Morning Report for this date, Company G was in St. Avold, France, conducting unit training.

18. The company was still in St. Avold.

19. Vincent Carl Anuskiewicz was from Shamokin, Pennsylvania. Both of his parents immigrated from Poland in 1905.

Chapter 3

1. In a 1981 letter to a fellow veteran, my father wrote, "Another character popped to mind. Sylvester Anderson. Do you remember him? When we had to maneuver at night, he was out scout. When I first met him, my heart sank. He was a lanky, tow-headed soldier wearing steel-rimmed spectacles. His hearing was impaired. His nose dripped, and he had a hacking cough. It's disconcerting to move in the darkness with a guy going 'cough-cough-cough.' The remarkable thing about him was his uncanny sense of direction. One look at the terrain, and he would mold his hands in some way to help him remember. And in pitch black night, he led us over the terrain, all the while gently coughing into a handkerchief." Anderson was from Eau Claire, Wisconsin, the son of a Norwegian immigrant farming family.

2. Company G of the 317th did move in the direction of Bastogne, but remained twenty miles west of Bastogne. The 2nd Battalion of the 318th entered Bastogne on 28 December, as part of the larger effort to relieve the surrounded 101st Airborne.

3. The Morning Report for Company G listed Moors as MIA on this date, 23 December 1944.

4. Frank J. Coputo was later transferred to the Battalion HQ Company.

5. "Nobody ever fastened the chin strap on his helmet in the front lines, for the blasts from nearby bursts had been known to catch helmets and break people's necks." Pyle, *Brave Men*, p. 444.

6. The Morning Report's Record of Events for 23 December 1944 states, "Company moved out of town of Mullendorf, Luxembourg, at 0800 and marched about 5 miles to high ground 2 mi NE Feulen. Company was stopped by enemy small arms fire. Company reorganized and after dark supported by 4 tanks withdrew after tanks were trapped." According to an After Action interview with Lt Col William Boydstun, this action occurred during an attack on Welscheid.

7. William Koedam was from Hull, Iowa.

8. Dad had a three-day pass to Nancy, France. From the 4th to the 9th of January, Company G was three miles north of Feulen, Luxembourg. Nancy is about one hundred miles south of Feulen.

9. Pfc. John Buehler was from Sebwaing, Michigan. His brother Carl had been wounded earlier that winter.

10. The Battalion Headquarters Company Morning Report for 21 January 1945, states, "Battalion HQ located in village of Tadler, Luxembourg. The mission was to seize and hold the bridges at Dirbach, Luxembourg. At 1400, the Battalion moving from SW encountered enemy approximately 400 yards from Dirbach and a fire fight resulted [Company E]. Terrific artillery, mortar, and machine gun fire held up our advance. As fire fight continued, many casualties were inflicted on our force. The commanding officer and other key personnel were wounded. At 1730 orders were received to withdraw to our original positions under cover of darkness. Due to the difficult terrain the attack was carried out over, the evacuation of the wounded was difficult and a hazardous problem. Complete platoons are being drafted as litter bearers. Weather cold and clear." All names in my father's writings are real, with the exception of Alfred Miller. Perhaps Dad did not remember or concealed his identity on purpose.

11. After 21 January, until the end of the month, the regiment continued attacking to the northeast, toward the Sauer River separating Luxembourg and Germany. The Company G Morning Report on 26 January states, "Departed from Lellingen at 0530 hrs by foot traveling NE cross country over mountainous terrain. Took 2 PWs enroute. Reached objective. Discovered German ammunition dumps. Beat off three attacks by enemy combat patrols. Received heavy artillery & mortar fire. Ammunition dumps destroyed by enemy before withdrawing." The Report for the 27th states, "Company left position at 0400 hrs by foot traveling NE cross country. Mission to take Mon Schmitz [Schmitzbierg] and high ground. Company was held up in a draw by superior firepower of enemy auto weapons and snipers. Attacked through snow 2 ft deep at 2200 hrs. Encountered heavy enemy and small arms fire. One platoon reached edge of town but was forced to withdraw. Occupied and organized high ground." By the end of January, when this letter was written, the entire regiment had moved to another sector and was in Oberglabach, Luxembourg.

12. On this day, the company was in Diekirch, Luxembourg.

13. On 21 January, Company E was almost destroyed, and Smith was switched from G to E Company to help rebuild. He returned to G Company six weeks later.

14. My father served Captain McDonnell in Company E until early April, when Dad moved back to George Company. In a 1981 letter to a fellow veteran, my father wrote, "Oddly enough, and I don't' know why—I didn't get along with McDonnell. Either he was strange or I was. With him I maintained strict military courtesy. He couldn't find fault with my work as that was kept up with scrupulous care—we just weren't compatible, that's all. His best shot—I was nominated for a Silver Star, but he had it reduced to an Oak Leaf Cluster to my Bronze Star." That is, instead of the higher level commendation, Dad received two Bronze Stars.

15. The company was still in Diekirch, Luxembourg.

16. On 12 February, the Company crossed the Sauer river at Dillingen, Luxembourg, and on 14 February seized Bollendorf, Germany. After the war, Smith wrote in a letter to a former comrade, "I quit believing the radio and paper when they announced that Bollendorf and a few other towns were taken in February before we actually got there, and you can imagine our surprise when they nearly beat our pants off when we tried to enter the town. From then on, I waited to see, before I believed a thing I heard."

17. The Morning Report for the next day, 19 February 1945, states, "Company left village at 0400, marched 1000 yards to Nusbaum and attacked village under cover of darkness. Gained control of a section of town. Platoons are engaged in clearing houses. 41 prisoners taken. Sustained direct fire from 3 enemy tanks until they were scattered by artillery & our TDs. Weather cool, scattered showers."

18. Captain George F. McDonell assumed command of Company E on 6 February 1945.

19. In postwar correspondence with other veterans, my father mentioned the poor level of literacy among soldiers. He wrote about helping them with grammar and spelling in their letters and official reports. A special study states, "Beginning 15 May 1941, the ability to read, write, and compute as commonly prescribed in the fourth grade in grammar school became the standard for induction. Those men who had not completed the fourth grade were eligible for induction only upon passing the Minimum Literacy Test prescribed by the War Department. This standard remained in effect until 1 August 1942, when the Army began to accept illiterates in numbers not to exceed 10 percent of all white and 10 percent of all Negro registrants accepted in any one day." Ulysses Lee, "The Employment of Negro Troops," Center of Military History of the US Army, Washington, DC, 2000, https://history.army.mil/books/wwii/11-4/chapter9.htm.

20. Bill Mauldin, a young infantryman in the 45th Division, won a Pulitzer Prize for his World War II cartoons.

21. The Morning Report for 26 February states, "Company left Mettendorf, Germany, at 1800 hrs by foot traveling north to Berg. No opposition. Moved out of Berg at 2145 hrs for Oberweis. Company was advance element of Battalion. Traveled approximately 4 miles. Took approximately 25 PWs. Went into billets. Company left Oberweis traveling north as flank guard for Battalion. Crossed Prum River, arrived in Wissmannsdorf." On the date of this letter, Company E was still in Wissmannsforf, and the Morning Report

states, "Company on alert awaiting orders. Care & cleaning of equipment & personal hygiene."

22. Company E was in Ehlenz, Germany, from the 2nd to 10th of March 1945.

23. Lt. Col. Henry G. Fischer served as commander of the 317th Infantry Regiment from 4 December 1944 until the end of the war.

Chapter 4

1. St. Valentinkirche in Oberndorf, Germany. Since his last letter, Company E had moved its command post twelve times in fifteen days, traveling by foot and truck, encountering little resistance, and moving steadily closer to the Rhine River. Morning Reports for 16 and 17 March state, "Company departed bivouac area vicinity of Gerimerath at 1700 and marched all night to present position," and, "Company located in Lochweiler, Germany, clearing houses and mopping up behind 10th Armored."

2. This may refer to the fight at Teting-sur-Nied on 25 November. The flag has a corner marker "Mörchingen," the German name of the French town Morhange, about twelve miles from Teting-sur-Nied.

3. Among German defenders at Mainz were German youth support groups with paramilitary training. One of the youth was Hermann O. Pfrengle, who was at Mainz and who later wrote of his experiences in *Forget That You Have Been Hitler Soldiers*, Burd Street Press, Shippensburg, PA, 2001.

4. The Company Morning Report for 28 March states, "Company departed Mainz, Germany at 2230 hrs 27 Mar 45. Hiked to Rhine River, approx. 3 miles. Arrived 0030 hrs. Loaded Company in assault boats at 0200 to cross Rhine River. Encountered intense opposition from German 20mm & 50 cal machine gun fire, causing heavy casualties. Made landing on east bank of Rhine River and advanced, clearing houses and defensive positions. Objective taken at 0800."

5. The army established a US Riviera Recreational Area in Nice. In April, the After Action Report for the 317th Infantry Regiment, S-1 (Personnel), contained this statement: "A quota of three-day passes to Paris, France, were issued and 7-day furloughs granted to the Riviera, France." The seven days included travel each way.

6. "Lend-Lease" refers to a law passed in 1941, "An Act to Promote the Defense of the United States," which allowed lending or leasing vital supplies to military allies and ended US neutrality.

7. Avondale was a newly developed upper-class section of Jacksonville, Florida.

8. Lines have been erased here, no doubt by a blushing Elizabeth.

9. While Dad was on furlough, Company E moved from Gudensberg through Kassel to Hausen, a distance of about 100 miles, meeting little resistance. Upon his return on 8 April, he was reassigned back to Company G, which was then in Bufleben, Germany. Other elements of the 2nd Battalion did have trouble near Kassel while their sister regiments captured the city in heavy fighting. The 4 April After Action Report states that the 2nd Battalion met "40 to 60 SS infantry" outside Kassel, and "the entire force was killed or captured."

10. On 11 April, anticipating the arrival of US troops, German guards fled and inmates took charge. That afternoon, the 6th Armored Division entered the camp. Infantry of the 80th Division were nearby, and the event described in this letter happened the next day. There are many sources of detailed information about the liberation of Buchenwald, including the US Holocaust Memorial Museum website, at www.ushmm.org.

11. The day before encountering Buchenwald, 11 April 1945, the Morning Report for Company G states (and the After Action Report confirms), "Company left Tiefthal, Germany, at 1730 hrs 10 April 1945 to attack Gispersleben Germany. Met stiff opposition on hill west of town. Enemy used small arms, machine guns, and direct fire weapons. Attack continued into town and encountered small arms fire. Counterattacked by 3 German tanks & about 200 Infantry. Repulsed attack and took 3 PWs. Took about 80 PWs in operation. Town cleared and outposted by 2200 hrs."

12. This was in Bad Kostritz, Germany.

13. This event occurred on 15 April. The Morning Report for Company G states, "Co. left Weimar Germany at 1000 hrs 15 Apr 45 by truck. Arrived at Hermsdorf Germany at 1200 hrs. Company attacked east & cleared woods to village of Reichardsdorf taking 40 PWs. Company then advanced to Bad Kostritz." Forty years later, Lt. Andrew Z. Adkins and his son completed a memoir, *You Can't Get Much Closer Than This: Combat with Company H, 317th Infantry Regiment, 80th Division* (Havertown, PA: Casemate, 2015), in which he wrote, "We got into Bad Kostritz about five o'clock in the afternoon. G Company came strolling in with their bag of prisoners. Sgt. Smith (their first Sgt. from Jacksonville) was mad as hell and he had the Krauts, about 30 of them, marching in step at rigid attention" (p. 227).

14. In June 1942, in retaliation for the murder of a senior SS leader named Reinhard Heydrich, German soldiers destroyed the Czech village of Lidice. All men were shot, and women were sent to Ravensbruck concentration camp. A few children were spared and raised by German families.

15. This atrocity is unconfirmed. It may have happened during the action at Gispersleben on 11 April.

16. German citizens' image of Americans was evidently affected by Hollywood movies and their own propaganda.

17. No letter remains from the day before. If Dad's words were shockingly amorous, perhaps Elizabeth destroyed that entire letter.

18. Not surprisingly, my father's letters from the latter half of April seem to indicate notable mood swings. He goes from shockingly amorous (the missing letter) and describing his comrades and himself in very testosterone-charged terms; to describing feeling "down" and "indifferent"; then back to playful comments, humor, and admiring the German countryside. While the week in the Riviera was a welcome respite, how jarring and surreal it must have been to go from the bloody Rhine crossing almost immediately to a week of leisure on the Riviera—then just as abruptly back into action, albeit somewhat less lethal action. Dad's letters in late April demonstrate considerable self-awareness of the effects of his experiences on his state of mind.

19. Company G was still in Bad Kostritz. Morning Reports for the Division band list

up to fifty-eight members. Presumably the band was present for this parade, but no band unit Morning Reports are available for the month of April.

20. He had been in Mettendorf on the 25th of February.

21. The next day, Company G left Bad Kostritz by truck to Berglesau, about one hundred miles.

22. Dogpatch was the fictional home of the characters in Al Capp's comic strip *Li'l Abner*, set in an impoverished location in the hilly backcountry of the American South.

23. Nuremberg is the location of the Zeppelinfeld, the large gathering place used for Nazi rallies and a central location for a 1934 Nazi Party rally that was filmed and titled *Triumph of the Will*.

24. Company G Morning Report for this day states, "Company maintaining security guard and conducting training. Company took hot showers and had hot meals. Morale excellent. Weather cool."

25. This letter was written on the day Hitler died in Berlin.

26. Evidence of lampshades made of human skin from Nazi prisoners is disputed. See Mark Jacobson, *The Lampshade: A Holocaust Detective Story from Buchenwald to New Orleans*, New York, Simon & Schuster, 2010. Dad's secondhand account of prisoner treatment are also unverified.

27. On this day, Company G was in Dingolfing. After leaving Nuremberg, the Company and the 317th Infantry Regiment reported no serious resistance from the enemy until the surrender on 7 May.

28. Company G was still in Dingolfing, Germany.

29. On 4 May, Company G moved to Timelkam, Austria, where the day before, the 2nd Battalion HQ Morning Report mentioned small arms resistance and snipers. On the date of this letter, Company G was in Grunberg, Austria. After crossing the Rhine River in late March, the 80th Division crossed central Germany quickly, then turned south to Austria in pursuit of a suspected German redoubt in the Alps. Apparently, the US army moved so fast that they overtook any chance of a Nazi last stand.

30. The Morning Report for this day states, "Company received message of cessation of hostilities 1550 hours 7 May 45. After a short prayer of Thanksgiving Company entrucked at Hofern Austria and rode approximately 30 miles to Spital am Pyhrn, Austria. Company arrived at 2130 and went into billets. Mission to guard and protect property and direct traffic of Axis prisoners to proper destination. Weather mild. Morale excellent."

Chapter 5

1. At the war's end, it had been 218 days since Dad was assigned to Company G. Since he left home, his mother, Carrie Mai, had remarried and moved to her new husband's farm near Williston, Florida.

2. The Morning Report for 2nd Battalion HQ Company for this date states, "Battalion now attached to Task Force Smythe with mission as follows: Occupation, outposting, and securing of Spital, to furnish adequate guard on the gold reserves of the Hungarian National Bank and to establish road blocks at each end of town to keep all enemy person-

nel south of that point. Two collecting points are activated for the collection, disposition, and guarding of all enemy arms, equipment, and material, also all displaced personnel and German soldiers." The Battalion's final S-2 Intelligence Report for May 1945 adds this information, "At the close of World War II, new problems arose in the form of nuisance activity by die-hard SS troops, i.e., wire cutting, threats to civilians, petty theft, and the handling of displaced persons. Troops continuing to resist in small groups have been hunted down with excellent help from civilian mountain guides; civilians have also been instrumental in apprehending SS personnel and leading Nazi politicians. Road blocks manned by alert guards have also netted numerous suspicious persons and SS troops."

3. A Hungarian shipment of valuables, many taken from Hungarian Jews, was intercepted by the US Army. Litigation about disposition and ownership continued until 2005, when a settlement allocated over $25 million for Holocaust survivors and Holocaust memory projects. "United States Settles World War II–Era Hungarian Gold Train Claims," *American Journal of International Law*, 100, no. 1, 2006, pp. 220–22, www.jstor.org/stable/3518845.

4. Mortimer Snerd was a slow-witted puppet in Edgar Bergen's popular ventriloquism act.

5. His words, "But I guess I would be pretty 'hot' too if my wife and children (if I had any) and my parents had been slaughtered or been taken into slavery to some godforsaken place," perfectly described the trials associated with being Black in America. Dad did not pause to make the obvious comparison, probably because as a white southerner who grew up in the era of Jim Crow, it never occurred to him. Today, those words leap off the page.

6. My father's faith in "the way Americans operate" was not uncommon, but Americans who had been subject to enslavement, lynching, segregation, and dispossession of all kinds know that America was not a place of assured safety. For some background on how rosy but inaccurate memories of national history prevent national healing, see Susan Neiman, *Learning from the Germans: Race and the Memory of Evil*, Farrar, Straus and Giroux, New York, 2019.

7. The Morning Report on 11 May for the 2nd Battalion of the 317th Regiment confirms that Major General Horace McBride, commander of the 80th Division, and XX Corps commander Lt. General Walton H. Walker did meet Russian Major General Pavel Voskresenskii at the bridge over the Enns River at Liezen. Perhaps Smith wrote about another occasion.

8. Company G left St. Gallen on this day and spent a few days back in Spital, Austria, before moving to Grossreifling, Austria, also on the Enns River. The 317th Regiment controlled a line along the Enns River from Liezen to Rettenstein.

9. When war ceased, the millions of US service members in Europe performed police and security work, but they had time on their hands. At the end of May 1945, the last monthly After Action Personnel Report for the 317th Infantry Regiment stated, "For the entertainment of the Regiment, movies were shown at every available opportunity. Reading and writing material were distributed and also a supply of items from the Regimental Post Exchange. Individual rolls of film were collected for developing and censorship. American Red Cross Club mobiles visited the units and the men were served coffee and

donuts. A quota of three day passes to Paris and Thionville, France, was issued and seven day furloughs granted to the Riviera. A quantity of athletic equipment was distributed for the recreation of the men of the regiment and softball games played at every available opportunity. A quota of 200 men were permitted to attend the lake resort at Grunden [Grundelsee] every other day. Quantities of beer were obtained. A plan of competitive sports was organized with passes to Paris, Thionville and the Riviera as rewards to the winning groups." Throughout the summer of 1945, organized sports was a major way to keep soldiers occupied.

10. This is his remembrance of 4 October 1944, when he was assigned to Company G. Obviously, this was information he chose not to share with his wife at the time. They crossed the Seille River on 8 November 1944.

11. In Europe, a total of twenty-nine Americans were executed for rape under military justice. Of these, twenty-five were Black, or 87 percent. For all crimes, fifty-five American servicemen were executed in England alone, and of those, forty were Black, even though white servicemen outnumbered Black by more than ten to one. See J. Robert Lilly, *Taken by Force: Rape and American G.I.s in Europe during World War II*, Palgrave Macmillan, New York, 2007. Also, Anna Mulrine Grobe, "Why Do Black Troops Face a Harsher Form of Military Justice?" *The Christian Science Monitor*, 17 July 2020, www.csmonitor.com/USA/ Military/2020/0720/why-do-black-troops-face-a-harsher-form-of-military-justice.

12. In the Morning Report of 25 January 1945, the status of Joseph Moors was changed from MIA to KIA as of 23 December 1945.

Chapter 6

1. In his memoir *War as I Knew It* (Bantam Books, 1947), General Patton recorded many visits to the 80th Division during wartime. After the war, the general wrote, "Whenever we turned the 80th Division on anything, we always knew that the objective would be attained" (p. 266). Sergeant Smith thought that the general drove his troops harder than necessary, resulting in too many casualties.

2. At the editor's request, an archivist at the Library of Congress searched the Patton Collection but did not find a copy of this letter. Perhaps it was a standard statement from Patton's press office.

3. Edward D. Sumskis, 1921–2003. In the 1940 census, he lived in Cleveland and worked in a machine shop before the war.

4. This was the seventh film in Frank Capra's *Why We Fight* series.

5. In a 1984 letter to a fellow veteran, my father wrote, "In St. Avold, to avoid time bombs in buildings, about eighteen of us were crammed into one room of a house. Boy! When you're packed in like we were you get to know each other well. One unforgettable character was Shima. He was forever seeking to lure females down the primrose path, and they were determined he wouldn't. Unfortunately, we were compelled to listen to his exploits. He sought to be friendly with a young female member of the household that only spoke German. He conned our interpreter, Decker, to plead his case with her. She

was engaged to a German she met when the Germans occupied the town, and Decker tried to explain to Shima that he was barking up the wrong tree. But Shima wouldn't listen, and we had to hear about his attempts night after night."

6. Lieutenant Julius Borys had been assigned to Company G on 9 April 1945, as a platoon leader.

7. The Morning Report of 25 December 1944 listed PFC George Shima as "lost to hospital" along with six other enlisted men in Company G.

8. The 80th Division Operational History reported 3,180 killed in action and died of wounds and 17,959 overall casualties, including wounded and missing. The division strength averaged 14,000 officers and enlisted men.

9. This is a reference to Steinbach Castle, Lohr am Main.

10. The Oak Leaf Cluster is the designation for a second award of the same kind—in this case a second Bronze Star. This award was common. Eightieth Division soldiers were awarded 3,357 Bronze Stars, 671 Silver Stars, 48 Distinguished Services Crosses, and 4 Medals of Honor.

RECOMMENDED READING

Fussell, Paul, *The Boys' Crusade: The American Infantry in Northwest Europe, 1944–1945*, Modern Library, New York, 2003.

———, *Wartime: Understanding Behavior in the Second World War*, Oxford University Press, New York, 1989.

Liebling, A. J., *Liebling Abroad*, Playboy Press, New York, 1981.

———, *The Road Back to Paris*, Doubleday, Doran & Co., Garden City, NY, 1944.

March, William, *Company K*, University of Alabama Press, Tuscaloosa, 1989.

Neiman, Susan, *Learning from the Germans: Race and the Memory of Evil*, Farrar, Straus and Giroux, New York, 2019.

Pfrengle, Hermann O., *Forget That You Have Been Hitler Soldiers: A Youth's Service to the Reich*, Burd Street Press, Shippensburg, PA, 2001.

Pyle, Ernie, *Here Is Your War*, Consolidated Book Publishers, Chicago, 1943.

Remarque, Erich Maria, *All Quiet on the Western Front*, Little, Brown, and Company, Boston, 1929.

Samet, Elizabeth D., *Looking for the Good War: American Amnesia and the Violent Pursuit of Happiness*, Farrar, Straus and Giroux, New York, 2021.

INDEX

CPSIA information can be obtained
at www.ICGtesting.com
Printed in the USA
LVHW081308150922
728310LV00001B/1